HARCOURT
Math

Harcourt School Publishers

Orlando • Boston • Dallas • Chicago • San Diego

www.harcourtschool.com

For permission to reprint copyrighted material, grateful acknowledgment is made to the following sources:

Aladdin Paperbacks, an imprint of Simon & Schuster Children's Publishing Division: Cover illustration by Ron Barrett from *Benjamin's 365 Birthdays* by Judi Barrett. Illustration copyright © 1974 by Ron Barrett. Cover illustration by Nancy Winslow Parker from *The Goat in the Rug* as told to Charles L. Blood & Martin Link by Geraldine. Illustration copyright © 1976 by Nancy Winslow Parker. Cover illustration by Ray Cruz from *Alexander, Who Used to be Rich Last Sunday* by Judith Viorst. Illustration copyright © 1978 by Ray Cruz.

Dial Books for Young Readers, a division of Penguin Putnam Inc.: Cover illustration by Devis Grebu from *The King's Chessboard* by David Birch. Illustration copyright © 1988 by Devis Grebu. Cover illustration by Patricia MacCarthy from *17 Kings and 42 Elephants* by Margaret Mahy. Illustration copyright © 1987 by Patricia MacCarthy.

Four Winds Press: Cover illustration by Cyndy Szekeres from *The 329th Friend* by Marjorie Weinman Sharmat. Illustration copyright © 1979 by Cyndy Szekeres.

Greenwillow Books, a division of William Morrow & Company, Inc.: Cover illustration by Donald Crews from *Each Orange Had 8 Slices: A Counting Book* by Paul Giganti, Jr. Illustration copyright © 1992 by Donald Crews. Cover illustration by Donald Crews from *How Many Snails? a Counting Book* by Paul Giganti, Jr. Illustration copyright © 1988 by Donald Crews.

Harcourt, Inc.: Cover illustration from *The Twelve Circus Rings* by Seymour Chwast. Copyright © 1993 by Seymour Chwast. Cover illustration from *How Big Were the Dinosaurs?* by Bernard Most. Copyright © 1994 by Bernard Most.

HarperCollins Publishers: Cover illustration from *Arthur's Funny Money* by Lillian Hoban. Copyright © 1981 by Lillian Hoban. Cover illustration by S. D. Schindler from *BETCHA!* by Stuart J. Murphy. Illustration copyright © 1997 by S. D. Schindler. Cover illustration by George Ulrich from *Divide and Ride* by Stuart J. Murphy. Illustration copyright © 1997 by George Ulrich. Cover illustration by John Speirs from *A Fair Bear Share* by Stuart J. Murphy. Illustration copyright © 1998 by The Big Cheese Design, Inc. Cover illustration by Steven Kellogg from *If You Made a Million* by David M. Schwartz. Illustration copyright © 1989 by Steven Kellogg. Cover illustration by Jon Buller from *Ready, Set, Hop!* by Stuart J. Murphy. Illustration copyright © 1996 by Jon Buller.

Henry Holt and Company, LLC: Cover illustration from *The Empty Pot* by Demi. Copyright © 1990 by Demi. Cover illustration from *Measuring Penny* by Loreen Leedy. Copyright © 1997 by Loreen Leedy.

Houghton Mifflin Company: Cover illustration by Bonnie MacKain from *One Hundred Hungry Ants* by Elinor J. Pinczes. Illustration copyright © 1993 by Bonnie MacKain.

Hyperion Books for Children: Cover illustration by Carol Schwartz from *Sea Sums* by Joy N. Hulme. Illustration © 1996 by Carol Schwartz.

Little, Brown and Company Inc.: Cover illustration from *The Village of Round and Square Houses* by Ann Grifalconi. Copyright © 1986 by Ann Grifalconi.

North-South Books Inc., New York: Cover illustration from *A Birthday Cake for Little Bear* by Max Velthuijs, translated by Rosemary Lanning. Copyright © 1988 by Nord-Süd Verlag AG, Gossau Zurich, Switzerland.

Philomel Books, a division of Penguin Putnam Inc.: Cover illustration from *Anno's Math Games II* by Mitsumasa Anno. Copyright © 1982 by Kuso Kobo; translation and special contents of this edition copyright © 1989 by Philomel Books. Cover illustration by Mitsumasa Anno from *Anno's Mysterious Multiplying Jar* by Masaichiro and Mitsumasa Anno. Text translation copyright © 1983 by Philomel Books; copyright © 1982 by Kuso Kobo.

Scholastic Inc.: Cover illustration by Susan Guevara from *The King's Commissioners* by Aileen Friedman. A Marilyn Burns Brainy Day Book. Copyright © 1994 by Marilyn Burns Education Associates. Published by Scholastic Press, a division of Scholastic Inc. Cover photograph from *Eating Fractions* by Bruce McMillan. Copyright © 1991 by Bruce McMillan. SCHOLASTIC HARDCOVER is a registered trademark of Scholastic Inc.

Simon & Schuster Books for Young Readers, an imprint of Simon & Schuster Children's Publishing Division: Cover illustration from *Clocks and More Clocks* by Pat Hutchins. Copyright © 1970 by Pat Hutchins. Cover illustration by Sharon McGinley-Nally from *Pigs Will Be Pigs* by Amy Axelrod. Illustration copyright © 1994 by Sharon McGinley-Nally.

Viking Penguin, a division of Penguin Putnam Inc.: Cover illustration by Leo and Diane Dillon: from *The Hundred Penny Box* by Sharon Bell Mathis. Illustration copyright © 1975 by Leo and Diane Dillon.

Albert Whitman & Company: Cover illustration from *Two of Everything* by Lily Toy Hong. © 1993 by Lily Toy Hong.

© Harcourt

Senior Author

Evan M. Maletsky
Professor of Mathematics
Montclair State University
Upper Montclair, New Jersey

Mathematics Advisor

David G. Wright
Professor of Mathematics
Brigham Young University
Provo, Utah

Authors

Angela Giglio Andrews
Math Teacher, Scott School
Naperville District #203
Naperville, Illinois

Jennie M. Bennett
Instructional Mathematics Supervisor
Houston Independent School District
Houston, Texas

Grace M. Burton
Chair, Department of Curricular Studies
Professor, School of Education
University of North Carolina at Wilmington
Wilmington, North Carolina

Howard C. Johnson
Dean of the Graduate School
Associate Vice Chancellor for Academic Affairs
Professor, Mathematics and Mathematics
* Education*
Syracuse University
Syracuse, New York

Lynda A. Luckie
Administrator/Math Specialist
Gwinnett County Public Schools
Lawrenceville, Georgia

Joyce C. McLeod
Visiting Professor
Rollins College
Winter Park, Florida

Vicki Newman
Classroom Teacher
McGaugh Elementary School
Los Alamitos Unified School District
Seal Beach, California

Janet K. Scheer
Executive Director
Create A Vision
Foster City, California

Karen A. Schultz
College of Education
Georgia State University
Atlanta, Georgia

Program Consultants and Specialists

Janet S. Abbott
Mathematics Consultant
California

Elsie Babcock
Director, Mathematics and
* Science Center*
Mathematics Consultant
Wayne Regional Educational
  Service Agency
Wayne, Michigan

William J. Driscoll
Professor of Mathematics
Department of Mathematical
  Sciences
Central Connecticut State
  University
New Britain, Connecticut

Lois Harrison-Jones
Education and Management
* Consultant*
Dallas, Texas

Arax Miller
Curriculum Coordinator and
* English Department*
* Chairperson*
Chamlian School
Glendale, California

Rebecca Valbuena
Language Development
* Specialist*
Stanton Elementary School
Glendora, California

iii

Unit 1
CHAPTERS 1–6

NUMBERS, OPERATIONS, AND DATA

© Harcourt

Unit 2

CHAPTERS 7–10

MONEY AND TIME

© Harcourt

Unit Wrap Up

© Harcourt

Unit 3
CHAPTERS 11–16

2-DIGIT ADDITION AND SUBTRACTION

© Harcourt

Unit Wrap Up

© Harcourt

Unit 4
CHAPTERS 17–20

GEOMETRY AND MEASUREMENT

Unit Wrap Up

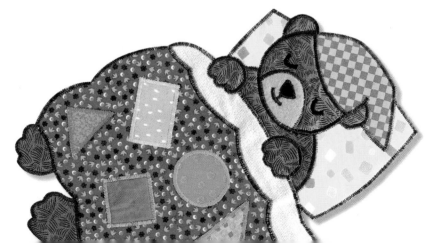

Unit 5
CHAPTERS 21–24

NUMBER SENSE AND FRACTIONS

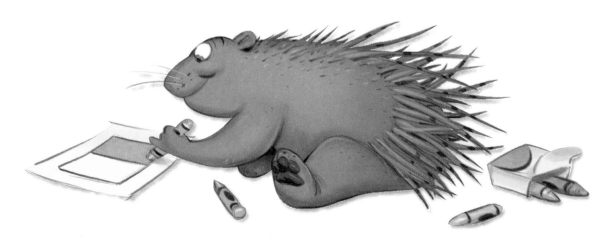

Unit 6

CHAPTERS 25–30

3-DIGIT ADDITION AND SUBTRACTION, MULTIPLICATION AND DIVISION

Unit Wrap Up

$7.00

© Harcourt

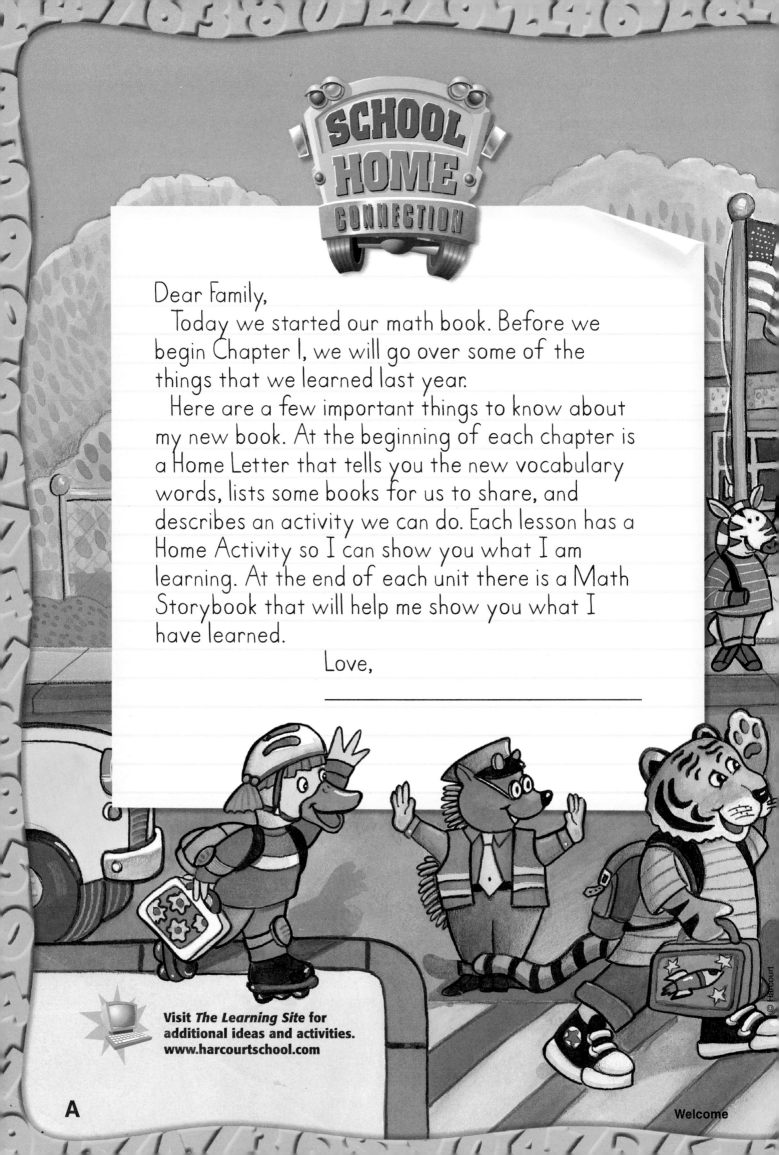

SCHOOL HOME CONNECTION

Dear Family,

Today we started our math book. Before we begin Chapter 1, we will go over some of the things that we learned last year.

Here are a few important things to know about my new book. At the beginning of each chapter is a Home Letter that tells you the new vocabulary words, lists some books for us to share, and describes an activity we can do. Each lesson has a Home Activity so I can show you what I am learning. At the end of each unit there is a Math Storybook that will help me show you what I have learned.

Love,

_____

Visit *The Learning Site* for additional ideas and activities. www.harcourtschool.com

A

Welcome

Getting Ready for Grade 2

Hi! Welcome to second grade. Let's show your teacher some of the things you learned last year.

School Bus

◆ **HOME ACTIVITY** • In *Getting Ready*, your child will review ones and tens of the place value system, add and subtract basic facts, and measure and locate objects in space. Your child will describe data and solve simple problems.

Name _____

Count by twos. Color each number .
Count by fives. Circle each number.

1

1	2	3	4	5	6	7	8	9	10
11	12	13	14	15	16	17	18	19	20
21	22	23	24	25	26	27	28	29	30
31	32	33	34	35	36	37	38	39	40
41	42	43	44	45	46	47	48	49	50

Circle the statements that are correct.

2

$83 > 81$	$46 = 40 + 6$	$5 = 50$
$59 > 95$	$75 > 45$	$32 > 31$

C

Skip-Count

Name _____

Write the number that tells how many.

1

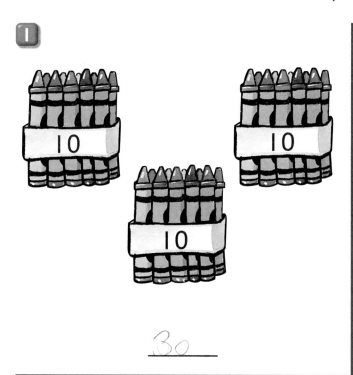

_30_

2

_____

Draw base ten blocks to show how many.

3

| 14 | 41 | 50 |

© Harcourt

Name _____

Add or subtract.

4 + 2 = _____   10 − 2 = _____   7 + 2 = _____

6 + 1 = _____   9 − 1 = _____   9 − 2 = _____

8 + 2 = _____   7 − 3 = _____   9 + 1 = _____

7 + 3 = _____   8 − 4 = _____   5 + 5 = _____

4 + 4 = _____   8 − 8 = _____   10 − 4 = _____

4 + 5 = _____   10 − 3 = _____   9 − 6 = _____

6 + 3 = _____   6 − 4 = _____   6 + 2 = _____

8 + 0 = _____   9 − 5 = _____   10 − 7 = _____

E   **Addition and Subtraction**

Name _____

Use ⚪. Draw them.
Write the number sentence.

Three boys. Three girls.
How many children in all?

1

_____ ◯ _____ = _____ children

Write the number sentence.

There are 9 birds. 4 birds leave.
How many birds are left?

2

_____ ◯ _____ = _____ birds

Problem Solving

F

Name _____

About how long is the string? Use ⊂▭⊃.

1 ▨▨▨▨▨▨▨▨▨▨▨▨▨▨▨▨▨▨▨▨▨▨▨▨▨▨▨▨   ___ ⊂▭⊃

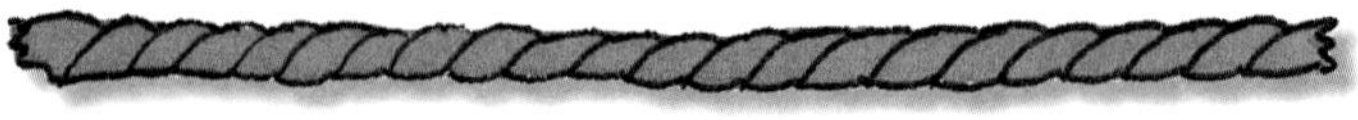

2 ▨▨▨▨▨▨▨▨▨▨▨▨▨▨▨▨▨▨▨▨▨▨▨▨▨▨▨▨▨▨▨▨   ___ ⊂▭⊃

Use the chart.
Make a bar graph.

3

Favorite Colors	
red	JHT III
yellow	III
blue	JHT I

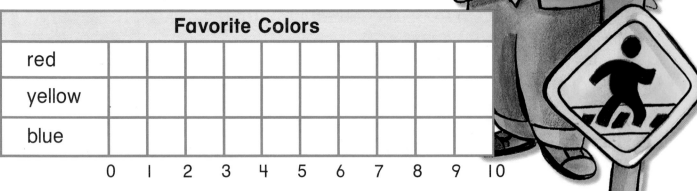

Favorite Colors										
red										
yellow										
blue										

        0   1   2   3   4   5   6   7   8   9   10

Measurement and Graphing

© Harcourt

Name _____

Follow the directions.

1️⃣ Draw a red square.

2️⃣ Draw a large green triangle above the red square.

3️⃣ Draw a small blue circle below the red square.

Use the same shapes to make a different pattern. Draw your new pattern.

4️⃣

Patterns

Talk About
How do you know
Tell how you solved

Name _____

Show a way to solve this problem.

I have some teddy bears. I gave 3 of them away. Now I have 7. How many teddy bears did I have to start?

I had __10__ teddy bears to start.

bout It

ow that your answer makes sense?
this problem.

CHAPTER 1 Addition Strategies

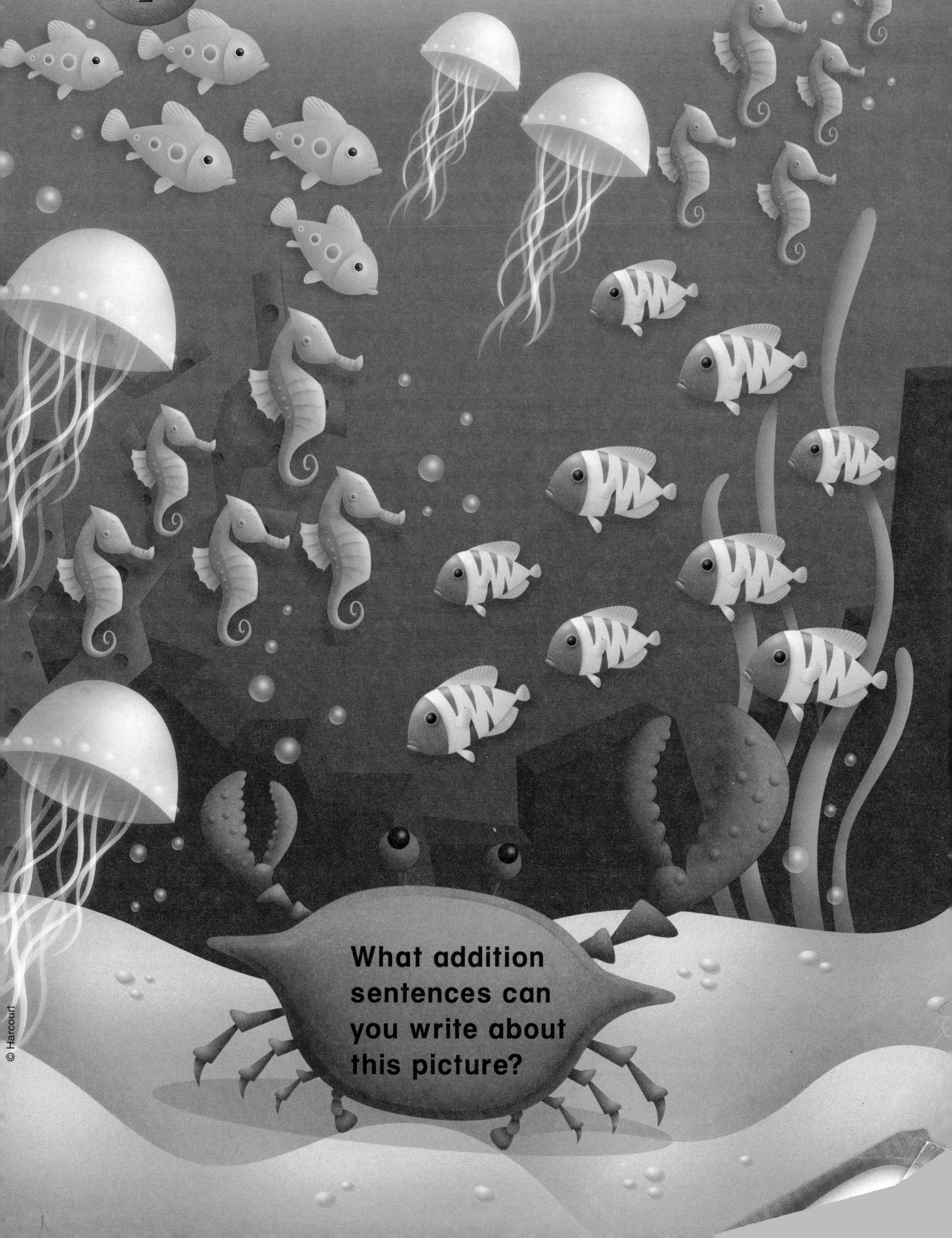

What addition sentences can you write about this picture?

SCHOOL HOME CONNECTION

Dear Family,
   Today we started Chapter 1. We will learn addition facts to 20. We will also learn addition strategies to help us solve problems. Here is the math vocabulary and an activity for us to do together at home.

Love,

_____

My Math Words
doubles plus one
sum

Vocabulary

doubles plus one Addition facts whose sums are one more than the sum of a doubles fact

doubles
$7 + 7 = 14$

doubles plus one
$7 + 8 = 15$

sum The sum is the answer when numbers are added.

ACTIVITY

Fold a piece of paper into four sections, and write one of these problems in each section.

$3 + 6 =$ ___ $4 + 3 =$ ___

$5 + 2 =$ ___ $7 + 3 =$ ___

Have your child draw pictures to find each sum.

Books to Share

To read about addition with your child, look for these books in your local library.

Two of Everything, by Lily Toy Hong, Albert Whitman, 1993.

The Pig in the Pond, by Martin Waddell, Candlewick, 1996.

Visit *The Learning Site* for additional ideas and activities.
www.harcourtschool.com

Name _____

Follow the directions.

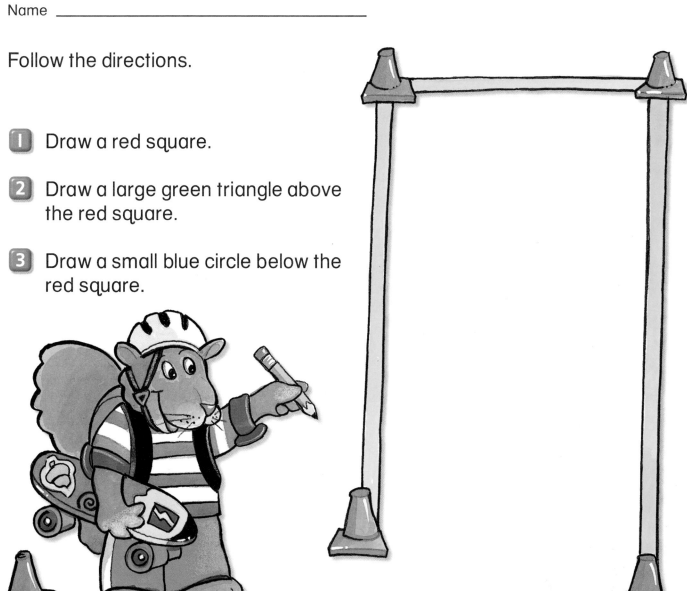

1 Draw a red square.

2 Draw a large green triangle above the red square.

3 Draw a small blue circle below the red square.

Use the same shapes to make a different pattern.
Draw your new pattern .

4

Patterns

Name _____

Show a way to solve this problem.

I have some teddy bears. I gave 3 of them away. Now I have 7. How many teddy bears did I have to start?

I had __10__ teddy bears to start.

Talk About It

How do you know that your answer makes sense?
Tell how you solved this problem.

I

> Changing the **order** of the **addends** does not change the **sum**.

> Any number plus **zero** **equals** the same number.

$8 + 4 =$ __12__

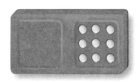

$9 + 0 =$ __9__

$4 + 8 =$ __12__

$0 + 9 =$ __9__

Write the sum.

1
$5 + 4 =$ __9__
$4 + 5 =$ __9__

2
$10 + 0 =$ __10__
$0 + 10 =$ __10__

3
$7 + 5 =$ __12__
$5 + 7 =$ __12__

4
$6 + 4 =$ __10__
$4 + 6 =$ __10__

5
$3 + 9 =$ __12__
$9 + 3 =$ __12__

6
$0 + 11 =$ __11__
$11 + 0 =$ __11__

7
$0 + 8 =$ __8__
$8 + 0 =$ __8__

8
$4 + 7 =$ __11__
$7 + 4 =$ __11__

9
$6 + 0 =$ __6__
$0 + 6 =$ __6__

Talk About It ▪ Reasoning

What happens to the sum when you change the order of the addends?
What happens when you add a number to zero?

 5 +2 = 7

2 +5 = 7

0 +5 = 5

 5 +0 = 5

Write the sum.

1
3 +2 = 5

2 +3 = 5

2
12 + 0 = 12

0 +12 = 12

3
4 +1 = 5

1 +4 = 5

4
6 +3 = 4

3 +6 = 9

5
8 +2 = 10

2 +8 = 10

6
6 +5 = 8

5 +6 = 11

Problem Solving ▪ Visual Thinking

7 Color these cubes to show $3 + 6 = 9$.

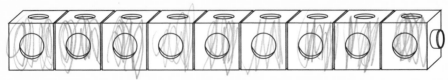

Tell how you would change the colors to show $6 + 3 = 9$.

HOME ACTIVITY • Have your child use small objects to show an addition fact. Change the order of the addends, and have your child show the new fact.

4 four

Chapter 1

© Harcourt

Name _____

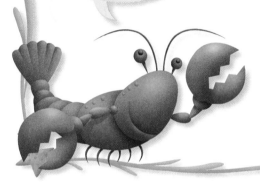

Start with the **greater** number. **Count on** to find the sum.

Say 8.
Count on 1.
9
The sum is 9.

$$\begin{array}{r} 8 \\ +1 \\ \hline 9 \end{array}$$

Say 8.
Count on 2.
9, 10
The sum is 10.

$$\begin{array}{r} 8 \\ +2 \\ \hline 10 \end{array}$$

Say 8.
Count on 3.
9, 10, 11
The sum is 11.

$$\begin{array}{r} 8 \\ +3 \\ \hline 11 \end{array}$$

Circle the greater number.
Count on to find the sum.

1.

$$\begin{array}{r} 9 \\ +1 \\ \hline \end{array} \qquad \begin{array}{r} 9 \\ +2 \\ \hline \end{array} \qquad \begin{array}{r} 9 \\ +3 \\ \hline \end{array} \qquad \begin{array}{r} 2 \\ +7 \\ \hline \end{array} \qquad \begin{array}{r} 8 \\ +2 \\ \hline \end{array} \qquad \begin{array}{r} 3 \\ +9 \\ \hline \end{array}$$

2.

$$\begin{array}{r} 7 \\ +1 \\ \hline \end{array} \qquad \begin{array}{r} 2 \\ +7 \\ \hline \end{array} \qquad \begin{array}{r} 7 \\ +3 \\ \hline \end{array} \qquad \begin{array}{r} 1 \\ +8 \\ \hline \end{array} \qquad \begin{array}{r} 2 \\ +9 \\ \hline \end{array} \qquad \begin{array}{r} 2 \\ +10 \\ \hline \end{array}$$

3.

$$\begin{array}{r} 10 \\ +3 \\ \hline \end{array} \qquad \begin{array}{r} 8 \\ +3 \\ \hline \end{array} \qquad \begin{array}{r} 2 \\ +6 \\ \hline \end{array} \qquad \begin{array}{r} 8 \\ +1 \\ \hline \end{array} \qquad \begin{array}{r} 3 \end{array}$$

HOME ACTIVITY

Talk About It ■ Reasoning

Why is it easier to start with the greater number when counting on?

Chapter 1 • Addition Strategies

Practice

$3 + 9 = 12$

Circle the greater number.
Count on to find the sum.

1 $3 + 9 = \underline{12}$

2 $9 + 2 = \underline{\hspace{1cm}}$

3 $1 + 9 = \underline{\hspace{1cm}}$

4 $2 + 9 = \underline{\hspace{1cm}}$

5 $7 + 2 = \underline{\hspace{1cm}}$

6 $10 + 1 = \underline{\hspace{1cm}}$

7 $1 + 4 = \underline{\hspace{1cm}}$

8 $4 + 2 = \underline{\hspace{1cm}}$

9 $3 + 4 = \underline{\hspace{1cm}}$

10 $3 + 10 = \underline{\hspace{1cm}}$

11 $1 + 8 = \underline{\hspace{1cm}}$

12 $9 + 2 = \underline{\hspace{1cm}}$

13 $6 + 2 = \underline{\hspace{1cm}}$

14 $4 + 3 = \underline{\hspace{1cm}}$

15 $2 + 8 = \underline{\hspace{1cm}}$

16 $6 + 1 = \underline{\hspace{1cm}}$

17 $2 + 5 = \underline{\hspace{1cm}}$

18 $10 + 2 = \underline{\hspace{1cm}}$

Problem Solving ■ Mental Math

Find the sum.

19 Rob has 7 shirts. Ed has 2 more than Rob. How many shirts does Ed have?

_____ shirts

20 Susan has 3 pennies. Mary has 5 more than Susan. How many pennies does Mary have?

_____ pennies

Have your child tell an addition story for each picture in this lesson.

Name _Sophia_

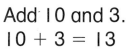

Make a Ten

Add 8 + 5.

Use a ten frame. Put in 8 counters. Put 5 counters outside.	Then **make a ten**. Move 2 counters to fill the ten frame. 8 + 2 = 10	Add 10 and 3. 10 + 3 = 13
	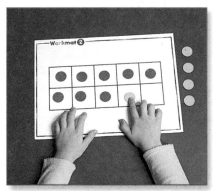	

$$\begin{array}{r} 8 \\ +5 \\ \hline \end{array}$$

$$\begin{array}{r} 10 \\ +\ 3 \\ \hline 13 \end{array}$$

Use a ten frame and ⬤ to make a ten.
Find the sum.

1.

$$\begin{array}{r} 8 \\ +5 \\ \hline 13 \end{array} \quad \begin{array}{r} 7 \\ +6 \\ \hline 13 \end{array} \quad \begin{array}{r} 6 \\ +9 \\ \hline 15 \end{array} \quad \begin{array}{r} 4 \\ +6 \\ \hline 10 \end{array} \quad \begin{array}{r} 8 \\ +4 \\ \hline 12 \end{array} \quad \begin{array}{r} 8 \\ +6 \\ \hline 14 \end{array}$$

2.

$$\begin{array}{r} 3 \\ +7 \\ \hline 10 \end{array} \quad \begin{array}{r} 9 \\ +2 \\ \hline 11 \end{array} \quad \begin{array}{r} 7 \\ +7 \\ \hline 14 \end{array} \quad \begin{array}{r} 4 \\ +8 \\ \hline 12 \end{array} \quad \begin{array}{r} 5 \\ +7 \\ \hline 12 \end{array} \quad \begin{array}{r} 9 \\ +8 \\ \hline 12 \end{array}$$

3.

$$\begin{array}{r} 8 \\ +7 \\ \hline 51 \end{array} \quad \begin{array}{r} 9 \\ +4 \\ \hline 13 \end{array} \quad \begin{array}{r} 5 \\ +9 \\ \hline 14 \end{array} \quad \begin{array}{r} 6 \\ +6 \\ \hline 12 \end{array} \quad \begin{array}{r} 4 \\ +7 \\ \hline 11 \end{array} \quad \begin{array}{r} 8 \\ +3 \\ \hline 12 \end{array}$$

Talk About It ▪ Reasoning

When you set up an addition problem, why do
you put the greater number in the ten frame?

$$\begin{array}{r} 5 \\ +8 \\ \hline ? \end{array}$$

Think
10
+3

Use a ten frame and ⬤ to find the sum.

1

5	8	9	5	9	8
+8	+6	+6	+9	+8	+7
13	14	15	16	17	15

2

9	8	9	7	3	7
+2	+4	+7	+7	+8	+6
11	12	16	14	11	13

3

5	4	4	9	5	8
+7	+9	+7	+3	+6	+2
12	13	11	12	11	10

4

6	7	9	8	9	4
+5	+9	+4	+8	+5	+6
11	16	13	16	14	10

Problem Solving ▪ Visual Thinking

Draw a picture of how you would use a ten frame to solve this problem.

5 Megan has 10 shells. 7 shells are pink and the rest are orange. How many orange shells does Megan have?

_____3_____ orange shells

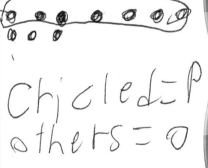

Chicled=P
others=0

 HOME ACTIVITY • Ask your child how he or she used a ten frame to find the sums on this page.

© Harcourt

Add 3 Numbers  Algebra

You can add three numbers in different ways.

Choose two numbers to add first.
Look for facts you know.

$7 + 2 + 3 = 12$	$7 + 2 + 3 = 12$	$7 + 2 + 3 = 12$
$9 + 3 = 12$	$7 + 5 = 12$	$10 + 2 = 12$

Circle the addends you add first. Write the sum.

$8 + 1$ $6 + 3$

1. $(6 + 2) + 1 = \underline{9}$ $6 + (2 + 1) = \underline{9}$

2. $(5 + 3) + 4 = \underline{12}$ $(5 + 3) + 4 = \underline{12}$

3. $(4 + 2) + 7 = \underline{13}$ $(4 + 2) + 7 = \underline{13}$

4. $(4 + 5) + 4 = \underline{13}$ $(4 + 5) + 4 = \underline{13}$

5. $(6 + 6) + 2 = \underline{14}$ $(6 + 6) + 2 = \underline{14}$

6. $6 + (7 + 3) = \underline{16}$ $(6 + 7) + 3 = \underline{16}$

Talk About It ■ Reasoning

How do you decide which two addends to add first?

Write the sum.

1

```
  3          3              3              3
  8 ——→ 11   8 ——→ 15       8 ——→ 10       8 ——→ 10
 +7        + 7             +7   + 3         +7   + 8
           ‒‒‒             ‒‒‒  ‒‒‒         ‒‒‒  ‒‒‒
            18                   18               18
```

2

```
  5        9        1        1        6        3
  4        8        7        8        1        7
 +5       +1       +7       +1       +7       +2
 ‒‒       ‒‒       ‒‒       ‒‒       ‒‒       ‒‒
 14       18       15       10       14       12
```

3

```
  2        4        2        5        5        9
  7        5        8        2        3        1
 +2       +4       +5       +5       +3       +7
 ‒‒       ‒‒       ‒‒       ‒‒       ‒‒       ‒‒
 11       14       15       12       11       17
```

Problem Solving ■ Reasoning

4 Draw grapes on the 3 plates.

Ari eats the grapes on the first two plates and Jane eats the grapes on the third plate. How many grapes do they eat altogether? 16

_____ grapes

If Ari eats the grapes on the first plate and Jane eats the grapes on the other two plates, how many grapes do they eat altogether? 16

_____ grapes

Are your answers the same? Why or why not?

8 grapes

5 grapes

6 grapes

HOME ACTIVITY • Ask your child how he or she decided which two addends to add first.

Name _____

UNDERSTAND ⟩ PLAN ⟩ SOLVE ⟩ CHECK

Solve.

Kim finds 3 shells on Monday.
She finds double that many shells on Tuesday.
How many shells does she find in all?
Here are some steps to help you
solve the problem.

UNDERSTAND

Read the problem. Draw a line
under what you want to find out.
Circle the facts that are given.

PLAN

You can draw a picture to find out
how many shells Kim finds in all.

SOLVE

Draw  to show how many shells
Kim finds on Monday.
Draw to show how many shells
Kim finds on Tuesday.

Write a number sentence to go with the picture.

$$\underline{3} + \underline{6} = \underline{9}$$ shells

CHECK

Read the problem again.
Tell a classmate how your picture shows the answer.

Use the four steps to solve the problem.
Draw a picture. Write a number sentence.

1 Sam collects 5 brown shells and 4
white shells. How many shells
does he collect?

$5 + 4 = 9$ ____ shells

2 Nan sees 8 crabs. Then 4 crabs
join them. How many crabs
does Nan see altogether?

_____ ◯ _____ ◯ _____ crabs

3 Pat sees 6 large starfish and 4 small
starfish. How many starfish
does he see in all?

_____ ◯ _____ ◯ _____ starfish

4 Gina catches 9 fish. Bob catches
double that number. How many
fish does Bob catch?

_____ ◯ _____ ◯ _____ fish

Write About It

Make up an addition story about goldfish in a bowl.
Draw a picture to show your story.

HOME ACTIVITY • Have your child explain the four steps he or she would use to solve a problem.

Name _____

CHECK ▪ Concepts and Skills

Write the sum.

1 $5 + 0 = $ _____

$0 + 5 = $ _____

Circle the greater number.
Count on to find the sum.

2 $\begin{array}{r} 7 \\ +2 \\ \hline \end{array}$ $\begin{array}{r} 3 \\ +6 \\ \hline \end{array}$ $\begin{array}{r} 4 \\ +1 \\ \hline \end{array}$

Write the sum. Write the doubles-plus-one sum.

3 $4 + 4 = $ _____

$4 + 5 = $ _____

4 $6 + 6 = $ _____

$6 + 7 = $ _____

Use a ten frame and ⬤
to make a ten. Find the sum.

5 $\begin{array}{r} 9 \\ +5 \\ \hline \end{array}$ $\begin{array}{r} 6 \\ +8 \\ \hline \end{array}$ $\begin{array}{r} 8 \\ +7 \\ \hline \end{array}$

Circle the addends you add first.
Write the sum.

6 $\begin{array}{r} 3 \\ 3 \\ +5 \\ \hline \end{array}$ $\begin{array}{r} 2 \\ 6 \\ +4 \\ \hline \end{array}$ $\begin{array}{r} 6 \\ 5 \\ +3 \\ \hline \end{array}$

CHECK ▪ Problem Solving

Draw a picture to solve.
Write a number sentence.

7 Jon has 7 red crayons.
He has 4 blue crayons.
How many crayons
does he have in all?

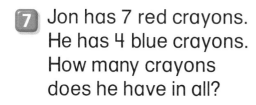 

_____ ◯ _____ = _____ crayons

© Harcourt

Name _____

Choose the best answer for questions 1–4.

1 Which numbers have the same sum as 1 + 2?

4 + 1   1 + 4   2 + 1   6 + 2
○   ○   ○   ○

2 Which numbers have the same sum as 0 + 5?

5 + 0   0 + 4   5 + 1   1 + 6
○   ○   ○   ○

3 What is the sum?   4 + 1 + 4 = _____

6   9   10   12
○   ○   ○   ○

4 Dan has 6 fish in his fish tank. He adds 4 more.
How many fish are in the fish tank now?

2 fish   3 fish   9 fish   10 fish
○   ○   ○   ○

Show What You Know

5 Draw a picture of doubles.
Write the number sentence.

Draw the doubles-plus-one.
Write the number sentence.

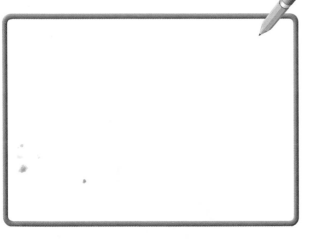

____○____○____   ____○____○____

CHAPTER 2 Subtraction Strategies

What fact family is shown by the horses in this picture?

SCHOOL HOME CONNECTION

Dear Family,
 Today we started Chapter 2. We will subtract from numbers up to 20. Here is the math vocabulary and an activity for us to do together at home

 Love,

 _____

Vocabulary

A **fact family** is a group of addition and subtraction facts that use the same numbers.

Here is the fact family for 7, 8, and 15:

$$7 + 8 = 15 \qquad 8 + 7 = 15$$
$$15 - 7 = 8 \qquad 15 - 8 = 7$$

Ask your child to write fact families.

difference The answer to a subtraction problem is the difference.

Visit *The Learning Site* for additional ideas and activities. www.harcourtschool.com

ACTIVITY

Place 20 small objects in a paper bag. Have your child remove some of the objects and say how many are left in the bag. Have your child look in the bag to count, and then have him or her say and write the subtraction sentence. Repeat with fewer than 20 objects.

Books to Share

To read about addition and subtraction with your child, look for these books in your local library.

Sea Sums, by Joy Hulme, Hyperion Books, 1996.

Window, by Jeannie Baker, HarperCollins, 1991.

© Harcourt

6 blue   7 red

13 in all

> 6, 7, and 13 are the numbers in this **fact family**.

$$\underline{6} + \underline{7} = \underline{13} \quad | \quad \underline{7} + \underline{6} = \underline{13}$$

$$\underline{13} - \underline{6} = \underline{7} \quad | \quad \underline{13} - \underline{7} = \underline{6}$$

Write the fact family for the set of numbers.

1   8   9

17

_____ + _____ = _____   _____ + _____ = _____

_____ − _____ = _____   _____ − _____ = _____

2   6   8

14

_____ + _____ = _____   _____ + _____ = _____

_____ − _____ = _____   _____ − _____ = _____

Talk About It ■ Reasoning

How many different number sentences can you write for the set of numbers 6, 6, and 12? Why?

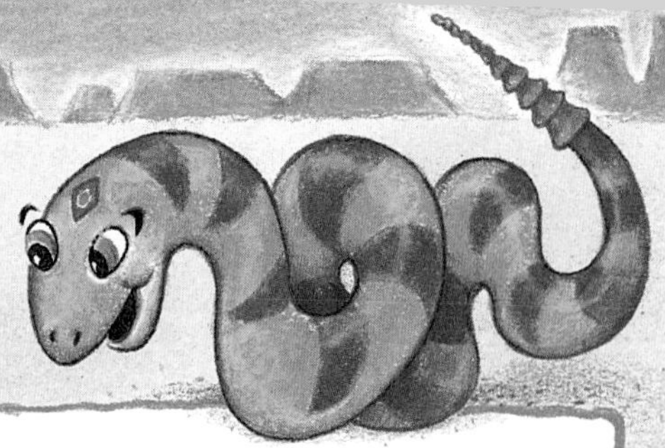

Write the fact family for the set of numbers.

1

```
    4
 +  8
 ‾‾‾‾
   12
```

```
    8
 +  4
 ‾‾‾‾
   12
```

12
8   4

```
   12
 -  8
 ‾‾‾‾
    4
```

```
   12
 -  4
 ‾‾‾‾
    8
```

2

```
 +
 ‾‾‾‾
```

```
 +
 ‾‾‾‾
```

16
9   7

```
 -
 ‾‾‾‾
```

```
 -
 ‾‾‾‾
```

3

```
 +
 ‾‾‾‾
```

```
 +
 ‾‾‾‾
```

15
7   8

```
 -
 ‾‾‾‾
```

```
 -
 ‾‾‾‾
```

4

```
 +
 ‾‾‾‾
```

```
 +
 ‾‾‾‾
```

11
4   7

```
 -
 ‾‾‾‾
```

```
 -
 ‾‾‾‾
```

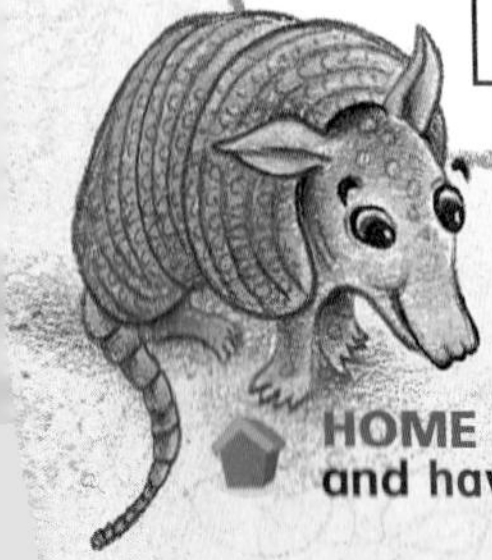

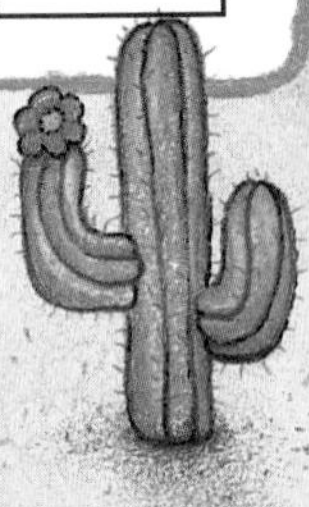

HOME ACTIVITY • Give your child the numbers 5, 7, and 12, and have him or her write the fact family.

UNDERSTAND > PLAN > SOLVE > CHECK

Problem Solving
Use Logical Reasoning

Which statements equal 9?
Which statements do not?

Knowing the mental math strategies can help you solve the problem.

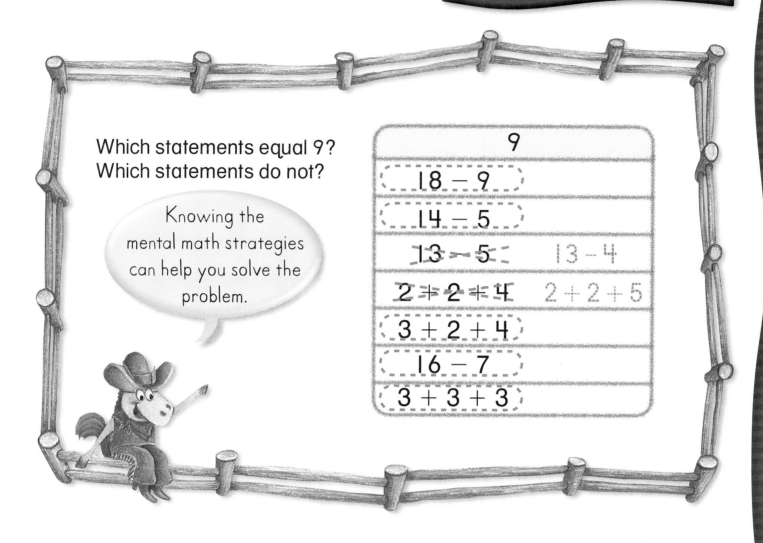

9
18 − 9
14 − 5
13 − 5   13 − 4
2 + 2 + 4   2 + 2 + 5
3 + 2 + 4
16 − 7
3 + 3 + 3

Circle the statements that equal the number at the top. Cross out others. Correct those statements.

1
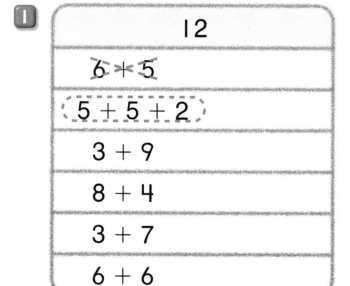

12
6 + 5
5 + 5 + 2
3 + 9
8 + 4
3 + 7
6 + 6

2
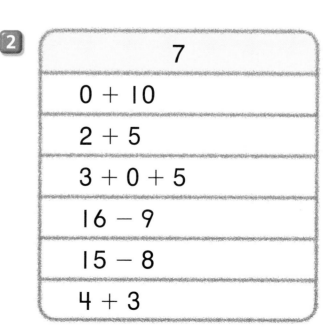

7
0 + 10
2 + 5
3 + 0 + 5
16 − 9
15 − 8
4 + 3

© Harcourt

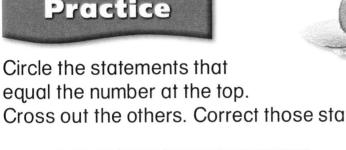

Practice

Circle the statements that equal the number at the top.
Cross out the others. Correct those statements.

1

14
(14 + 0)
7 + 9
17 − 3
7 + 4 + 2
14 − 0
7 + 7

2

11
1 + 5 + 5
5 + 6
12 − 1
6 + 2 + 2
6 + 6
14 − 3

3

10
13 − 3
10 + 1
5 + 5
7 + 4
15 − 5
11 − 1

4

6
4 + 2 + 2
6 − 0
10 − 3
12 − 7
3 + 3
5 + 1

Algebra

Write + or −. Make each equal 6.

5 13 ◯ 7   4 ◯ 2   14 ◯ 8   2 ◯ 2 ◯ 2

© Harcourt

🏠 **HOME ACTIVITY** • Ask your child to show three ways to get a sum of 10 and three ways to get a difference of 10.

Chapter 2

Name _____

CHECK ▪ Concepts and Skills

Subtract.

1 $3 - 3 =$ **0** $7 - 0 =$ **7** $8 - 0 =$ _____

2 $9 - 9 =$ **0** $11 - 0 =$ _____ $12 - 12 =$ _____

Count back to find the difference.

3 $7 - 2 =$ _____ $8 - 1 =$ _____ $5 - 3 =$ _____

Use . Add or subtract.

4
$$\begin{array}{r} 7 \\ +2 \\ \hline \end{array}$$
$$\begin{array}{r} 9 \\ -2 \\ \hline \end{array}$$
$$\begin{array}{r} 6 \\ +3 \\ \hline \end{array}$$
$$\begin{array}{r} 9 \\ -6 \\ \hline \end{array}$$

5 Write the fact family for the set of numbers.

6   5

11

_____ + _____ = _____

_____ − _____ = _____

_____ + _____ = _____

_____ − _____ = _____

CHECK ▪ Problem Solving

6 Circle the statements that equal the number at the top. Cross out the others. Correct those statements.

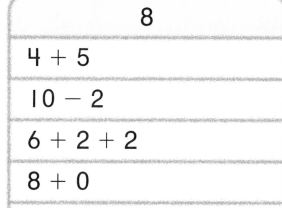

8
$4 + 5$
$10 - 2$
$6 + 2 + 2$
$8 + 0$
$9 - 1$
$16 - 8$

© Harcourt

Name _____

Choose the best answer for questions 1–5.

1   9 − 9 = _____

0   9   18   19
○   ○   ○   ○

2   5 − 0 = _____

0   5   10   11
○   ○   ○   ○

3 Which addition fact can help you solve this subtraction fact?

8 − 2 = 6

3 + 5 = 8   7 + 1 = 8   6 + 2 = 8   6 − 2 = 4
○   ○   ○   ○

4 Which is **not** a way to make 13?

14 − 1   6 + 7   10 + 3   12 − 1
○   ○   ○   ○

5 Ricco sees 14 cows in a field. Five of the cows are brown.
The rest are white. How many cows are white?

8   9   10   19
○   ○   ○   ○

Show What You Know

6 Color some of the cubes blue and some red.
Write the number sentences that are in the fact family.

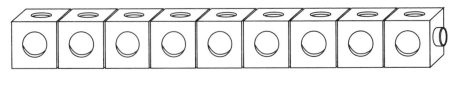

_____ ○ _____ ○ _____   _____ ○ _____ ○ _____

 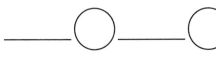

© Harcourt

Each team has 10 runners. How many from each team have not crossed the finish line?

Finish

SCHOOL HOME CONNECTION

Dear Family,
    Today we started Chapter 3. We will practice addition and subtraction strategies. Here is the math vocabulary and an activity for us to do together at home.

    Love,

_____

My Math Words

missing number

Vocabulary

A **missing number** is a number missing from the first part of an addition or subtraction sentence.

For example, in 7 + _____ = 15, the missing number is 8.

Give your child some problems like this to solve.

ACTIVITY

Read a book to your child, and ask him or her to make up a number problem about the characters in the story. Your child should draw a picture of the problem and then write a number sentence to solve.

Books to Share

To read about addition and subtraction with your child, look for these books in your local library.

Ready, Set, Hop!,
by Stuart J. Murphy,
HarperCollins, 1996.

Animals on Board,
by Stuart J. Murphy,
HarperCollins, 1998.

Each Orange Had 8 Slices,
by Paul Giganti Jr.,
William Morrow & Company, 1999.

Visit *The Learning Site* for additional ideas and activities.
www.harcourtschool.com

© Harcourt

Addition Facts

Add in any order.
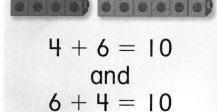
4 + 6 = 10
and
6 + 4 = 10

Use doubles.
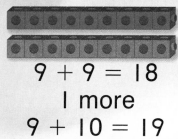
9 + 9 = 18
1 more
9 + 10 = 19

Make a ten.

10 + 6 = 16
so
9 + 7 = 16

Count on.
8 + 3 = 11

5 6 7 8 9 10 11 12

Say 8. Count on 3.
9, 10, 11

Add zero.
10 + 0 = 10

Add three numbers.
6 + 4 + 3 = 13
10 + 3 = 13

Write the sum.

1

10	1	7	5	8	2
+1	+10	+5	+7	+2	+8
11	11				

2

7	7	8	9	9	9
+7	+8	+8	+8	+9	+10

3

10	8	9	9	7	6
+3	+2	+1	+3	+1	+0

4 7 + 2 + 5 = _____

5 4 + 6 + 6 = _____

Talk About It ▪ Reasoning

Choose one of the rows. What strategy did you use to solve each problem? Explain your thinking.

© Harcourt

Write the sum.

1 Use doubles.

8	16
5	
10	
9	

2 Use doubles plus one.

6	
8	
4	

3 Add 0.

12	
5	
10	
7	

4 Count on 1.

7	
4	
11	
9	

5 Count on 2.

8	
10	
7	
5	

6 Count on 3.

7	
8	
9	
10	

Problem Solving ▪ Reasoning

7 Sharon made a ten to find the sums. What mistake did she make each time? Correct her mistakes.

$$\begin{array}{r} 9 \\ +8 \\ \hline 16 \end{array} \qquad \begin{array}{r} 9 \\ +5 \\ \hline 13 \end{array} \qquad \begin{array}{r} 9 \\ +6 \\ \hline 14 \end{array}$$

HOME ACTIVITY • Each day, work with your child to practice facts with a given sum. For example, on Monday, practice all of the facts with a sum of 15.

© Harcourt

$7 + \underline{} = 15$ 	 $15 - 7 = \underline{}$

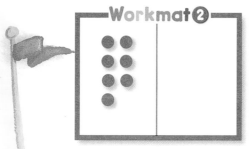

You can use subtraction to find the missing number

$7 + \underline{8} = 15$ 	 $15 - 7 = \underline{8}$

Write the missing number. Use counters if you need to.

1 $6 + \underline{4} = 10$ 	 $10 - 6 = \underline{}$

2 $\underline{} + 9 = 12$ 	 $12 - 9 = \underline{}$

3 $7 + \underline{} = 14$ 	 $14 - 7 = \underline{}$

4 $\underline{} + 5 = 11$ 	 $11 - 5 = \underline{}$

5 $8 + \underline{} = 16$ 	 $16 - 8 = \underline{}$

6 $\underline{} + 9 = 13$ 	 $13 - 9 = \underline{}$

7 $6 + \underline{} = 15$ 	 $15 - 6 = \underline{}$

Talk About It ■ Reasoning

Glen had 15 marbles. He gave some to a friend.
If he has 9 left, how many did he give to his friend? How do you know?

© Harcourt

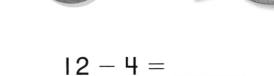

Write the missing number.
Use counters if you need to.

1 4 + __8__ = 12   12 − 4 = _____

2 _____ + 7 = 10   10 − 7 = _____

3 9 + _____ = 16   16 − 9 = _____

4 _____ + 4 = 11   11 − 4 = _____

5 6 + _____ = 14   14 − 6 = _____

6 _____ + 9 = 18   18 − 9 = _____

7 6 + _____ = 14   14 − 6 = _____

8 4 + _____ = 13   13 − 4 = _____

Algebra

Solve.

9 16 − ■ = 8   **10** 5 + ■ = 12   **11** 13 − ■ = 9

■ = _____   ■ = _____   ■ = _____

HOME ACTIVITY • Put 20 small items in a bag. Have your child remove some, count them, and tell how many are left in the bag. Repeat.

© Harcourt

Name _____

There are many ways to subtract.

Subtract zero and all.

$$\begin{array}{r} 13 \\ -\ 0 \\ \hline 13 \end{array} \qquad \begin{array}{r} 10 \\ -10 \\ \hline 0 \end{array}$$

Count back.

$$\begin{array}{r} 12 \\ -\ 3 \\ \hline 9 \end{array}$$

Say 12.
Count back 3.
11, 10, 9

Use doubles.

$$\begin{array}{r} 9 \\ +9 \\ \hline 18 \end{array} \quad \text{so} \quad \begin{array}{r} 18 \\ -\ 9 \\ \hline 9 \end{array}$$

Use addition.

$$8 + 6 = \underline{\ 14\ }$$
$$14 - 6 = \underline{\ 8\ }$$

Subtract.
Choose a strategy.

1

$$\begin{array}{r} 9 \\ -1 \\ \hline 8 \end{array} \qquad \begin{array}{r} 10 \\ -\ 5 \\ \hline \end{array} \qquad \begin{array}{r} 13 \\ -\ 5 \\ \hline \end{array} \qquad \begin{array}{r} 9 \\ -3 \\ \hline \end{array} \qquad \begin{array}{r} 8 \\ -2 \\ \hline \end{array} \qquad \begin{array}{r} 15 \\ -15 \\ \hline \end{array}$$

2

$$\begin{array}{r} 10 \\ -\ 3 \\ \hline \end{array} \qquad \begin{array}{r} 15 \\ -\ 0 \\ \hline \end{array} \qquad \begin{array}{r} 12 \\ -12 \\ \hline \end{array} \qquad \begin{array}{r} 11 \\ -\ 1 \\ \hline \end{array} \qquad \begin{array}{r} 12 \\ -\ 0 \\ \hline \end{array} \qquad \begin{array}{r} 16 \\ -\ 8 \\ \hline \end{array}$$

3

$$\begin{array}{r} 11 \\ -\ 3 \\ \hline \end{array} \qquad \begin{array}{r} 7 \\ -1 \\ \hline \end{array} \qquad \begin{array}{r} 15 \\ -\ 8 \\ \hline \end{array} \qquad \begin{array}{r} 14 \\ -\ 3 \\ \hline \end{array} \qquad \begin{array}{r} 17 \\ -\ 9 \\ \hline \end{array} \qquad \begin{array}{r} 18 \\ -\ 9 \\ \hline \end{array}$$

Talk About It ■ Reasoning

For which problems did you use doubles?
Explain your thinking.

Practice

Solve.
Color the doubles facts 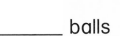.
Color the count-back
facts 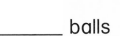.
Color the all and zero
facts any way you like.

$$18 - 9$$

$$13 - 0$$

$$14 - 0$$

$$12 - 6$$

$$13 - 3$$

$$14 - 7$$

$$16 - 8$$

$$15 - 1$$

$$17 - 2$$

$$10 - 5$$

$$19 - 19$$

$$15 - 15$$

$$18 - 3$$

Problem Solving ▪ Visual Thinking

Use the picture to solve.

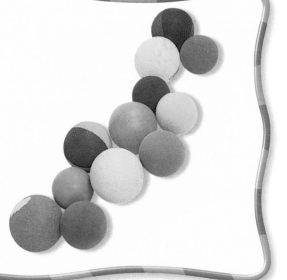

1. What if there were 8 fewer balls? How many balls would there be? _____ balls

2. What if there were 5 fewer balls? How many balls would there be? _____ balls

© Harcourt

🏠 **HOME ACTIVITY** • Each day, work with your child to practice subtracting from a given number. For example, on Monday, practice subtracting from 15.

Name _____

Problem Solving
Write a Number Sentence

There were 15 girls at the game.
Then 6 girls went home.
How many girls were still at the game?

 UNDERSTAND

What do you want to find out?

 PLAN

You can write a number sentence to solve the problem.

 SOLVE

You can draw a picture or make a model.
Then write a number sentence to solve.

 $$15 \ominus 6 = 9$$
girls

 CHECK

Does your answer make sense? Explain.

Draw a picture or make a model.
Write a number sentence to solve.

1 After the game, 9 girls and
7 boys had a picnic. How many
children were at the picnic?

 ____ ◯ ____ = ____
children

2 In the yard, 9 girls played catch.
Then 8 more girls joined them.
How many girls played catch?

 ____ ◯ ____ = ____
girls

Chapter 3 • Addition and Subtraction Practice

© Harcourt

Draw a picture or make a model.
Write a number sentence to solve.

1 At the game, 7 girls and 5 boys cheered. How many children cheered at the game?

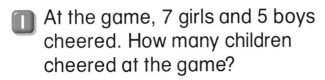

$7 \oplus 5 = 12$

children

2 There were 5 wooden bats and 8 metal bats. How many bats were there in all?

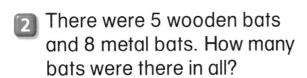

____ ◯ ____ = ____

bats

3 There were 16 girls and 8 boys playing ball. How many more girls than boys were playing ball?

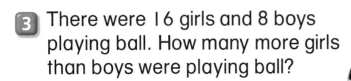

____ ◯ ____ = ____

more girls

4 At the game, 4 girls sat together. Then 9 more girls joined them. How many girls were sitting together?

____ ◯ ____ = ____

girls

Write About It

Make up an addition story or a subtraction story.
Draw a picture to show your story.

🏠 **HOME ACTIVITY** • Make up a story problem for your child to solve.

Name _____

CHECK ▪ Concepts and Skills

Write the sum.

1
$$\begin{array}{r} 4 \\ +4 \\ \hline \end{array}$$
$$\begin{array}{r} 6 \\ +3 \\ \hline \end{array}$$
$$\begin{array}{r} 0 \\ +2 \\ \hline \end{array}$$
$$\begin{array}{r} 5 \\ +3 \\ \hline \end{array}$$
$$\begin{array}{r} 9 \\ +1 \\ \hline \end{array}$$
$$\begin{array}{r} 1 \\ +6 \\ \hline \end{array}$$

2 $4 + 7 + 4 =$ _____ $1 + 9 + 3 =$ _____

Write the missing number. Use counters if you need to.

3

$7 +$ _____ $= 13$

$13 - 7 =$ _____

4

$8 +$ _____ $= 11$

$11 - 8 =$ _____

5

_____ $+ 9 = 12$

$12 - 9 =$ _____

Subtract. Choose a strategy.

6
$$\begin{array}{r} 5 \\ -0 \\ \hline \end{array}$$
$$\begin{array}{r} 10 \\ -5 \\ \hline \end{array}$$
$$\begin{array}{r} 7 \\ -7 \\ \hline \end{array}$$
$$\begin{array}{r} 14 \\ -7 \\ \hline \end{array}$$
$$\begin{array}{r} 7 \\ -2 \\ \hline \end{array}$$
$$\begin{array}{r} 9 \\ -2 \\ \hline \end{array}$$

CHECK ▪ Problem Solving

Draw a picture or make a model.
Write a number sentence to solve.

7 There are 9 apples and 4 oranges in the bowl. How many apples and oranges are in the bowl?

_____ ◯ _____ = _____

Name _____

Choose the best answer for questions 1–7.

1 5 + 3 = _____

   1 ○   8 ○   9 ○   10 ○

2 9 − 3 = _____

   6 ○   7 ○   8 ○   9 ○

3 3 + 7 + 6 = _____

   9 ○   10 ○   15 ○   16 ○

4 11 − _____ = 11

   0 ○   10 ○   11 ○   19 ○

5 8 + _____ = 11

   1 ○   2 ○   3 ○   4 ○

6 17 + 0 = _____

   0 ○   7 ○   17 ○   19 ○

7 There are 9 kick balls and 5 soccer balls in a bag.
How many kick balls and soccer balls are there in the bag?

   4 ○   6 ○   13 ○   14 ○

Show What You Know

8 Write a number less than 9 in the blank.
Color the marbles to match the problem.
Write a number sentence.

Joe had _____ marbles.
He found some more marbles.
Then he had 12 marbles.
How many marbles did he find?

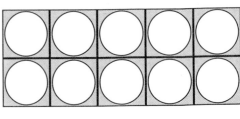

_____ ◯ _____ ◯ _____ marbles

© Harcourt

tens	ones	teen words
10 ten 20 twenty	1 one 2 two	11 eleven 12 twelve
30 thirty 40 forty	3 three 4 four	13 thirteen 14 fourteen
50 fifty 60 sixty	5 five 6 six	15 fifteen 16 sixteen
70 seventy 80 eighty	7 seven 8 eight	17 seventeen 18 eighteen
90 ninety	9 nine	19 nineteen

Read the number.
Write the number in different ways.

1 ninety-six

_9_ tens _6_ ones

_90_ + _6_

_96_

2 eighteen

____ ten ____ ones

____ + ____

____

3 sixty-two

____ tens ____ ones

____ + ____

____

4 fourteen

____ tens ____ ones

____ + ____

____

5 seventy

____ tens ____ ones

____ + ____

____

6 eighty-one

____ tens ____ one

____ + ____

____

7 twenty-three

____ tens ____ ones

____ + ____

____

8 fifty-seven

____ tens ____ ones

____ + ____

____

9 thirteen

____ ten ____ ones

____ + ____

____

Talk About It ▪ Reasoning

In what three ways can you show the number 85?

Read the number.
Write the number in different ways.

1 twenty-five

__2__ tens __5__ ones

__20__ + __5__

__25__

2 thirty-three

____ tens ____ ones

____ + ____

____

3 ninety-one

____ tens ____ one

____ + ____

____

4 fifty-eight

____ tens ____ ones

____ + ____

____

5 forty-seven

____ tens ____ ones

____ + ____

____

6 seventy-four

____ tens ____ ones

____ + ____

____

Mixed Review

About how many are in the first jar?
Circle the best estimate.

7

more than 50

about 50

© Harcourt

 HOME ACTIVITY • Name any number from 1 to 99, for example, 76. Have your child write that number as tens and ones (7 tens 6 ones), in expanded notation (70 + 6), and as a number in standard form (76).

Chapter 4

UNDERSTAND > PLAN > SOLVE > CHECK

Problem Solving
Make Reasonable Estimates

Carol carries her books to school. About how many books could Carol carry?

Circle the number that makes the most sense.

(5)   50   100

Carol could carry about __5__ books.

Circle the most reasonable estimate.

1 The Smiths went away on a short vacation. About how many days might they be away?

5   50   100

2 Carmen put pennies in this jar. About how many pennies might she have?

3   30   100

3 Larry has a handful of marbles. About how many marbles might he have?

10   40   100

4 Hojin has a small fishbowl. About how many fish might he have?

5   20   100

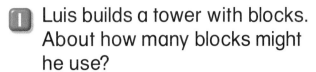

Circle the most reasonable estimate.

1 Luis builds a tower with blocks. About how many blocks might he use?

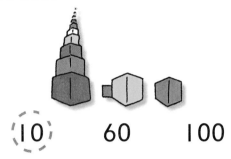

(10)   60   100

2 Emma invited the entire class to her party. About how many children might that be?

5   20   100

3 Greg carried a bag of apples. About how many apples might be in the bag?

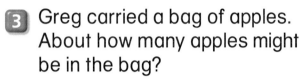

10   50   100

4 Jenny buys a bunch of grapes. About how many grapes might be in a bunch?

5   30   100

5 Kim's stamp book is full. About how many stamps might she have?

10   20   100

6 All the second-grade classes will go on a trip. About how many buses might they use?

5   50   100

Write About It

Write a story problem like the ones on this page.
Ask a classmate to solve your problem.

HOME ACTIVITY • Ask your child how many apples you should buy at the store—10, 40, or 100. Talk about which answer makes the most sense.

© Harcourt

Name _____

CHECK ■ Concepts and Skills

Count the spots.
Write how many tens.
Then write how many ones.

1 _____ tens = _____ ones

Circle the value of the blue digit.

2   2<u>4</u>

4 or 40

Circle the value of the blue digit.

3   3<u>7</u>   <u>1</u>2

7 or 70   1 or 10

Read the number. Write the number in different ways.

4 twenty-four

_____ tens _____ ones

_____ + _____

_____

5 thirty-seven

_____ tens _____ ones

_____ + _____

_____

CHECK ■ Problem Solving

Circle the most reasonable estimate.

6 Akio packs apples in his family's lunches.
About how many apples might he pack?

5   30   100

Name _____

Choose the best answer for questions 1–4.

1 There are 10 spots on each ladybug.
How many spots are there in all?

60	70	80	90
○	○	○	○

2 What is the value of the
underlined digit?

7<u>3</u>

3	7	30	70
○	○	○	○

3 Which number matches
the words?

thirty-one

31	13	3	30
○	○	○	○

4 Which addition fact can help you solve this subtraction fact?

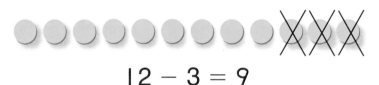

$12 - 3 = 9$

$9 - 3 = 6$	$4 + 8 = 12$	$9 + 3 = 12$	$7 + 5 = 12$
○	○	○	○

Show What You Know

5 Draw blocks. Show tens and ones.
Write the number in three different ways.

_____ tens _____ ones

_____ + _____

_____

© Harcourt

Number Patterns, Compare and Order

MOVIE

What number patterns do you see in this picture?

Dear Family,
    Today we started Chapter 5. We will compare numbers and put them in order. We will also learn about number patterns. Here is the math vocabulary and an activity for us to do together at home.

Love,

_____

My Math Words
greater than >
less than <

Vocabulary

greater than (>) and **less than (<)**
Symbols used to compare two numbers.

49 > 34   34 < 49

49 is greater than 34.
34 is less than 49.

Give your child three grocery items with prices of less than $1.00. Have your child line up the three items in order by price, from greatest to least and then from least to greatest.

Books to Share

To read about ordering numbers with your child, look for these books in your local library.

The Twelve Circus Rings,
by Seymour Chwast,
Harcourt, Brace & Company, 1996.

Seven Blind Mice,
by Ed Young,
Penguin Putnam, 1992.

Clams All Year,
by Maryann Cocca-Leffler,
Bantam Doubleday Dell, 1998.

© Harcourt

Visit *The Learning Site* for additional ideas and activities. www.harcourtschool.com

Compare Numbers: >, <, or = 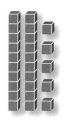 Algebra

23 is greater than 13. | 18 is less than 24. | 25 is equal to 25.

23 > 13   18 < 24   25 = 25

Write greater than, less than, or equal to. Then write
>, <, or =.

 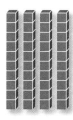

1 23 is _less than_ 32.

23 (<) 32

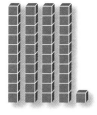

2 40 is _____ 41.

40 ( ) 41

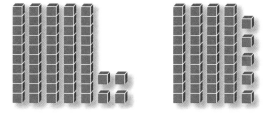 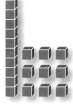

3 54 is _____ 45.

54 ( ) 45

4 19 is _____ 19.

19 ( ) 19

Talk About It ▪ Reasoning

How do you know that 35 is greater than 23?

Write greater than, less than, or equal to. Then write >, <, or =.

1 98 is ~~greater than~~ 89.

   98 (>) 89

2 5 is _____ 15.

   5 ( ) 15

3 35 is _____ 38.

   35 ( ) 38

4 60 is _____ 59.

   60 ( ) 59

5 27 is _____ 27.

   27 ( ) 27

6 76 is _____ 67.

   76 ( ) 67

7 56 is _____ 36.

   56 ( ) 36

8 31 is _____ 31.

   31 ( ) 31

Problem Solving ▪ Reasoning

Solve.
Show how you solved the problem.

9 Carlos is thinking of a number.
It is between 20 and 40.
It is 10 less than 40.
What number is it? _____

HOME ACTIVITY • Have your child compare the prices of two grocery items that cost less than $1.00 each and tell which price is greater.

Name _____

Order Numbers: Before, After, Between

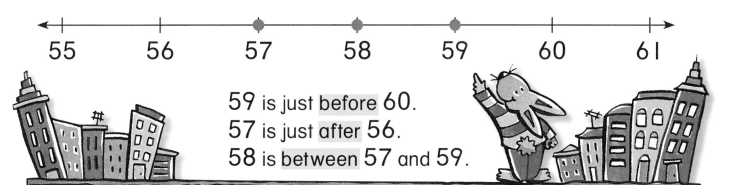

55   56   57   58   59   60   61

59 is just **before** 60.
57 is just **after** 56.
58 is **between** 57 and 59.

Write the number that is just before,
just after, or between.

1 | 26   _27_   28

2 | 50   51   _____

3 | 35   _____   37

4 | 89   _____   91

5 | 14   _____   16

6 | _____   31   32

7 | 38   39   _____

8 | 83   _____   85

9 | _____   80   81

10 | 8   9   _____

11 | 17   18   _____

12 | _____   44   45

Talk About It ▪ Reasoning

How would you use before, after, and
between to tell about these numbers?

89
90
91

Practice

Write the number that is just after, just before, or between.

	after		**before**		**between**

1. 34, _35_   _39_ , 40   55, _56_ , 57

2. 10, _____   _____ , 25   42, _____, 44

3. 98, _____   _____ , 8   75, _____, 77

4. 27, _____   _____ , 88   28, _____, 30

5. 50, _____   _____ , 61   9, _____, 11

6. 19, _____   _____ , 30   97, _____, 99

7. 79, _____   _____ , 33   26, _____, 28

8. 45, _____   _____ , 49   84, _____, 86

Mixed Review

9. Write the fact family for the set of numbers.

   6   7   13

_____ + _____ = _____   _____ + _____ = _____

_____ − _____ = _____   _____ − _____ = _____

HOME ACTIVITY • Say a number. Have your child say the numbers that come just before and just after that number.

Name ____________________

Even and Odd

If each cube is in a pair, the number is **even**.
If one cube is left over, the number is **odd**.

1	2	3	4	5	6	7	8	9	10
odd	even	odd	even	odd	even	odd	even	odd	even

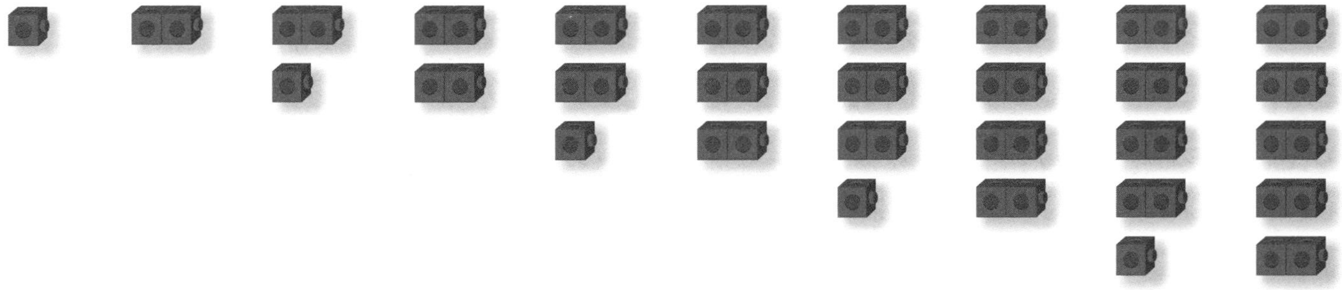

Show the number of cubes.
Snap the cubes together in pairs.
Write even or odd.

1. 12 even
2. 25 ____________
3. 19 ____________
4. 16 ____________
5. 14 ____________
6. 27 ____________
7. 30 ____________
8. 13 ____________
9. 28 ____________
10. 31 ____________

Talk About It ■ Reasoning

Look at the last digit of each number. How does it help you know whether the number is even or odd? Would a number ending in 0 be even or odd?

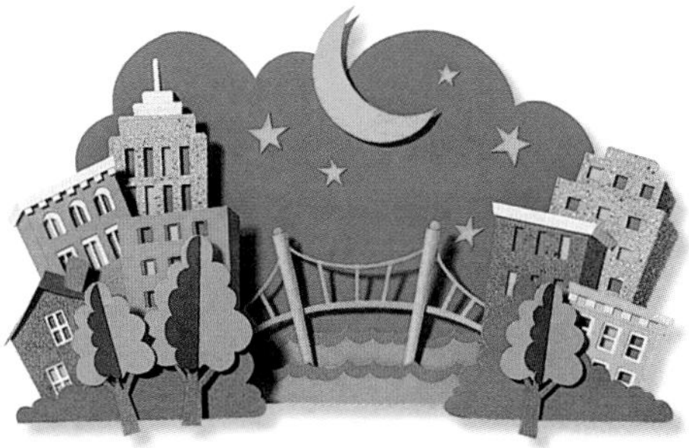

Practice

Show the number of .
Write even or odd.

For 2-digit numbers, build each ten and then snap the ones together in pairs.

1 21 ___odd___

2 24 _____

3 18 _____

4 22 _____

5 36 _____

6 29 _____

7 20 _____

8 23 _____

9 35 _____

10 27 _____

11 39 _____

12 34 _____

13 45 _____

14 40 _____

15 38 _____

16 41 _____

Problem Solving ▪ Number Sense

17 How can you tell that a number that ends with 5, such as 85, is odd?

Use cubes to prove your answer.

HOME ACTIVITY • Give your child 20 small objects. Have him or her show you a number of objects between 1 and 20 and then tell you if the number is even or odd.

Name _____

CHECK ▪ Concepts and Skills

Use the pictograph to answer the questions.

Our Favorite Subjects	
reading	🧍 🧍 🧍
math	🧍 🧍 🧍 🧍 🧍
science	🧍 🧍 🧍 🧍

Key: Each 🧍 stands for 5 children.

1. How many people like reading best? _____

2. How many people like math best? _____

3. How many more children like math than science? _____

CHECK ▪ Problem Solving

Use the tally table to fill in the bar graph.

Our Favorite Sports	
basketball	IIII
football	III
baseball	I
soccer	IIII

Our Favorite Sports				
basketball				
football				
baseball				
soccer				

0   I   2   3   4

Use the graph to answer the questions.

4. How many more children like soccer than baseball? _____

5. How many children in all like football or basketball? _____

© Harcourt

Choose the best answer for questions 1–3.

1 The graph shows favorite animals.
How many children in all chose dogs or birds?

Our Favorite Animals	
cats	🐱 🐱 🐱
dogs	🐕 🐕 🐕 🐕
birds	🐦 🐦 🐦

3   7   8   11
○   ○   ○   ○

2 Skip count. Which number is missing?

3, 6, 9, ___, 15, 18

21   14   12   11
○   ○   ○   ○

3 What is the sum?

2 + 3 + 8 = ___

5   10   11   13
○   ○   ○   ○

Show What You Know

4 Use red, green, and yellow. Color the apples.

Fill in the tally table. Fill in the bar graph.

Color of Apples		
Color	**Tally**	**Total**
Red		
Green		
Yellow		

Color of Apples										
Red										
Green										
Yellow										

0 1 2 3 4 5 6 7 8 9 10

© Harcourt

Name _____

Crack the Codes

Use your skills to find the answers to these riddles. First, solve each problem. Then match each number to the letter. Good luck!

a	b	c	d	e	f	g	h	i	j	k	l	m
1	2	3	4	5	6	7	8	9	10	11	12	13

n	o	p	q	r	s	t	u	v	w	x	y	z
14	15	16	17	18	19	20	21	22	23	24	25	26

What type of ship never sinks?

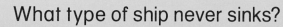

9 −3	9 +9	5 +4	0 +5	16 −2	3 +1	10 +9	12 −4	6 +3	8 +8

What sings and flies but doesn't swim?

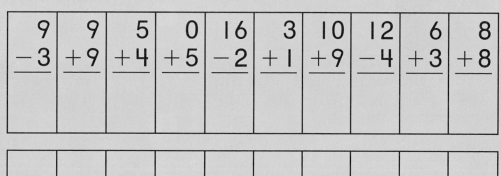

10 −9		4 +4	26 −5	6 +7	15 −2	8 +1	10 +4	3 +4	10 −8	8 +1	11 +7	13 −9

Stretch Your Thinking ☐ Make up a riddle in code for your classmates to solve.

© Harcourt

Name _____

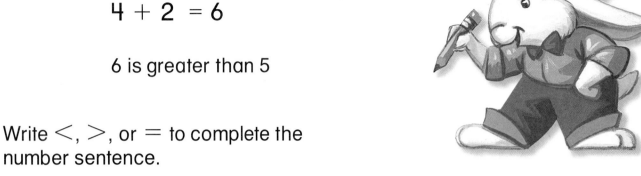

$$4 + 2 \enspace \bigcirc{>} \enspace 5$$

$$4 + 2 = 6$$

6 is greater than 5

Write $<$, $>$, or $=$ to complete the number sentence.

1 $5 + 1 \enspace \bigcirc \enspace 6$ **2** $10 + 2 \enspace \bigcirc \enspace 13$

3 $8 - 3 \enspace \bigcirc \enspace 2$ **4** $7 - 3 \enspace \bigcirc \enspace 4$

5 $6 + 3 \enspace \bigcirc \enspace 5 + 3$ **6** $4 + 2 \enspace \bigcirc \enspace 1 + 5$

7 $10 - 7 \enspace \bigcirc \enspace 14 - 11$ **8** $9 - 3 \enspace \bigcirc \enspace 4 - 2$

9 $1 + 15 \enspace \bigcirc \enspace 17 - 1$ **10** $8 + 3 \enspace \bigcirc \enspace 7 + 5$

11 $14 - 7 \enspace \bigcirc \enspace 15 - 7$ **12** $18 + 3 \enspace \bigcirc \enspace 24 - 3$

Name _____

Skills and Concepts

Add or subtract.

1 10 + 0 = _____

0 + 10 = _____

2 9 + 9 = _____

9 + 10 = _____

3 9 + _____ = 16

4 4 + 5 + 1 = _____

5 13 − 13 = _____

6 12 − 2 = _____

7 Write the fact family for the set of numbers.

6, 7, 13

_____ + _____ = _____   _____ − _____ = _____

_____ + _____ = _____   _____ − _____ = _____

8 Write how many tens and ones in three different ways.

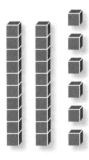

_____ tens _____ ones = _____

_____ + _____ = _____

_____

9 Circle the value of the underlined digit.

<u>8</u>2

8 or 80

Good Work

10 Read the number. Write the number in different ways.

sixty-two

_____ tens + _____ ones

_____ + _____

_____

11 Write the correct position of the bee.

     _____

first

12 Write greater than, less than, or equal to.

28 is _____ 30

28 ◯ 30

13 Show the number of . Write odd or even.

_____

14 Use the tally table. How many children chose oranges?

_____ children

Our Favorite Fruits	
apple	ll
bananas	llll
oranges	llll ll

Each **l** stands for 1 child's vote.

Problem Solving

15 Use the graph. How many children in all like apples or bananas?

_____ children

Our Favorite Fruits							
apple							
bananas							
oranges							
1	2	3	4	5	6	7	8

Study Guide and Review • Unit 1

© Harcourt

Veggie Soup

Paul wants to use at least one of each type of vegetable to make his soup.

Write how many of each vegetable Paul can use if he chooses 15 vegetables.

_____ | _____ | _____ | _____

Show your work.

Technology

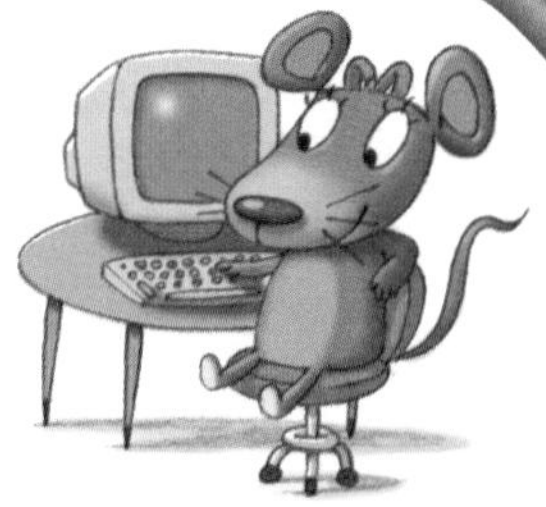

Name ___________________________

The Learning Site • Addition Surprise

1. Go to **www.harcourtschool.com.**
2. Click on 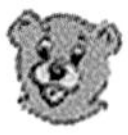 .
3. Drag the sums into the table.
4. What picture did you find?

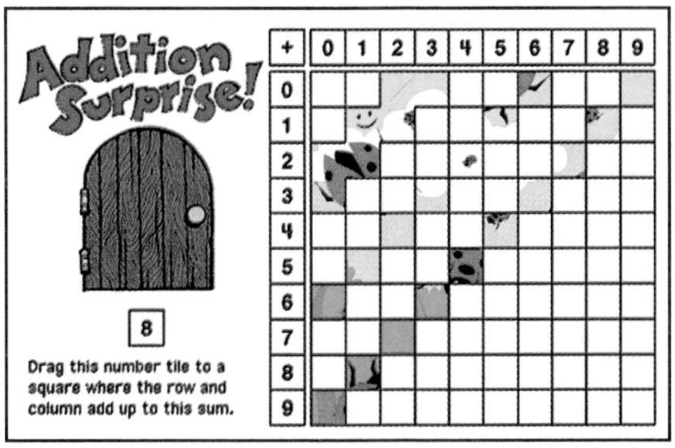
Addition Surprise!
8
Drag this number tile to a square where the row and column add up to this sum.
+ 0 1 2 3 4 5 6 7 8 9
0 1 2 3 4 5 6 7 8 9

Practice and Problem Solving

Write the missing number.

1. $5 + 3 =$ ____
2. $3 + 7 =$ ____
3. ____ $+ 9 = 18$
4. $4 +$ ____ $= 12$
5. First there were 6 birds.
   Then _____ birds came.
   Now there are 15 birds.
6. First, there were _____ birds.
   Then 4 birds came.
   Now there are 12 birds.

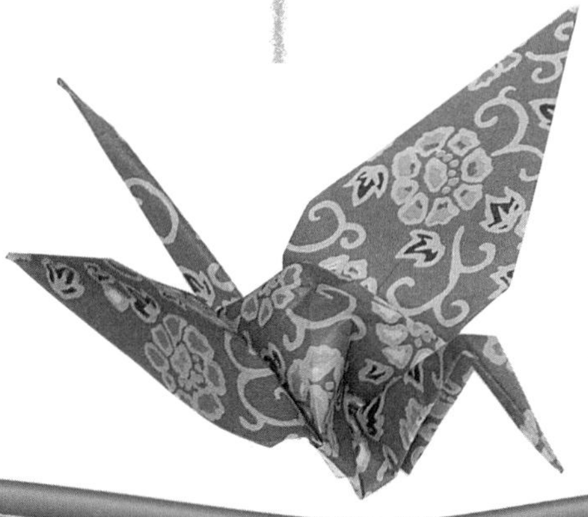

Name _____

PROBLEM SOLVING ON LOCATION

In Our Nation's Capital

Washington, D.C., is the capital of our country. Tourists like to visit many interesting places there.

Which of these places would you and your classmates most like to visit?

Capitol Building

National Air and Space Museum

Washington Monument

White House

Fill in the tally table to show the votes. Use the tally table to fill in the graph.

Places We Would Like to Visit		
	Tally	**Total**
White House		
Capitol Building		
Washington Monument		
National Air and Space Museum		

Places We Would Like to Visit												
White House												
Capitol Building												
Washington Monument												
National Air and Space Museum												

0 2 4 6 8 10 12 14 16 18 20 22 24

Name _____

PROBLEM SOLVING ON LOCATION

In the Forest

Many kinds of animals live in South Carolina. Here are just a few you might see in the state parks and forests there.

deer

robin

beaver

turkey

dragonfly

black bear

bee

Sort these animals.
Write each name where
you think it belongs.

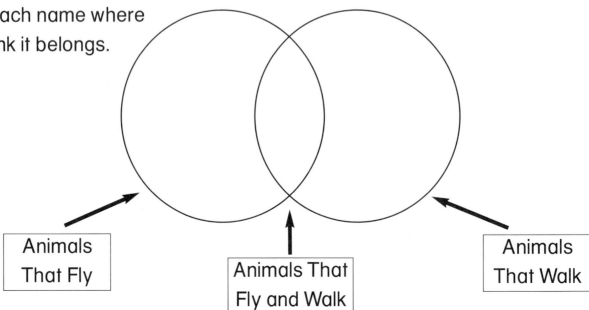

Animals That Fly

Animals That Fly and Walk

Animals That Walk

Oranges
50¢

Cheese

75¢

Corn
25¢

HONEY
75¢

Tomatoes
2 for 25¢

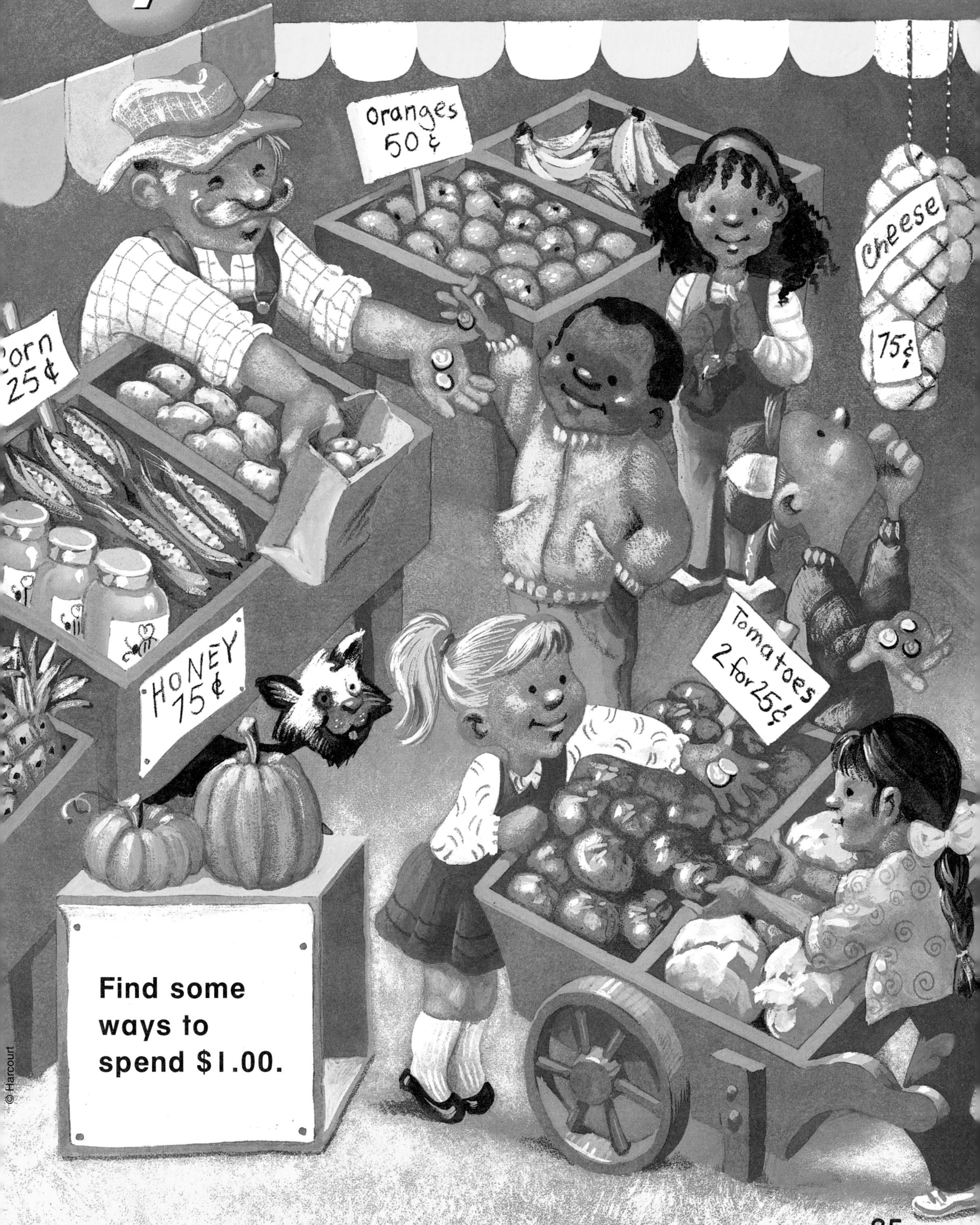

Find some
ways to
spend $1.00.

© Harcourt

SCHOOL HOME CONNECTION

Dear Family,
   Today we started Chapter 7. We will count with coins to $1.00, using combinations of pennies, nickels, dimes, quarters, and half-dollars. Here are the math vocabulary words and an activity for us to do together at home.

Love, Sophie

Sophia

My Math Words
half-dollar
one dollar

 **Vocabulary**

half-dollar A coin worth 50¢

one dollar A bill worth 100¢

Visit The Learning Site for additional ideas and activities.
www.harcourtschool.com

 **ACTIVITY**

Ask your child to choose one grocery item that costs $1.00 or less. Have him or her use pennies, nickels, dimes, and quarters to show what coins could be used to buy the item.

Books to Share

To read about money with your child, look for these books in your local library.

If You Made a Million,
by David M. Schwartz,
William Morrow, 1994.

Alexander Who Used to Be Rich Last Sunday,
by Judith Viorst,
Aladdin, 1980.

Lilly's Purple Plastic Purse,
by Kevin Henkes,
William Morrow, 1998.

Name _____

CHECK ▪ Concepts and Skills

Count on to find the total amount.

_____ ¢, _____ ¢, _____ ¢, _____ ¢, _____ ¢, _____ ¢ ☐ ¢

Draw and label the coins in order from greatest to least value. Write the total amount.

_____

Use coins. Show $1.00 with the coins named.
Draw and label the coins. Write the amount.

3 dimes

_____

CHECK ▪ Problem Solving

Use coins to show the price.
Draw the coins you used.

4 John buys honey.
What coins can he use?

© Harcourt

Name _____

Choose the best answer for questions 1-3.

1 What is the total amount?

30¢	47¢	50¢	52¢
○	○	○	○

2 David has these coins. Which toy can he buy?

 75¢  95¢  70¢ 90¢

○	○	○	○

3 Which numbers have the same sum as 7 + 2?

0 + 7	1 + 7	2 + 7	3 + 4
○	○	○	○

Show What You Know

4 Write a price that is less than $1.00.
Draw coins to show the price. Put the
coins in order from greatest to least value.

© Harcourt

CHAPTER 8 Using Money

What are some different coins you could use to buy the doll? Which way uses the fewest coins?

SCHOOL HOME CONNECTION

Dear Family,
   Today we started Chapter 8. We will learn to show amounts of money. We will also learn to compare prices and to make change. Here is the math vocabulary and an activity for us to do together at home

Love,

_____

My Math Word
change

Vocabulary

change The difference between the price of an item and the amount you give the clerk. The clerk will give back change.

38¢

39¢,   40¢

2¢ **change**

Visit *The Learning Site* **for additional ideas and activities. www.harcourtschool.com**

ACTIVITY

As you and your child shop, let him or her pick out an item that costs $1.00 or less. Give your child more than enough coins to buy the item. Ask him or her to choose the coins needed to pay for the item.

Books to Share

To read more stories about money with your child, look for these books in your local library.

Arthur's Funny Money, by Lillian Hoban, HarperCollins, 1981.

The Donkey and the Rock, by Demi, Henry Holt, 1999.

Market Day, by Eve Bunting, HarperCollins, 1999.

© Harcourt

Name _____

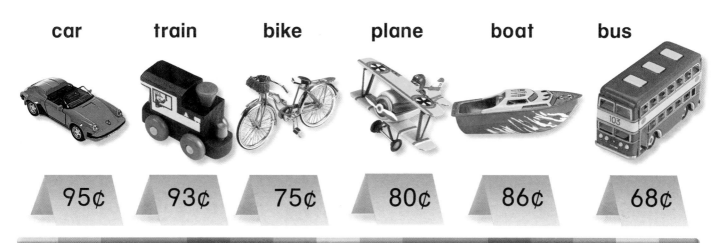

car	train	bike	plane	boat	bus
95¢	93¢	75¢	80¢	86¢	68¢

Write the amount. Write the names and prices of toys you could buy.

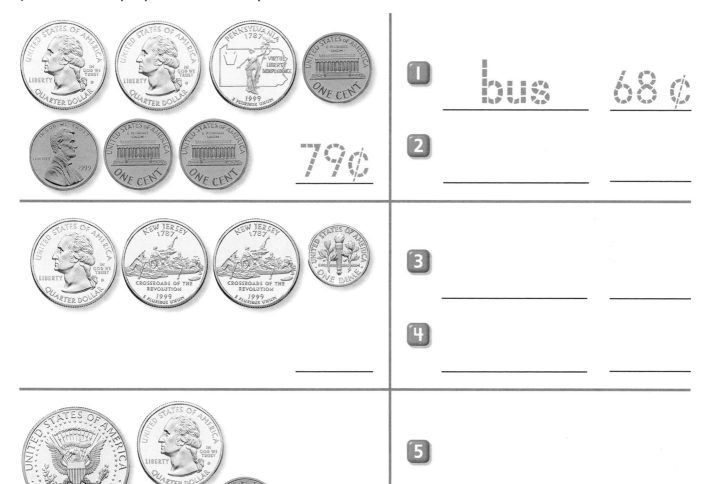

79¢

1 bus   68¢

2 _____ _____

3 _____ _____

4 _____ _____

5 _____ _____

6 _____ _____

Talk About It ▪ Reasoning

Would you be able to buy the car if you have 89¢? Why or why not?

© Harcourt

duck	giraffe	ladybug	tiger	lizard
65¢	70¢	90¢	79¢	85¢

Write the amount. Write the names and prices of toys you could buy.

75¢

1  giraffe 70¢

2 _____ _____

_____

3 _____ _____

4 _____ _____

_____

5 _____ _____

6 _____ _____

Algebra

7 You save 5¢ each day.
You start on Monday.
On Friday, how much have you saved? _____

Monday	Tuesday	Wednesday	Thursday	Friday

HOME ACTIVITY • Ask your child to count out loud each group of coins.

© Harcourt

Name _____

Count on from the price to find the change.
Start with pennies and then use nickels or dimes.

1 You have 25¢. You buy

17¢

18¢, _19¢_, _20¢_, _25¢_

Your change is _8¢_ .

---

2 You have 50¢. You buy

37¢

38¢, _____, _____, _____

Your change is _____ .

---

3 You have 40¢. You buy

33¢

34¢, _____, _____

Your change is _____ .

---

4 You have 30¢. You buy

21¢

22¢, _____, _____, _____, _____

Your change is _____ .

Talk About It ▪ Reasoning

How do you know if you have gotten the right amount of change?

Chapter 8 • Using Money

one hundred seventeen **117**

Count on from the price to find the change.
Start with pennies first, then use nickels or dimes.

1 You have 50¢. You buy

38¢

39¢, 40¢, 50¢

Your change is __12¢__.

2 You have 75¢. You buy

62¢

_____, _____, _____, _____

Your change is _____.

3 You have 50¢. You buy

36¢

_____, _____, _____, _____, _____

Your change is _____.

Problem Solving ▪ Reasoning

Solve.

4 Hans buys a toy that costs 23¢. He gives the clerk some money and gets 2¢ change. How much money did Hans give the clerk?

The toy costs _____.

Hans gets _____ change.

Hans gave the clerk _____.

HOME ACTIVITY • When you buy items that cost less than 99¢, help your child count on from the price of the item to the amount given to the clerk to figure out the change you should get.

© Harcourt

Name _____

Problem Solving
Make a List

There are 5 coins in Ana's bag.
None of the coins is greater than 5¢.
What coins could there be?
Make a list to find out.

Check to make sure the total sum of coins is always five.

nickels	pennies	total amount
5	0	25¢

Talk About It ▪ Reasoning

If you know all the coins are nickels,
how will your list change?

Check to make sure the total number of coins you use is always three.

There are 3 coins in Ana's bag. None of the coins is greater than 10¢. What coins could there be? Make a list to find out.

dimes	nickels	pennies	total amount
3	0	0	30¢

Write About It

Suppose you know that at least one of the coins is a penny. Explain how your list will change.

HOME ACTIVITY • Put three coins (none greater than 10¢) into a bag. Ask your child to make a list of the possible combinations of coins in the bag.

© Harcourt

Name _____

CHECK ▪ Concepts and Skills

Use coins. Show the amount of money
in two ways. Draw and label each coin.

1
83¢

Write the amount. Then show the same amount
with the fewest coins. Draw and label each coin.

2

Count on from the price to find
the change.

3 You have 30¢. You buy

22¢

23¢, _____, _____, _____

Your change is _____.

CHECK ▪ Problem Solving

Solve.

4 Ana has 2 coins in her bag.
None of the coins is greater
than 5¢. What coins could
there be? Make a list to
find out.

nickels	pennies	total amount

Name _____

Choose the best answer for questions 1–3.

1 What is the total amount?

27¢   67¢   47¢   90¢
○   ○   ○   ○

2 Jacob bought a ball that cost 62¢. He paid 65¢.
What should he say to count his change?

65   64, 65   63, 64, 65   65, 66, 67
○   ○   ○   ○

3 What is the total amount of money?

Half-Dollar	Dimes	Nickels	Pennies	Total
1	1	2	3	?

73¢   72¢   70¢   48¢
○   ○   ○   ○

Show What You Know

4 Write an amount that is less than $1.00. Draw coins to show the amount in two different ways.

Telling Time

2:30

To	Track	Time
San Diego	2	2:00
Detroit	4	2:30
Boise	3	3:00
Orlando	1	8:45

How many minutes until the next train leaves? Ask other questions about time.

© Harcourt

SCHOOL HOME CONNECTION

Dear Family,
   Today we started Chapter 9. We will learn how to tell time. Here is the math vocabulary and an activity for us to do together at home.

Love,

_____

Vocabulary

minute A unit used to measure time. There are 60 minutes in one hour.

hour Another unit used to measure time. There are 60 minutes in one hour and 24 hours in one day.

digital clock A clock that shows digits for the hour and the minutes after the hour.
For example: 7:35 and 12:05

digital clock

 Visit *The Learning Site* for additional ideas and activities.
www.harcourtschool.com

ACTIVITY

Ask your child to tell you what time a favorite TV show starts and what time the show ends. Have him or her tell you how long the show lasts.

Books to Share

To read about telling time with your child, look for these books in your local library.

Clocks and More Clocks, by Pat Hutchins, Simon & Schuster, 1994.

The Boy Who Stopped Time, by Anthony Taber, Margaret K. McElderry Books, 1993.

Tuesday, by David Wiesner, Houghton Mifflin, 1997

© Harcourt

Time After the Hour

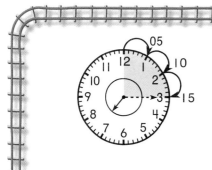
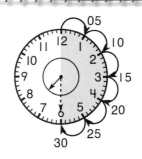
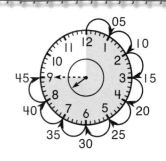

7:15

15 minutes after 7
quarter past 7

7:30

30 minutes after 7
half past 7

7:45

45 minutes after 7
quarter to 8

Draw the minute hand to show the time.
Write the time.

1 45 minutes after 10

10:45

2 quarter past 3

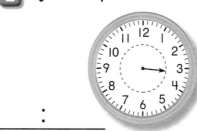

___ : ___

3 30 minutes after 4

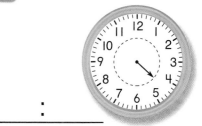

___ : ___

4 45 minutes after 6

___ : ___

5 15 minutes after 11

___ : ___

6 half past 8

___ : ___

7 45 minutes after 2

___ : ___

8 half past 12

___ : ___

9 quarter past 5

___ : ___

Talk About It ▪ Reasoning

Look at the clocks at the top of the page. How do
they show why you could say that 7:30 is half past 7?

Draw the minute hand to show the time.
Write the time.

1 25 minutes after 6

6:25

2 10 minutes after 12

:
_____

3 45 minutes after 3

:
_____

4 quarter past 1

:
_____

5 20 minutes after 6

:
_____

6 half past 5

:
_____

7 30 minutes after 4

:
_____

8 5 minutes after 12

:
_____

9 40 minutes after 10

:
_____

Problem Solving ▪ **Application**

Circle early or late.

10 Lunch is served at 12:30.
Juan gets there at 12:45.
Is Juan early or late?

early   late

11 Sue is meeting Karen at 7:00.
Sue gets there at 6:45.
Is Sue early or late?

early   late

© Harcourt

🏠 **HOME ACTIVITY** • Use a clock at home. At the start of different activities, ask your child to tell the time to the nearest quarter hour and time after the hour.

Name _____

Times after the half-hour are
often given as before the next hour.

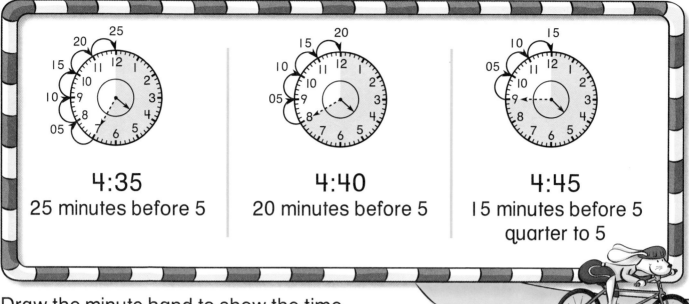

4:35	4:40	4:45
25 minutes before 5	20 minutes before 5	15 minutes before 5 quarter to 5

Draw the minute hand to show the time.
Write the time.

1 10 minutes before 5

4:50

2 quarter to 12

___ : ___

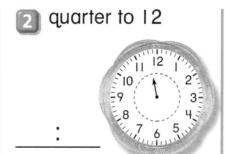

3 25 minutes before 4

___ : ___

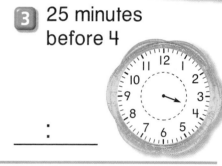

4 quarter to 10

___ : ___

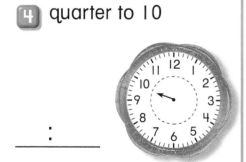

5 5 minutes before 6

___ : ___

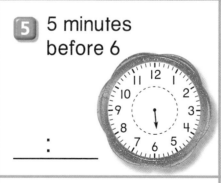

6 twenty minutes before 3

___ : ___

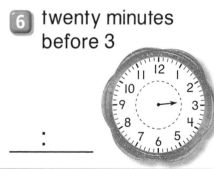

7 5 minutes before 7

___ : ___

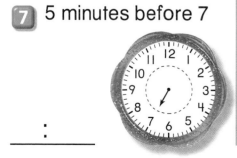

8 15 minutes before 9

___ : ___

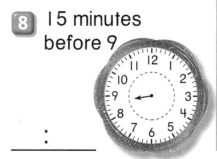

9 20 minutes before 5

___ : ___

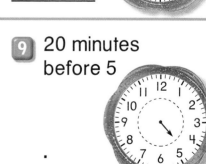

Talk About It ▪ Reasoning

How can 6:35 be before 7:00 and after 6:00?

Draw the minute hand to show the time.
Write the time.

1 5 minutes before 10

9:55

2 quarter to 11

____:____

3 20 minutes before 1

____:____

4 quarter to 6

____:____

5 10 minutes before 3

____:____

6 15 minutes before 6

____:____

7 25 minutes before 12

____:____

8 15 minutes before 9

____:____

9 quarter to 3

____:____

Algebra

10 Continue the pattern. Draw clock hands.

2:00   2:15   2:30   2:45   3:00

© Harcourt

HOME ACTIVITY • At times from the half-hour to the hour during the day, ask your child to tell the time before the hour.

Problem Solving
Use a Model

Draw the minute hand to show the time.
Write the time.

 30 minutes later

4:15

4:45

---

1  15 minutes later

10:00

_____:_____

---

2  5 minutes later

8:25

_____:_____

---

3  25 minutes later

3:40

_____:_____

Draw the minute hand to show the time.
Write the time.

1

9:05 _____

50 minutes later

9:55 _____

2

11:35 _____

35 minutes later

_____:_____

3

4:25 _____

10 minutes later

_____:_____

Problem Solving ▪ Estimating

Circle I second or I minute.

4 It takes about I second to sneeze. It takes about I minute to wash your hands. About how long does it take to tie your shoes?

I second   I minute

5 It takes about I second to blink your eyes. It takes about I minute to sharpen your pencil. About how long does it take to smile?

I second   I minute

© Harcourt

 HOME ACTIVITY • Have your child tell you the time every 5 minutes from 5 minutes to 55 minutes after the hour.

Name _____

CHECK ▪ Concepts and Skills

Write the time.

1

___ : ___

2

___ : ___

3

___ : ___

Draw the minute hand to show the time. Write the time.

4 20 minutes after 6

___ : ___

5 half past 5

___ : ___

6 5 minutes after 10

___ : ___

7 10 minutes before 8

___ : ___

8 quarter to 1

___ : ___

9 20 minutes before 4

___ : ___

Draw the minute hand to show the time. Write the time.

10

7:25

50 minutes later

___ : ___

© Harcourt

Choose the best answer for questions 1-4.

1 Shannece sees 12 kittens. Seven of them are black.
The rest are white. How many are white?

4   5   19   20
○   ○   ○   ○

2 What time does the clock show?

4:15   4:45
○   ○

4:30   4:50
○   ○

3 What time does the clock show?

quarter past 12   25 minutes after 12
○   ○

20 minutes after 12   half past 12
○   ○

4 What time does the clock show?

20 minutes before 10   30 minutes before 10
○   ○

25 minutes before 10   quarter to 10
○   ○

Show What You Know

5 Draw hands on the clock. Write the time.

Show a time that is 15 minutes past the hour.

_____ : _____

Show the time that is 30 minutes later.

_____ : _____

© Harcourt

Understanding Time

Write the month you think each picture shows.

SCHOOL HOME CONNECTION

Dear Family,
Today we started Chapter 10. We will use a calendar, learn about A.M. and P.M., and estimate time. Here is the math vocabulary and an activity for us to do together at home.

Love,

_____

My Math Words

A.M.
P.M.
month
day
date
week

Vocabulary

A.M. is used to label the time between midnight and noon.

P.M. is used to label the time between noon and midnight.

month
day

January						
Sunday	Monday	Tuesday	Wednesday	Thursday	Friday	Saturday
			1	2	3	4
⑤	6	7	8	9	10	11
12	13	14	15	16	17	18
⑲	20	21	22	23	24	25
26	27	28	29	30	31	

date

week

ACTIVITY

Help your child make a schedule of the activities that he or she does at home, such as homework, watching television, and helping with chores.

Books to Share

To read about time with your child, look for these books in your local library.

Benjamin's 365 Birthdays, by Judi Barrett, Aladdin, 1992.

Get Up & Go!, by Stuart J. Murphy, HarperCollins, 1996.

Morning, Noon, and Night, by Jean Craighead George, HarperCollins, 1999.

© Harcourt

Visit *The Learning Site* for additional ideas and activities. www.harcourtschool.com

Name _____

Problem Solving
Use a Model

The hour hand moves from 11 to 1 to show 2 hours. The minute hand moves around the clock 2 times.

The party starts at 11:00 A.M.
It is over at 1:00 P.M.
How much time has passed?

UNDERSTAND

What do you want to find out?

PLAN

You can use a model to solve the problem.

SOLVE

_2_ hours

CHECK

Does your answer make sense? Explain.

Use a to help solve the problem.
Write how much time has passed.

1 Jack starts playing the piano at 2:00 P.M. He plays until 2:20 P.M. How much time has passed?

_20_ minutes

2 School starts at 9:00 A.M. It ends at 3:00 P.M. How much time has passed?

_____ hours

3 Peter starts playing kickball at 3:30 P.M. He plays until 5:30 P.M. How much time has passed?

_____ hours

4 Judy starts her homework at 6:30 P.M. She finishes at 7:00 P.M. How much time has passed?

_____ minutes

Practice

Use a 🕐 to help solve the problem.
Write how much time has passed.

1 Rabbit got to the bus stop at
2:00 P.M. It is now 4:00 P.M.
How much time has passed?

___2___ hours

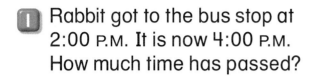

2 Rabbit's aunt puts the cake in
the oven at 2:15 P.M. She
takes it out at 2:45 P.M. How
much time has passed?

_____ minutes

3 Rabbit practices violin from
8:45 P.M. until 9:15 P.M. How
much time has passed?

_____ minutes

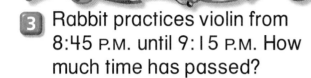

4 The soccer tournament
starts at 11:00 A.M. It is over
at 4:00 P.M. How much time
has passed?

_____ hours

5 Breakfast starts at 7:30 A.M.
It is over at 7:45 A.M. How
much time has passed?

_____ minutes

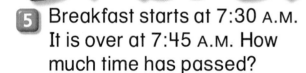

6 Rabbit sleeps from 9:00 P.M.
until 7:00 A.M. How much
time has passed?

_____ hours

7 Rabbit watches TV from 6:30
P.M. to 9:30 P.M. How much
time has passed?

_____ hours

8 The plane takes off at 2:00
P.M. It lands at 3:00 P.M. How
much time has passed?

_____ hour

Write About It

Write a story problem like those on this page. Give the starting time and
the ending time for an activity. Ask a classmate to solve your problem.

© Harcourt

🔺 **HOME ACTIVITY** • With your child, write down the starting and ending times for an activity you do. Find
out how much time passes while you do it. Repeat several times during the day.

Name _____

Use the **calendar** to answer the questions.

There are 7 days in 1 week.

NOVEMBER

Sunday	Monday	Tuesday	Wednesday	Thursday	Friday	Saturday
					1	2
3	4	5	6	7	8	9
10	11	12	13	14	15	16
17	18	19	20	21	22	23
24	25	26	27	28 Thanksgiving	29	30

1. What is the date of the third Tuesday? _November 19_

2. How many days are in this month? _30_

3. What is the day and date one week before Thanksgiving? _____, _____

4. What is the date one week after November 7? _____

5. On which day will the next month start? _____

Talk About It ▪ Reasoning

How does a calendar help you keep track of your activities?

Practice

Use the calendar to answer the questions.

January							February							March							April						
Su	M	T	W	Th	F	Sa	Su	M	T	W	Th	F	Sa	Su	M	T	W	Th	F	Sa	Su	M	T	W	Th	F	Sa
		1	2	3	4								1							1			1	2	3	4	5
5	6	7	8	9	10	11	2	3	4	5	6	7	8	2	3	4	5	6	7	8	6	7	8	9	10	11	12
12	13	14	15	16	17	18	9	10	11	12	13	14	15	9	10	11	12	13	14	15	13	14	15	16	17	18	19
19	20	21	22	23	24	25	16	17	18	19	20	21	22	16	17	18	19	20	21	22	20	21	22	23	24	25	26
26	27	28	29	30	31		23	24	25	26	27	28		23	24	25	26	27	28	29	27	28	29	30			
														30	31												

May							June							July							August						
Su	M	T	W	Th	F	Sa	Su	M	T	W	Th	F	Sa	Su	M	T	W	Th	F	Sa	Su	M	T	W	Th	F	Sa
				1	2	3	1	2	3	4	5	6	7			1	2	3	4	5						1	2
4	5	6	7	8	9	10	8	9	10	11	12	13	14	6	7	8	9	10	11	12	3	4	5	6	7	8	9
11	12	13	14	15	16	17	15	16	17	18	19	20	21	13	14	15	16	17	18	19	10	11	12	13	14	15	16
18	19	20	21	22	23	24	22	23	24	25	26	27	28	20	21	22	23	24	25	26	17	18	19	20	21	22	23
25	26	27	28	29	30	31	29	30						27	28	29	30	31			24	25	26	27	28	29	30
																					31						

September							October							November							December						
Su	M	T	W	Th	F	Sa	Su	M	T	W	Th	F	Sa	Su	M	T	W	Th	F	Sa	Su	M	T	W	Th	F	Sa
	1	2	3	4	5	6			1	2	3	4								1		1	2	3	4	5	6
7	8	9	10	11	12	13	5	6	7	8	9	10	11	2	3	4	5	6	7	8	7	8	9	10	11	12	13
14	15	16	17	18	19	20	12	13	14	15	16	17	18	9	10	11	12	13	14	15	14	15	16	17	18	19	20
21	22	23	24	25	26	27	19	20	21	22	23	24	25	16	17	18	19	20	21	22	21	22	23	24	25	26	27
28	29	30					26	27	28	29	30	31		23	24	25	26	27	28	29	28	29	30	31			
														30													

1 With which month does the year begin? January _____

2 Which month follows October? _____

3 Which month has the fewest days? _____

4 Which is the fifth month in the year? _____

5 What is the date one week after May 28? _____

🔷 **HOME ACTIVITY** • Point out a date on a calendar. Ask your child to tell you the days and dates one week before and one week after that date.

© Harcourt

About how long will it take?

to eat lunch

about 15 minutes

about 15 hours

Ask yourself which unit of time makes sense.

to play a soccer game

about 1 month

about 1 hour

About how long will it take?
Circle the reasonable estimate.

1 to take a trip

5 minutes   5 days

2 to paint a house

3 days   3 minutes

3 to brush your teeth

4 minutes   4 hours

4 to complete second grade

10 months   10 days

Talk About It ▪ Reasoning

What activities take hours to do?
What activities take minutes to do?

About how long will it take?
Circle the reasonable estimate.

1 to build a house

8 days   (8 months)

2 to walk the dog

10 minutes   10 hours

3 to eat dinner

30 minutes   30 days

4 to watch a game

2 weeks   2 hours

5 to count to 100

1 minute   1 week

6 to wash the car

1 month   1 hour

HOME ACTIVITY • Ask your child to estimate whether it would take minutes, hours, days, weeks, or months to sail around the world, watch a movie, and brush his or her teeth.

© Harcourt

Name _____

We tell time in minutes, hours, days, weeks, months, and years.

Time Relationships	
There are 60 minutes in 1 hour.	There are 24 hours in 1 day.
There are 7 days in 1 week.	There are 28, 30, or 31 days in 1 month.
There are 12 months in 1 year.	There are 52 weeks in 1 year.

Write **more than, less than,** or **the same as** for each sentence.

1 Mira went to live with her grandparents for one year. This is

the same as 52 weeks.

2 She was on the plane for 3 hours. This is

_____ 1 day.

3 Mira had some good friends after 7 days. This is

_____ 1 month.

4 Mira went home after 12 months. This is

_____ 1 year.

Talk About It ▪ **Reasoning**

Explain your answers to the questions on this page.

© Harcourt

Write more than, less than, or the same as for each sentence.

1 Every fall, Paulo plays soccer for 3 months. This is

__less than__ 52 weeks.

Time Relationships
There are 60 minutes in 1 hour.
There are 24 hours in 1 day.
There are 7 days in 1 week.
There are 28, 30, or 31 days in 1 month.
There are 12 months in 1 year.
There are 52 weeks in 1 year.

2 Before practice, Paulo warms up for 15 minutes. This is

_____ 1 hour.

3 The games last for about 2 hours. This is

_____ 60 minutes.

Problem Solving ▪ Visual Thinking

Estimate and write the time.

4 Tara started painting the fence at 8:00. It is 11:00 now. What time do you think she will finish? _____ : _____

HOME ACTIVITY • Suggest different activities and ask your child how long he or she estimates each would take.

© Harcourt

Name _____

CHECK ▪ Concepts and Skills

Write the correct time.
Circle A.M. or P.M.

1 make dinner

_____ : _____   A.M.   P.M.

About how long will it take?
Circle the reasonable estimate.

2 to wash your hands

I minute   I hour

Use a calendar to answer the question.

3 What is the date of the second
Friday in November?

_____

Write more than, less than, or the same as.

4 Mark's baby sister
is 6 weeks old.   This is _____ I month.

CHECK ▪ Problem Solving

Use a 🕐 to help solve the problem.
Write how much time has passed.

5 Annie starts playing a game at
4:15 P.M. She stops at 4:45 P.M.
How much time has passed?   _____ minutes

Name _____

Choose the best answer for questions 1–4.

1 Which would you do at 9:00 P.M.?

go to school	go to bed	eat dinner	plant flowers
○	○	○	○

2 Matthew slept from 10:00 P.M. until 8:00 A.M.
How much time passed?

8 minutes	8 hours	10 minutes	10 hours
○	○	○	○

3 Which is more than 1 hour?

16 minutes	72 minutes	60 minutes	26 minutes
○	○	○	○

4 What is the value of the underlined digit?

8<u>6</u>

6	60	8	80
○	○	○	○

Show What You Know

5 Use a 🕐. Complete the chart.
Choose your own times. Make Sara's baseball
game last longer than John's soccer game.

Games	Starting Time	Ending Time	How Long?
Sara's baseball game ⚾			
John's soccer game ⚽			

Grandma Rabbit's Birthday

written by Lucy Floyd
illustrated byTerri Chicko

This book will help me review time and money.

This book belongs to _____.

Rabbit was very excited. Today was Grandma Rabbit's birthday! "Grandma's birthday party is at 3:00," said Rabbit. "I must buy a gift for her! Let me see.

I have $___.___."

On the way to the store, Rabbit met
Toad. "Where are you going in such a hurry,
Rabbit?" asked Toad.

"Today is Grandma Rabbit's birthday,
and I must buy a gift for her!" said Rabbit.

"The party is at 3:00! My watch says ___:___."

Rabbit showed Toad his coins.
"You have too many coins," Toad said.
"You could lose some. Let me help
you. You have $1.00. I can make the
same amount with fewer coins. Trade
with me."

**Circle the coins that Toad can
trade with Rabbit.**

Rabbit went on his way and soon met Squirrel. "Where are you going in such a hurry, Rabbit?" asked Squirrel.

"Today is Grandma Rabbit's birthday, and I must buy a gift for her," said Rabbit.

"The party is at 3:00! My watch says ___:___."

Rabbit showed Squirrel his coins.
"You have too many coins," Squirrel said.
"You could lose some. Let me help you.
You have $1.00. I can make the same
amount with fewer coins. Trade with me."

**Circle the coins that Squirrel can trade
with Rabbit.**

Rabbit went on his way and soon met Chipmunk. "Where are you going in such a hurry, Rabbit?" asked Chipmunk.

"Today is Grandma Rabbit's birthday, and I must buy a gift for her," said Rabbit.

"The party is at 3:00! My watch says __:__."

Rabbit showed Chipmunk his coins. "You have too many coins," Chipmunk said. "You could lose some. Let me help you. You have $1.00. I can make the same amount with fewer coins. Trade with me."

Circle the coins that Chipmunk can trade with Rabbit.

Rabbit looked at all the things in the store. "I want to buy the very best gift for Grandma Rabbit," he said.

"My watch says ___:___."

How many minutes does Rabbit have

to get to the party?_____ minutes

"Hurray!" said Rabbit. "I got
to the birthday party on time, and
I have a gift for Grandma!"

Name _____

Discover the Date

Use your reasoning skills and the calendar clues to solve each case.

May

Sunday	Monday	Tuesday	Wednesday	Thursday	Friday	Saturday
		1	2	3	4	5
6	7	8	9	10	11	12
13	14	15	16	17	18	19
20	21	22	23	24	25	26
27	28	29	30	31		

Clue 1:
The date is a double.

Clue 2:
It is **not** an odd number.

Clue 3:
It is in the third week of May.

Clue 4:
It is the fourth day of the week.

What is the date? _____

Clue 1:
The date is **not** an even number.

Clue 2:
The digit in the tens place is even.

Clue 3:
It is not Sunday.

Clue 4:
It is in the last week of May. What is the date?

_____

Stretch Your Thinking □ Choose a date in May and make up clues that will help a classmate discover it.

© Harcourt

Name _____

If you toss a penny, is it more likely to land heads up or tails up?

My penny landed tails up!

My penny landed heads up!

Try it. You will need 1  🪙. Toss a penny 10 times.
For each toss, make a tally mark to show heads or tails.

Sides	Tally Marks	Totals
heads	𝍷𝍷𝍷𝍷 𝍷𝍷	7
tails	𝍷𝍷𝍷𝍷 𝍷𝍷𝍷 𝍷𝍷𝍷𝍷 𝍷𝍷	17

1. How many times did the coin land heads up? ____17____

2. How many times did the coin land tails up? ____7____

3. Did the coin land heads up or tails up more often? ___tails___

If you toss the penny 20 times, will it land more often on one side than the other? Write your prediction.

50/50 an equal chance

© Harcourt

Name _____

Stuck on You

Jane wants to buy these 2 stickers.

- She has 55¢ in her pocket.

- She has more than 3 coins, but less than 10 coins.

Show 2 ways Jane can have the coins in her pocket. How much money will Jane have left after she buys the stickers?

Show your work.

Technology

Name _____

Mighty Math Zoo Zillions • Count Money

1 Click .

2 Click ◻.

3 Click E.

4 Play 5 times.

Practice and Problem Solving

Use coins. Draw and label the coins to show the amount.

1

71¢

2 Use coins. Draw 2 ways to make 53¢.

Name _____

PROBLEM SOLVING ON LOCATION

In the Caves

Mammoth Cave, in Kentucky, is the longest group of connected caves in the world.

Tours and Times	
Historic Tour (1 hour long)	9:00, 10:00, 1:00
Frozen Niagara Tour (2 hours long)	9:00, 1:00
Violet City Tour (2 hours long)	10:00, 2:00
Wild Cave Tour (1 hour long)	9:00, 11:00, 3:00

Plan a day at Mammoth Cave. Go on each tour.

Complete the chart.

Tour	Start Time	End Time
Lunch	12:00	1:00

PROBLEM SOLVING ON LOCATION

At the Mint

Coins are made at the United States mints. The first mint in our country was in Philadelphia, Pennsylvania.

A coin press makes a different coin each day. It makes 4 coins every minute. Find out which coin it makes on each day.

penny   quarter   nickel   dime

Use coins. Draw to show your work.
Write the name of the coin.

On Monday, it makes
4¢ every minute.

On Tuesday, it makes
20¢ every minute.

_____

_____

On Wednesday, it makes
40¢ every minute.

On Thursday, it makes
$1.00 every minute.

_____

_____

© Harcourt

Name _____

Problem Solving
Make a Model

There are 27 children playing kickball on a playground. Then 13 children join the game. How many children in all are playing kickball?

UNDERSTAND

What do you want to find out?

PLAN

You can make a model to solve the problem.

SOLVE

tens	ones
2	7
+ 1	3
4	0

_40_ children

CHECK

Does your answer make sense? Explain.

Use Workmat 3 and ▤▤▤▤▤▤▤▤▤▤ ▪ .
Add. Regroup if you need to.
Write the sum.

1. At 12:00 in the lunchroom, there are 39 girls and 34 boys. How many children are eating lunch at 12:00?

_____ children

tens	ones
3	9
+ 3	4

2. In Ms. Dodge's class, 7 boys and 15 girls bring their lunch to school. How many children bring their lunch?

_____ children

tens	ones
	7
+ 1	5

© Harcourt

Use Workmat 3 and ▭▭▭▭▭▭▭▭ ▭ .
Add. Regroup if you need to.
Write the sum.

1 There are 10 boys and 12 girls
playing soccer on the field. How
many children are playing soccer?

_22_ children

tens	ones
1	0
+ 1	2
2	2

2 The Red Team scores 13 goals on
Monday and 8 on Tuesday. How many
goals does the team score in all?

_____ goals

tens	ones
+	

3 The soccer players eat 12 cheese
pizzas and 9 sausage pizzas. How
many pizzas do they eat?

_____ pizzas

tens	ones
+	

4 At the soccer party there are 29 blue
balloons and 37 red balloons. How
many balloons are there in all?

_____ balloons

tens	ones
+	

Write About It

Write a story about adding two numbers.
Both numbers are between 0 and 40.

© Harcourt

🏠 HOME ACTIVITY • Make up a problem like the ones on this page. Have your child use pennies and
dimes (see page 156) to solve the problem.

Name _____

CHECK ▪ Concepts and Skills

Add.

1

2	2 tens	20
+3	+3 tens	+30
	___ tens	

2

4	4 tens	40
+5	+5 tens	+50
	___ tens	

3 Count on to add.

$55 + 2 =$ _____ $30 + 42 =$ _____ $47 + 10 =$ _____

Use Workmat 3 and ▬▬▬▬▬▬ ▪ .

Show.	Add the ones. Are there 10 or more ones? If so, regroup 10 ones as 1 ten.	Write how many tens and ones.
4 25 + 16	Yes No	____ tens ____ ones
5 46 + 19	Yes No	____ tens ____ ones

CHECK ▪ Problem Solving

Use Workmat 3 and ▬▬▬▬▬▬ ▪ . Add.
Regroup if you need to. Write the sum.

6 13 children went to the soccer game.
18 children went to the baseball game.
How many children in all went to a game?

_____ children

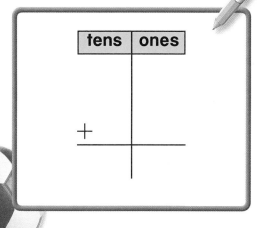

tens	ones
+	

Name _____

Choose the best answer for questions 1–5.

1
$$\begin{array}{r} 40 \\ +20 \\ \hline \end{array}$$

6   16   50   60
○   ○   ○   ○

2   72 + 4 = _____

76   80   81   112
○   ○   ○   ○

3 Which does the model show?

tens	ones

33 + 15   23 + 15
○

23 + 16   22 + 14
○   ○

4 Jasmine has 64 crayons. Kelli has 12 crayons. How many crayons do they have in all?

76   78   87   97
○   ○   ○   ○

5 Which number matches the words?
sixty-four

60   604   64   614
○   ○   ○

Show What You Know

6 Use red and blue. Color the tens.
Show two different ways. Write the numbers.

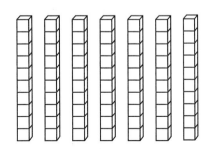

_____ tens + _____ tens = _____ tens

_____ + _____ = _____

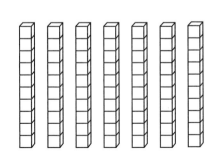

_____ tens + _____ tens = _____ tens

_____ + _____ = _____

© Harcourt

CHAPTER 12
2-Digit Addition

Make the addition problem that has the greatest sum.

SCHOOL HOME CONNECTION

Dear Family,
   Today we started Chapter 12. We will add more 2-digit numbers and learn how to estimate. Here is the math vocabulary and an activity for us to do together at home.

                    Love,
   _____

Vocabulary

estimate sums One way to find out *about* how many in all is to estimate. You can estimate by rounding each number to the closer ten and then adding the tens.

Estimate 39 + 23 as 40 + 20.

40 + 20 = 60

So 39 + 23 is about 60.

Visit *The Learning Site* for additional ideas and activities. www.harcourtschool.com

ACTIVITY

Give your child jars, cans, and boxes that contain up to 48 ounces of food. Ask your child to choose two of the items and add the ounces to find the total.

Books to Share

To read about addition with your child, look for these books in your local library.

17 Kings and 42 Elephants, by Margaret Mahy, Dial Books, 1990.

Pancakes, Pancakes, by Eric Carle, Aladdin, 1998.

E I E I O, by Gus Clarke, Lothrop, Lee & Shepard, 1993.

© Harcourt

Problem Solving
Estimate Sums

Carol saw 36 rain forest animals in the zoo. Charles saw 33 in a nature show. About how many rain forest animals did they see in all?

You **estimate** when you don't need an exact answer.

UNDERSTAND

What do you want to find out?

PLAN

You can estimate sums to solve the problem.

SOLVE

You can **round** numbers when you want to know about how many. When you round a number to the nearest ten, you can find the ten it is closer to on a number line.

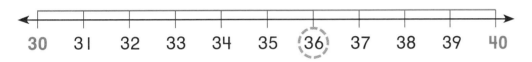

Circle 36 on the number line. 36 is closer to 40 than to 30.

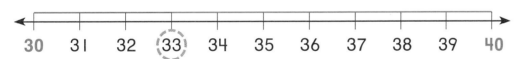

Circle 33 on the number line. 33 is closer to 30 than to 40.

Now, add your rounded numbers.

CHECK

Does your answer make sense? Explain.

When a number is halfway between 2 tens, round to the greater ten. You would round 15 to 20. Look at the number line. Which numbers would you round to 40?

estimate
40
+ 30
70

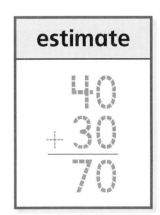

© Harcourt

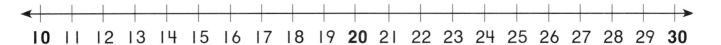

10 11 12 13 14 15 16 17 18 19 **20** 21 22 23 24 25 26 27 28 29 **30**

Use the number line to help you round.
Show your addition problem.

	estimate

1 Ian has 11 buttons. Erika gives him 17 buttons. About how many buttons does Ian have now?

about ___30___ buttons

$$\begin{array}{r} 10 \\ + 20 \\ \hline 30 \end{array}$$

2 Greg has 26 shells. He finds 21 more shells. About how many shells does Greg have in all?

about _____ shells

3 Bob has 19 stickers. Linda gives him 18 stickers. About how many stickers does Bob have now?

about _____ stickers

4 Pat earned 25¢ on Monday. She earned the same amount on Tuesday. Can she buy some marbles for 40¢?

_____

Write About It

Write a story about animals.
Add two numbers in your story.
Each number should be less than 50.

⬠ **HOME ACTIVITY** • Have your child practice estimating sums while you are at the supermarket. Pick two items with prices of up to 49¢. Ask your child to estimate the total price.

© Harcourt

Name _____

CHECK ▪ Concepts and Skills

Use Workmat 3 and 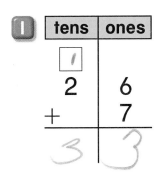.
Add. Regroup if you need to.

1	tens	ones
	1	
	2	6
+		7
	3	*3*

2	tens	ones
	☐	
	4	9
+		9

3	tens	ones
	☐	
	2	4
+1		8

4	tens	ones
	☐	
	4	3
+3		8

Use Workmat 3 and 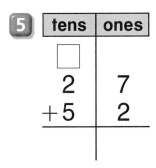.
Add. Regroup if you need to.

Rewrite the numbers in each problem.
Then add.

5	tens	ones
	☐	
	2	7
+5		2

6	tens	ones
	☐	
	3	8
+4		4

7 32 + 27

	tens	ones
	☐	
+		

8 74 + 8

	tens	ones
	☐	
+		

CHECK ▪ Problem Solving

Use the number line to help you round. Show your addition problem.

←─┼─→
10 11 12 13 14 15 16 17 18 19 **20** 21 22 23 24 25 26 27 28 29 **30**

9 Lee has 17 sports cards. Mike gives her 19 more cards. About how many sports cards does Lee have now?

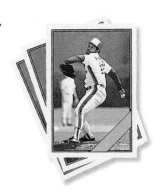

about _____ sports cards

estimate

© Harcourt

Name _____

Choose the best answer for questions 1–4.

1 Which is another way to write 29 + 44 = _____?

92	24	44	29
+44	+94	+92	+44
○	○	○	○

2

tens	ones
☐	
2	7
+1	2

15   35   39   41
○   ○   ○   ○

3

tens	ones
☐	
3	7
+1	4

50   51   60   61
○   ○   ○   ○

4 What time does the clock show?

6:20   6:25
○   ○

5:20   5:25
○   ○

Show What You Know

5 What numbers can you add to 56 without regrouping?
Write the numbers. Write the sums.

tens	ones		tens	ones		tens	ones		tens	ones
5	6		5	6		5	6		5	6
+			+			+			+	

© Harcourt

CHAPTER 13 Practice 2-Digit Addition

Write 2 addition problems. Regroup if you need to.

SCHOOL HOME CONNECTION

Dear Family,
   Today we started Chapter 13. We will practice adding 2-digit numbers and use mental math to solve problems. Here is the math vocabulary and an activity for us to do together at home.

                    Love,

   _____

Vocabulary

mental math A way to solve problems without using a pencil or paper.

$$
\begin{array}{r}
64 \\
+ 25 \\
\end{array}
$$

Add the tens.
$$
\begin{array}{r}
60 \\
+ 20 \\
\hline
80 \\
\end{array}
$$

Add the ones.
$$
\begin{array}{r}
4 \\
+ 5 \\
\hline
9 \\
\end{array}
$$

Find the sum.
$$
\begin{array}{r}
80 \\
+ 9 \\
\hline
89 \\
\end{array}
$$

Visit *The Learning Site* for additional ideas and activities. www.harcourtschool.com

ACTIVITY

Give your child a grocery receipt or ad from the newspaper. Have him or her find two items that each cost less than 50 cents and add their prices.

Books to Share

To read about addition with your child, look for these books in your local library.

The Hundred Penny Box, by Sharon Bell Mathis, Viking, 1975.

The Philharmonic Gets Dressed, by Karla Kuskin, HarperCollins, 1986.

Baseball's Greatest Hitters, by S. A. Kramer, Random House, 2000.

© Harcourt

Name _____

Janie saw 43 blue birds.
She saw 25 red birds.
How many birds did she see altogether?

Here is a way to add 43 + 25 in your head.
Adding in your head is called **mental math**.

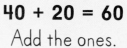

Think.
Add the tens.
40 + 20 = 60
Add the ones.
3 + 5 = 8
Then add the sums.
60 + 8 = 68

Janie saw __68__ birds.

Use mental math to add.

1 $19 + 21 = $ __40__

Think

$10 + 20 = 30$

$9 + 1 = 10$

$30 + 10 = 40$

2 $33 + 56 = $ _____

Think

___ + ___ = ___

___ + ___ = ___

___ + ___ = ___

3 $41 + 26 = $ _____

Think

___ + ___ = ___

___ + ___ = ___

___ + ___ = ___

4 $35 + 25 = $ _____

Think

___ + ___ = ___

___ + ___ = ___

___ + ___ = ___

Talk About It ▪ Reasoning

If you think $20 + 40 = 60$ and $7 + 3 = 10$, what two numbers are you adding?

Use mental math to add.

$$33 + 59 = \underline{\quad ? \quad}$$

Think.
Add the tens. **30 + 50 = 80**
Then add the ones. **3 + 9 = 12**
Add the sums. **80 + 12 = 92**

$$33 + 59 = \underline{92}$$

1 $45 + 13 = \underline{\quad\quad}$

Think

$$\underline{\quad} + \underline{\quad} = \underline{\quad}$$

$$\underline{\quad} + \underline{\quad} = \underline{\quad}$$

$$\underline{\quad} + \underline{\quad} = \underline{\quad}$$

2 $52 + 42 = \underline{\quad\quad}$

Think

$$\underline{\quad} + \underline{\quad} = \underline{\quad}$$

$$\underline{\quad} + \underline{\quad} = \underline{\quad}$$

$$\underline{\quad} + \underline{\quad} = \underline{\quad}$$

3 $61 + 29 = \underline{\quad\quad}$

Think

$$\underline{\quad} + \underline{\quad} = \underline{\quad}$$

$$\underline{\quad} + \underline{\quad} = \underline{\quad}$$

$$\underline{\quad} + \underline{\quad} = \underline{\quad}$$

Problem Solving ▪ Mental Math

Use mental math. Is the sum correct?
Circle Yes or No. Then write the correct sum.

4 $39 + 49 = 88$

Yes   No $\underline{\quad\quad}$

5 $67 + 24 = 81$

Yes   No $\underline{\quad\quad}$

🏠 **HOME ACTIVITY** • Have your child tell how he or she added the numbers for the exercises on this page.

© Harcourt

Name _____

Circle the problems in which you will need to regroup. Then add.

1

(28 + 47 = 75)

11
+56

14
+28

54
+ 9

37
+36

2
35
+29

14
+17

42
+36

16
+39

63
+ 4

3
26
+19

73
+24

54
+ 9

49
+18

21
+12

4
57
+17

39
+37

26
+36

5
48
+22

35
+49

61
+17

Talk About It ▪ **Reasoning**

How did you know which problems to circle?

Practice

Circle the problems in which you will need to regroup.
Then add.

1   13
  +39
  52

     25   67   19   73
   + 8   +20   +48   +13

2   17   33   19   14   73
  +46   + 3   +24   +28   +19

3   41   73   42   35   71
  +25   + 9   +39   +20   +19

4   25   29   47   79   17
  +37   +41   +25   + 3   +15

Problem Solving ▪ Estimation

5 You want a sum of about 60. Which 2 numbers would you add?

____ ____

6 You want a sum of about 90. Which 2 numbers would you add?

____ ____

| 28 |
| 47 |
| 59 |
| 8 |

HOME ACTIVITY • Have your child tell you how to add 2-digit numbers. Together, make up addition problems using the digits from your phone number. The sums should be 99 or less.

Chapter 13

© Harcourt

Name _____

Problem Solving
Make and Use a Graph

Some children at school are building birdhouses for a project. Use the chart to answer the questions.

Birdhouses Made

Kindergarten	7
First Grade	10
Second Grade	14
Third Grade	13

1. How many birdhouses in all did kindergarten and third grade make?

    20

2. How many birdhouses in all did second and third grade make?

    _____

3. Use the chart to complete the graph.

Birdhouses Made

	0	1	2	3	4	5	6	7	8	9	10	11	12	13	14	15
Kindergarten																
First Grade																
Second Grade																
Third Grade																

Use the graph to answer the questions.

4. How many birdhouses in all were made?

    _____

5. How many more birdhouses did second grade make than first grade?

    _____

6. How many more birdhouses would kindergarten need to make to equal the number made by second grade?

    _____

For a science project, three second-grade classes decided to learn about jungle animals.

1 How many children in all learned about gorillas and crocodiles?

_32_ children

elephant		13 children
gorilla		15 children
flamingo		10 children
tiger		12 children
crocodile		17 children

2 How many children in all learned about elephants and tigers?

_____ children

3 Complete the graph to show how many children learned about each animal.

Jungle Animals

	0	1	2	3	4	5	6	7	8	9	10	11	12	13	14	15	16	17
elephant																		
gorilla																		
flamingo																		
tiger																		
crocodile																		

Use the graph to answer the question.

4 How many children in all learned about jungle animals? _____ children

Write About It

What questions could you ask about the graph? Write some questions of your own.

© Harcourt

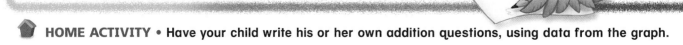

HOME ACTIVITY • Have your child write his or her own addition questions, using data from the graph.

Name _____

CHECK ▪ Concepts and Skills

Add.

1
tens	ones
1	6
+2	3

2
tens	ones
6	4
+1	7

Use mental math to add.

3 41 + 18 =

Think

____ + ____ = ____

____ + ____ = ____

____ + ____ = ____

Add.

4
$$21$$
$$+18$$

5
$$35$$
$$+26$$

6
$$17$$
$$+23$$

7
$$32$$
$$+61$$

8
$$53$$
$$+32$$

CHECK ▪ Problem Solving

9 Pat and Joe saw some birds at the park. They made a chart.

Complete the graph to show how many birds Pat and Joe saw.

Birds	
blue jays	9
crows	10
robins	12

Birds												
blue jays												
crows												
robins												

0　1　2　3　4　5　6　7　8　9　10　11　12

10 How many more crows than blue jays did Pat and Joe see? _____

11 How many birds did Pat and Joe see altogether? _____

© Harcourt

Name _____

Choose the best answer for questions 1–4 .

1
$$\begin{array}{r} 55 \\ +38 \\ \hline \end{array}$$

17   18   93   94
○   ○   ○   ○

2
$$\begin{array}{r} 66 \\ +23 \\ \hline \end{array}$$

89   83   49   43
○   ○   ○   ○

3 Which number tells how many children in all like sparrows or doves?

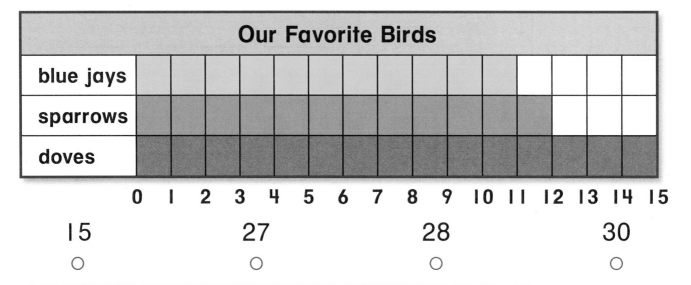

Our Favorite Birds

15   27   28   30
○   ○   ○   ○

4 Which is the tenth month of the year?

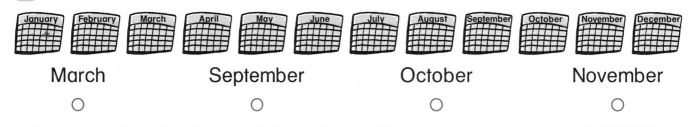

March   September   October   November
○   ○   ○   ○

Show What You Know

5 Use four of these numbers.
Write them in the boxes to make each sum.

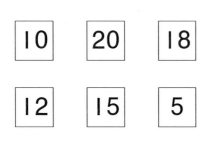

10   20   18
12   15   5

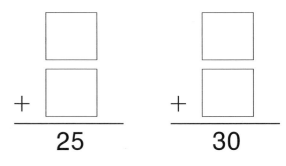

$$\begin{array}{r} \square \\ +\ \square \\ \hline 25 \end{array} \qquad \begin{array}{r} \square \\ +\ \square \\ \hline 30 \end{array}$$

© Harcourt

Name _____

CHECK ▪ Concepts and Skills

Subtract.

1

$5 - 1 =$ _____

$5 \text{ tens} - 1 \text{ ten} =$ _____ tens

$50 - 10 =$ _____

2

$9 - 3 =$ _____

$9 \text{ tens} - 3 \text{ tens} =$ _____ tens

$90 - 30 =$ _____

Choose a method to solve the problems.

3
$$\begin{array}{r} 45 \\ -10 \\ \hline \end{array}$$

4
$$\begin{array}{r} 89 \\ -\ 3 \\ \hline \end{array}$$

Use Workmat 3 and . Find the difference.

5

tens	ones
☐	☐
4	2
−1	6

6

tens	ones
☐	☐
2	3
−1	9

Use Workmat 3 and 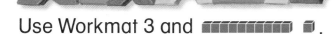.

Subtract.	Do you need to regroup?		Subtract. Write how many are left.
7 $21 - 6 =$ _____	Yes	No	_____ tens _____ ones
8 $49 - 7 =$ _____	Yes	No	_____ tens _____ones
9 $53 - 47 =$ _____	Yes	No	_____
10 $72 - 32 =$ _____	Yes	No	_____

© Harcourt

Name _____

Choose the best answer for questions 1–7.

1
$$\begin{array}{r} 80 \\ -50 \\ \hline \end{array}$$

30 ○   40 ○   120 ○   130 ○

2
$$\begin{array}{r} 73 \\ -\ 2 \\ \hline \end{array}$$

61 ○   63 ○   70 ○   71 ○

3
$$\begin{array}{r} 57 \\ -28 \\ \hline \end{array}$$

29 ○   31 ○   55 ○   85 ○

4
$$\begin{array}{r} 44 \\ -37 \\ \hline \end{array}$$

1 ○   7 ○   3 ○   81 ○

5
$$\begin{array}{r} 93 \\ -20 \\ \hline \end{array}$$

23 ○   53 ○   63 ○   73 ○

6
$$\begin{array}{r} 63 \\ -\ 5 \\ \hline \end{array}$$

56 ○   57 ○   58 ○   62 ○

7 Amanda has 5 pink erasers and 13 blue erasers in her pencil box. How many erasers are there in her pencil box?

5 ○   8 ○   17 ○   18 ○

Show What You Know

8 Complete each problem. Choose numbers that will **not** need to be regrouped.

_____ − 6 = _____   _____ − 7 = _____

_____ − 8 = _____   _____ − 9 = _____

© Harcourt

CHAPTER 15

2-Digit Subtraction

36 Bricks

36 Bricks

10 Tiles

10 Tiles

10 Tiles

10 Tiles

10 Tiles

99 Short Nails

47 Long Nails

What subtraction problems do you see at the construction site?

SCHOOL HOME CONNECTION

Dear Family,
 Today we started Chapter 15. We will look at more ways to subtract 2-digit numbers. Here is the math vocabulary and an activity for us to do together at home.

Love,

_____

My Math Words
estimate differences
rounding

Vocabulary

estimate differences Find *about* how many are left by rounding each number to the closer ten and then subtracting the tens.

Estimate 87 – 32 as 90 – 30.

90 – 30 = 60

So 87 – 32 is about 60.

rounding A way to estimate an answer. In this chapter, we round to the closer ten.

Visit *The Learning Site* for additional ideas and activities. www.harcourtschool.com

ACTIVITY

Cut paper into squares. On each square, write a number from 1-50. Have your child choose 2 squares and subtract the smaller number from the number on the other square. Continue until all the squares have been used.

Books to Share

To read about subtraction with your child, look for these books in your local library.

Alexander, Who Used to be Rich Last Sunday, by Judith Viorst, Simon & Schuster, 1988.

Caps for Sale, by Esphyr Slobodkina, HarperCollins, 1999.

© Harcourt

Name _____

CHECK ■ Concepts and Skills

Use Workmat 3 and 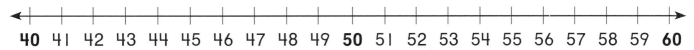 .
Subtract. Regroup if you need to.

Rewrite the numbers.
Then subtract.

1	tens	ones
	☐	☐
	6	5
	−3	8

2	tens	ones
	☐	☐
	8	8
	−5	3

3 43 − 28 = _____

tens	ones
−	

Subtract.

Subtract. Add to check.

4
```
  60
−25
```

5
```
  74
−45
```

6
```
  94
−67
```

CHECK ■ Problem Solving

Estimate by rounding. Then solve.

40 41 42 43 44 45 46 47 48 49 **50** 51 52 53 54 55 56 57 58 59 **60**

7 There are 58 toy cars in a bin.
Carl takes out 49 to play with.
How many toy cars are left
in the bin?

estimate	solve

_____ toy cars

Choose the best answer for questions 1–5.

1
$$63$$
$$-47$$

   16   17   27   110
   ○   ○   ○   ○

2
$$80$$
$$-79$$

   1   10   19   159
   ○   ○   ○   ○

3 Which is another way to write $47 - 9 =$ _____?

$$74 \quad 47 \quad 74 \quad 47$$
$$-19 \quad -9 \quad -9 \quad -19$$
 ○   ○   ○   ○

4 Which number is even?

  1   17   26   35
 ○   ○   ○   ○

5 There are 38 pencils in a cup. During a math lesson, the class uses 21 pencils from the cup. Which is the best estimate of how many pencils are left in the cup?

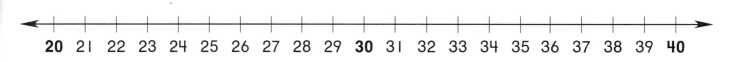

20 21 22 23 24 25 26 27 28 29 **30** 31 32 33 34 35 36 37 38 39 **40**

about 10   about 20   about 40   about 70
   ○   ○   ○   ○

Show What You Know

6 Write a subtraction problem.
Use numbers that have tens and ones.
Write an addition problem to check it.

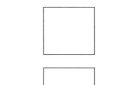

© Harcourt

CHAPTER 16 Practice 2-Digit Subtraction

19 Steps to Pond

Start

30 Steps to cave

27 Steps to Treasure

What subtraction stories can you write about this picture?

End

SCHOOL HOME CONNECTION

Dear Family,
   Today we started Chapter 16. We will subtract 2-digit numbers, use mental math, and add and subtract amounts of money. Here is the math vocabulary and an activity for us to do together at home.

Love,

_____

My Math Words

mental math

Vocabulary

mental math A way to subtract in your head without using pencil or paper.

$$\begin{array}{r} 36 \\ -17 \\ \hline ? \end{array}$$

Add more to make the smaller number a ten.

$$17 + 3 = 20$$

Add the same number to the larger number.

$$36 + 3 = 39$$

Subtract your answers.

So,

$$\begin{array}{r} 39 \\ -20 \\ \hline 19 \end{array} \qquad \begin{array}{r} 36 \\ -17 \\ \hline 19 \end{array}$$

Visit *The Learning Site* for additional ideas and activities. www.harcourtschool.com

ACTIVITY

Look at grocery store ads for items that cost 99¢ or less. Have your child use these numbers to write subtraction problems and find the differences.

Books to Share

To read about subtraction with your child, look for these books in your local library.

Anno's Math Games II, by Mitsumaso Anno, Putnam & Grosset Group, 1989.

Country Fair, by Elisha Cooper, HarperCollins, 1997.

Monster Money Book, by Loreen Leedy, Holiday House, 2000.

Name _____

CHECK ▪ Concepts and Skills

Find the difference.

	Add the same number to both numbers.	Subtract.	
1 $\begin{array}{r} 52 \\ -18 \\ \hline ? \end{array}$	52 + ____ = ____ 18 + ____ = ____	$\begin{array}{r} \square \\ -\ \square \\ \hline \square \end{array}$	So, $\begin{array}{r} 52 \\ -18 \\ \hline \square \end{array}$

Subtract. Choose a strategy.

2 $\begin{array}{r} 67 \\ -39 \\ \hline \end{array}$ | **3** $\begin{array}{r} 70 \\ -40 \\ \hline \end{array}$ | **4** $\begin{array}{r} 39 \\ -21 \\ \hline \end{array}$ | **5** $\begin{array}{r} 41 \\ -\ 8 \\ \hline \end{array}$

Circle the + or −. Then solve.

6 $\begin{array}{r} 33¢ \\ +27¢ \\ \hline \end{array}$ | **7** $\begin{array}{r} 82¢ \\ -45¢ \\ \hline \end{array}$ | **8** $\begin{array}{r} 87¢ \\ -\ 8¢ \\ \hline \end{array}$ | **9** $\begin{array}{r} 52¢ \\ +44¢ \\ \hline \end{array}$

CHECK ▪ Problem Solving

Add or subtract. Write the sum or difference.

10 You have 75¢. You buy a yo-yo. How much money do you have left?

You have $\begin{array}{r} \square \ ¢ \\ \bigcirc \quad \square \ ¢ \\ \hline \square \ ¢ \end{array}$

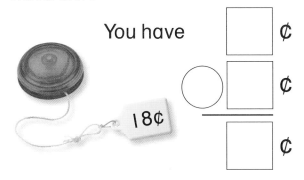
18¢

11 How much money would you need to buy a train car and a rope?

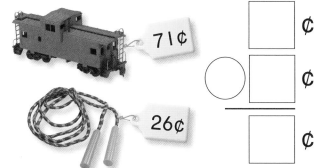
71¢
26¢

$\begin{array}{r} \square \ ¢ \\ \bigcirc \quad \square \ ¢ \\ \hline \square \ ¢ \end{array}$

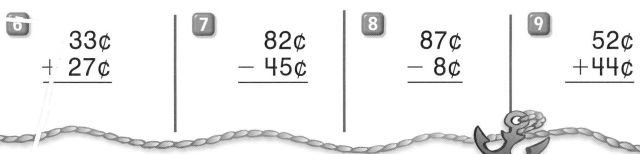

Name _____

Choose the best answer for questions 1–6.

1
$$34$$
$$-19$$

15   16   49   53
○   ○   ○   ○

2
$$75$$
$$-\;\;8$$

67   73   77   83
○   ○   ○   ○

3
$$97¢$$
$$-49¢$$

38¢   42¢   47¢   48¢
○   ○   ○   ○

4
$$9¢$$
$$+10¢$$

19¢   20¢   29¢   39¢
○   ○   ○   ○

5 Sarah wants to buy a baseball. She has 85¢. The baseball costs 99¢. Which tells how much more money Sarah will need to buy the baseball?

85¢ − 99¢   99¢ − 85¢   58¢ + 99¢   99¢ − 58¢
○   ○   ○   ○

6 How much money is shown?

55¢   56¢   66¢   65¢
○   ○   ○   ○

Show What You Know

7 Use these numbers. Write them in the boxes to make each difference.

| 44 | 15 | 12 | 59 |

$$\Box - \Box = 47 \qquad \Box - \Box = 29$$

The Picnic Lunch

written by Jo Sumara

illustrated by Ken Laidlaw

 This book will help me review 2-digit addition and subtraction.

This book belongs to _____.

Andy Ant could not believe his eyes.

Was it really a picnic?
It looked like a picnic.
It smelled like a picnic.
It was a picnic!

What luck! This was Andy's first day as a scout. He wanted everyone to be proud of him.

Andy yelled, "I found a picnic!"
"Yippee! Hooray!" the other ants shouted.
No one had found a picnic in a long
time. All the ants danced and cheered for
Andy. He felt very proud.

C

After Andy told the queen, she
gave orders to the ants. The ants
prepared for the picnic. 40 ants
and then 30 more lined up.

"Which way is the picnic?" asked
the ants. Andy pointed, and the ants
marched away.

D

How many ants were sent to the picnic? _____

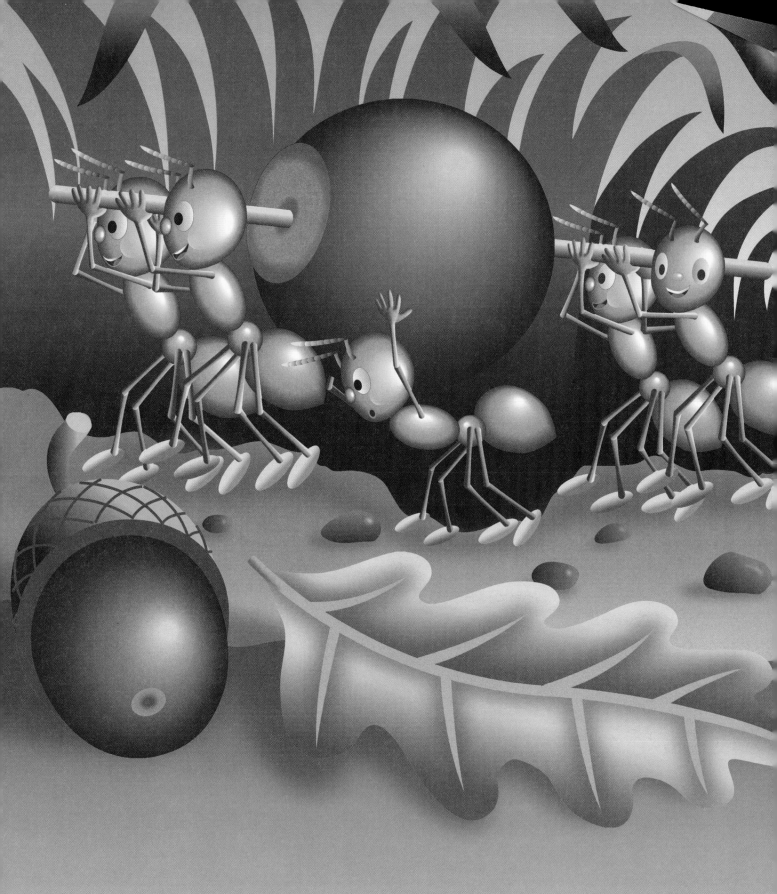

When the ants got to the picnic, they were amazed. There were so many foods to choose from. It took 5 ants to carry an olive. It took 20 of them to lift the cheese. They started the long, hard walk back home.

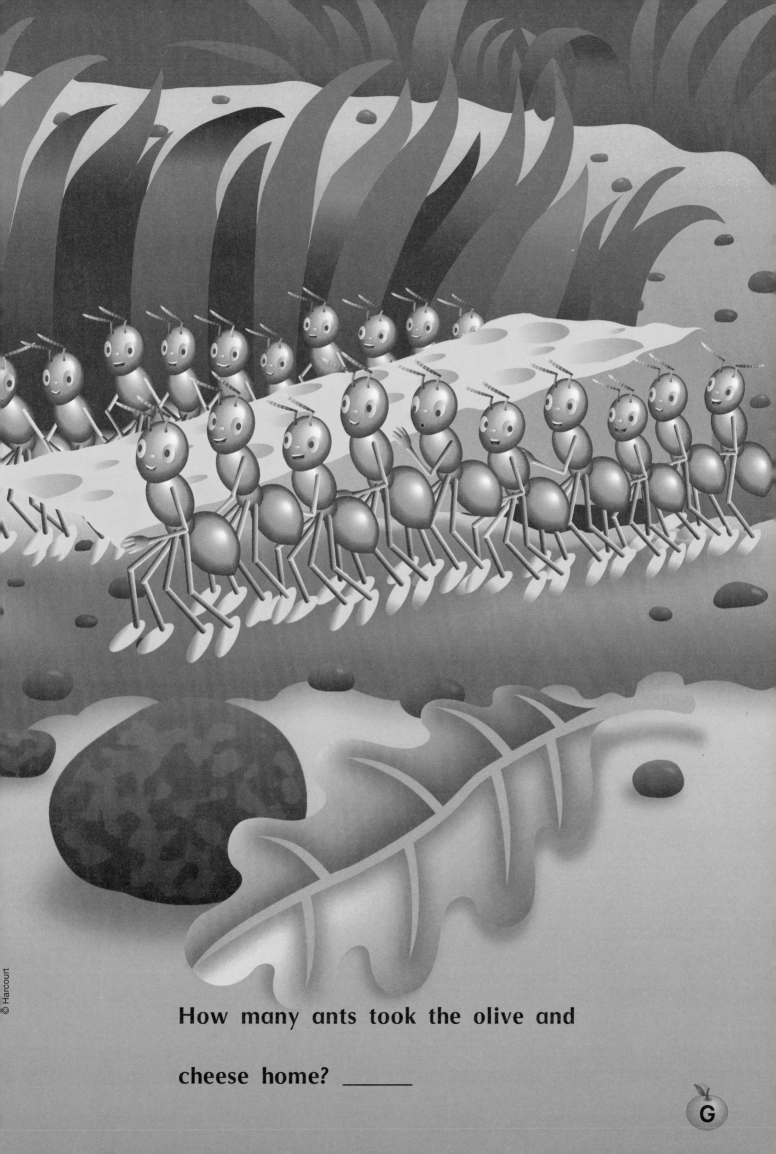

How many ants took the olive and

cheese home? _____

G

The queen sent 68 strong
ants to get the sandwich. It
turned out that 47 could pick
it up. What did the other
ants do?
They carried Andy!

H

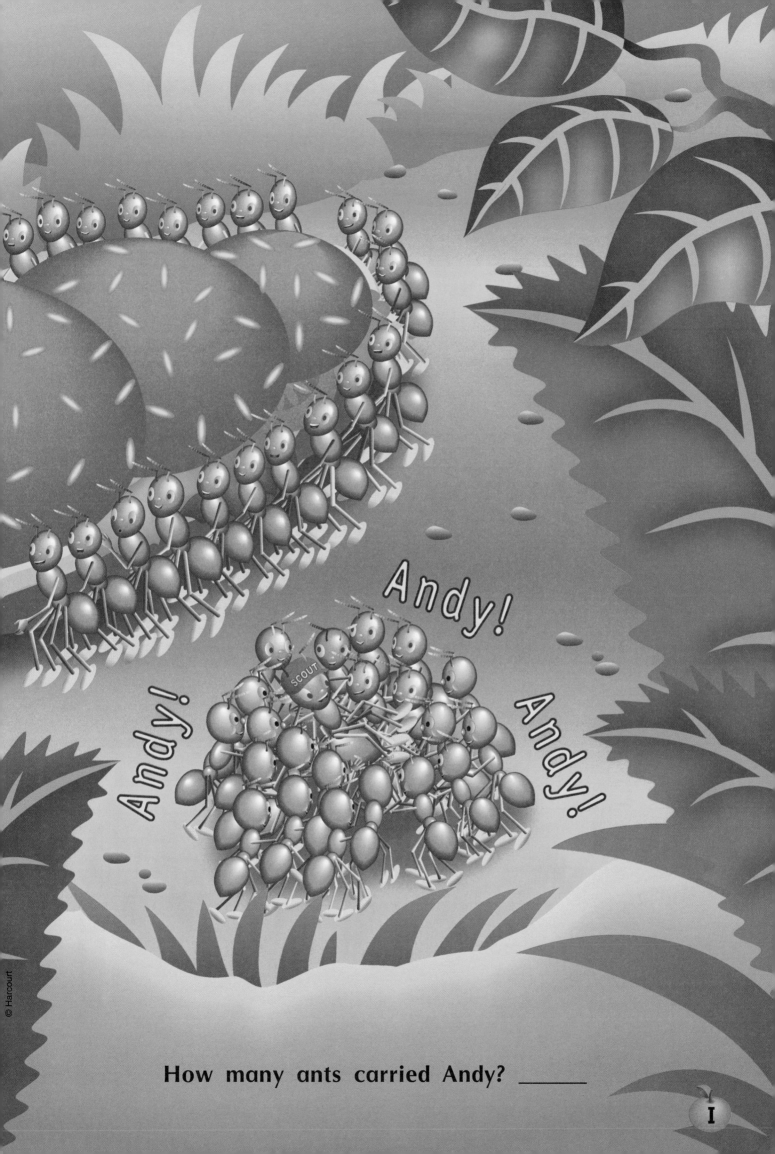

How many ants carried Andy? _____

At home, all the ants greeted
Andy. They were so proud of him.
"Hooray for Andy!" they cheered.
The queen invited her best scout to
sit at her table for the BIG picnic.

Name _____

A Stroll Through the Garden

Use your problem solving skills to write the missing sign. Draw a line to show the way out of the maze.

START

$83 \boxed{} 13 = 96$ $18 \boxed{} 36 = 54$

$\begin{array}{c} \boxed{} \\ \begin{array}{c} 12 \\ 14 \\ \hline 26 \end{array} \end{array}$

$13 \boxed{} 17 = 30$

$\begin{array}{c} \boxed{} \\ \begin{array}{c} 48 \\ 28 \\ \hline 20 \end{array} \end{array}$

$23 \boxed{} 19 = 42$

$11 \boxed{} 10 = 21$ $52 \boxed{} 24 = 76$

$\begin{array}{c} \boxed{} \\ \begin{array}{c} 41 \\ 18 \\ \hline 59 \end{array} \end{array}$

$3 \boxed{} 3 = 6$

$\begin{array}{c} \boxed{} \\ \begin{array}{c} 30 \\ 40 \\ \hline 70 \end{array} \end{array}$

$29 \boxed{} 68 = 97$

$\begin{array}{c} \boxed{} \\ \begin{array}{c} 19 \\ 19 \\ \hline 38 \end{array} \end{array}$

$13 \boxed{} 27 = 40$

$83 \boxed{} 27 = 56$

END

Stretch Your Thinking ▪ Draw a maze of your own for your classmates to solve.

© Harcourt

Name _____

The greatest sum is 5.

1	2	3

```
  1         2         1
+ 2       + 3       + 3
———       ———       ———
  3         5         4
```

Use each number one time in each problem.
Try to make the greatest possible sum.

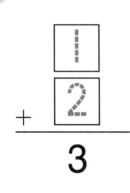

1	2	3	4

What is the greatest sum that you found? _____

© Harcourt

Name _____

Skills and Concepts

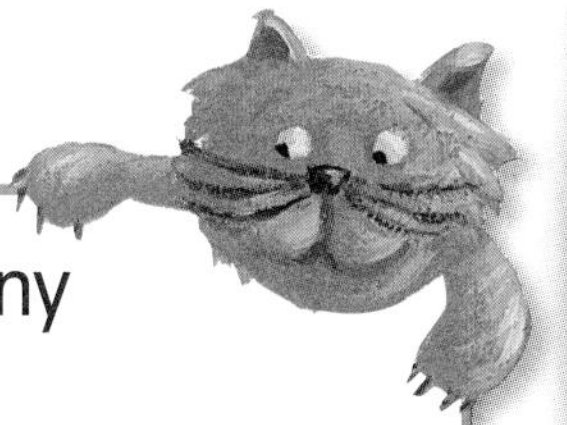

Use Workmat 3 and ▬▬▬▬▬▬▬ ▪. Add.

Show.	Join the ones. Can you make a ten? If so, regroup 10 ones as 1 ten.	Write how many in all.
1 56 + 4 = _____	Yes No	_____ tens _____ ones
2 17 + 16 = _____	Yes No	_____ tens _____ ones

Add.

3   62
       + 3

4   62
       + 30

5

tens	ones
☐	
3	7
+2	9

6

tens	ones
☐	
7	3
+1	7

7 Rewrite. Then add.

64 + 7

tens	ones
☐	
+	

8 Use mental math to add 28 + 65.

_____ + _____ = _____

_____ + _____ = _____

_____ + _____ = _____

Use Workmat 3 and ▭▭▭▭▭▭▭▭ ▢. Subtract.

Show.	Do you need to regroup?	Subtract the ones. Write how many tens and ones are left.
9 28 − 9 = _____	Yes No	_____ tens _____ ones
10 32 − 17 = _____	Yes No	_____ tens _____ ones

Subtract.

11
```
  74
−  2
```

12
```
  74
− 20
```

13

tens	ones
☐	☐
5	2
−3	6

14

tens	ones
☐	☐
4	0
−	3

15 Rewrite. Then subtract.

34 − 28

tens	ones
☐	☐
−	

16 Subtract. Add to check.

```
  22
− 14
```

Problem Solving

17 Jennifer wants to buy crayons for 45¢. She has 32¢. How much more money does she need?

45¢

_____ ¢

© Harcourt

Book Fair

Zack and his brother Jacob went to the book fair at the library.

- Zack had 52¢ and Jacob had 38¢.

- They put their money together and bought 2 items.

- They spent a total of 71¢.

Which 2 items could they have bought? How much change did they have left?

Show your work.

© Harcourt

Technology

Name _____

Calculator • Make the Next Number

Use a .

Add or subtract to get to each number.

$$23 \bigcirc \underline{\quad} = 53 \bigcirc \underline{\quad} = 31$$

Step 1

Think: 23 < 53, so add.

Press `ON/C` `2` `3` `+` `3` `0` `=` | 53 |.

Step 2

Think: 53 > 31, so subtract.

Press `-` `2` `2` `=` | 31 |.

So, 23 + 30 = 53 − 22 = 31

Practice and Problem Solving

Use a .

Add or subtract to get to each number.

1 $65 \bigcirc \underline{\quad} = 35 \bigcirc \underline{\quad} = 38 \bigcirc \underline{\quad} = 78$

Make your own.

2 $\underline{\quad} \bigcirc \underline{\quad} = \underline{\quad} \bigcirc \underline{\quad} = \underline{\quad}$

3 Talk About It Explain how to get from 23 to 73 to 78 to 68.

Name _____

PROBLEM SOLVING ON LOCATION

On the Trail

Pioneer families traveled by wagon and by foot on the Oregon trail. They carried with them all they owned.

blankets
10 pounds

corn
40 pounds

dried beef
20 pounds

tools
40 pounds

flour
30 pounds

oats
20 pounds

soap
10 pounds

beans
30 pounds

Each wagon holds 100 pounds. Find a way to load every item onto the wagons. Draw and label different ways.

Name _____

PROBLEM SOLVING ON LOCATION

On the Road

Chippewa National Forest, in Minnesota, is a favorite place for hiking, camping, swimming, boating, and fishing.

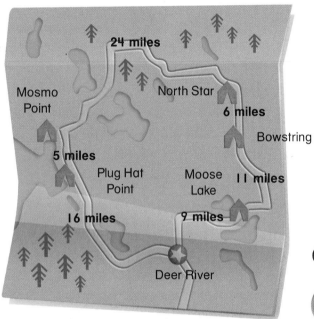

Chippewa National Forest

 = campsite

Plan a 5-day camping trip. Start at Deer River, and end at Deer River. Go on to a new campsite each day. Complete the chart.

	From	To	Miles
Day 1	Deer River		
Day 2			
Day 3			
Day 4			
Day 5			
Day 6		Deer River	
	Total miles traveled		

© Harcourt

Name ______________________________

UNDERSTAND › PLAN › SOLVE › CHECK

Problem Solving
Make a Model

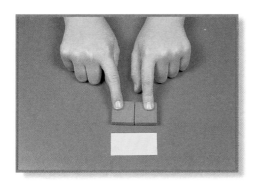

Chris wants to make a rectangle. How can he use 2 squares to make a rectangle?

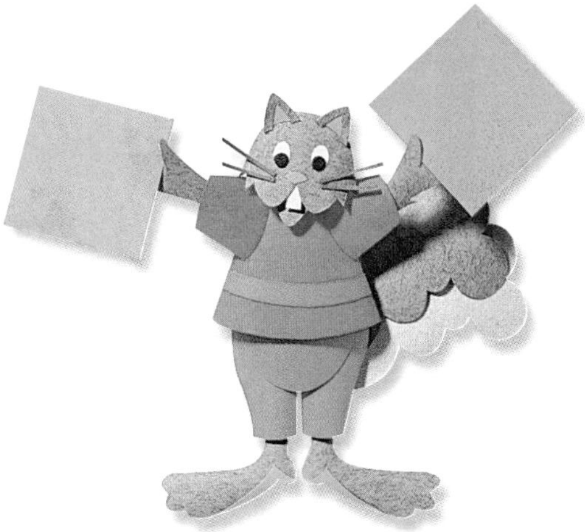

UNDERSTAND

What do you want to find out?

PLAN

You can make a model to solve the problem.

SOLVE

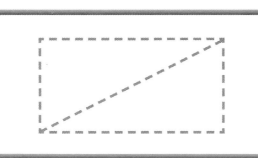

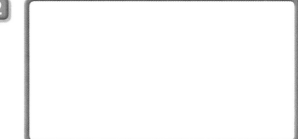

Use 2 squares to make a rectangle.

CHECK

Does your answer makes sense? Explain.

Use plane shapes. Put them together to make a new shape. Draw it. Write the name of the shape you made.

1

2 triangles

rectangle

2

2 rectangles

____

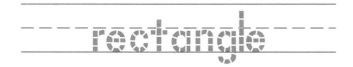

Draw a line or lines to separate the shape into new shapes.

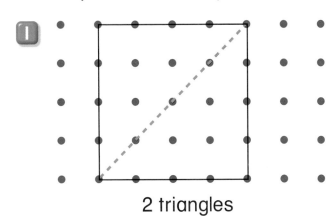

1 2 triangles

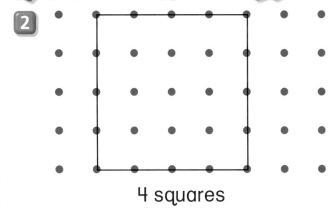

2 4 squares

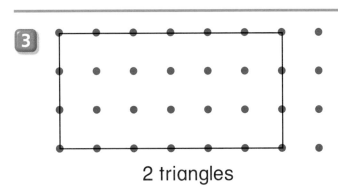

3 2 triangles

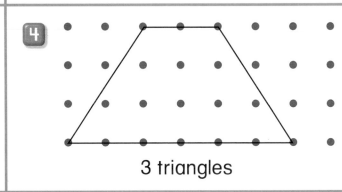

4 3 triangles

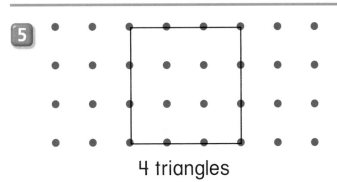

5 4 triangles

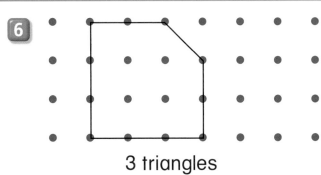

6 3 triangles

Mixed Review

Write <, >, or =.

7 37 ◯ 54   42 ◯ 42   83 ◯ 25

8 83 ◯ 99   94 ◯ 49   21 ◯ 78

🔷 **HOME ACTIVITY** • Draw and cut out a shape. Have your child draw lines on your figure and cut it apart to make and name new shapes.

© Harcourt

Name _____

You can move your box of crayons by turning it or flipping it.

You can **turn**.

You can **flip**.

Use ▰.
Put your ▰ on top of the first one.
Do not lift your ◣. Turn it to fit on top
of the second ◣. Trace the shape.

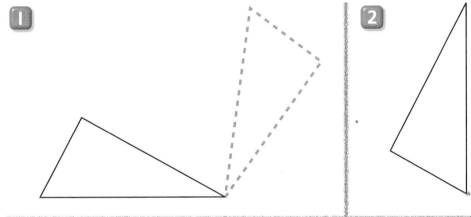

1

2

Put your ▰ on top of the first one.
Flip it to fit on top of the second ◣.
Trace the shape.

3

4

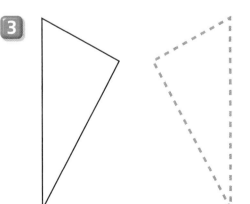

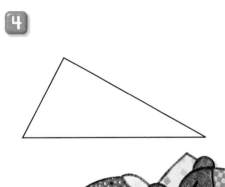

© Harcourt

Talk About It ▪ **Reasoning**
How is a turn different from a flip?

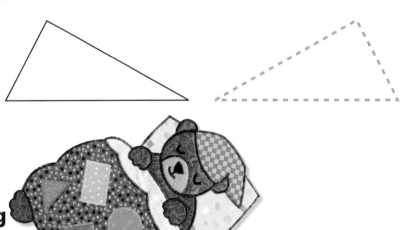

Use 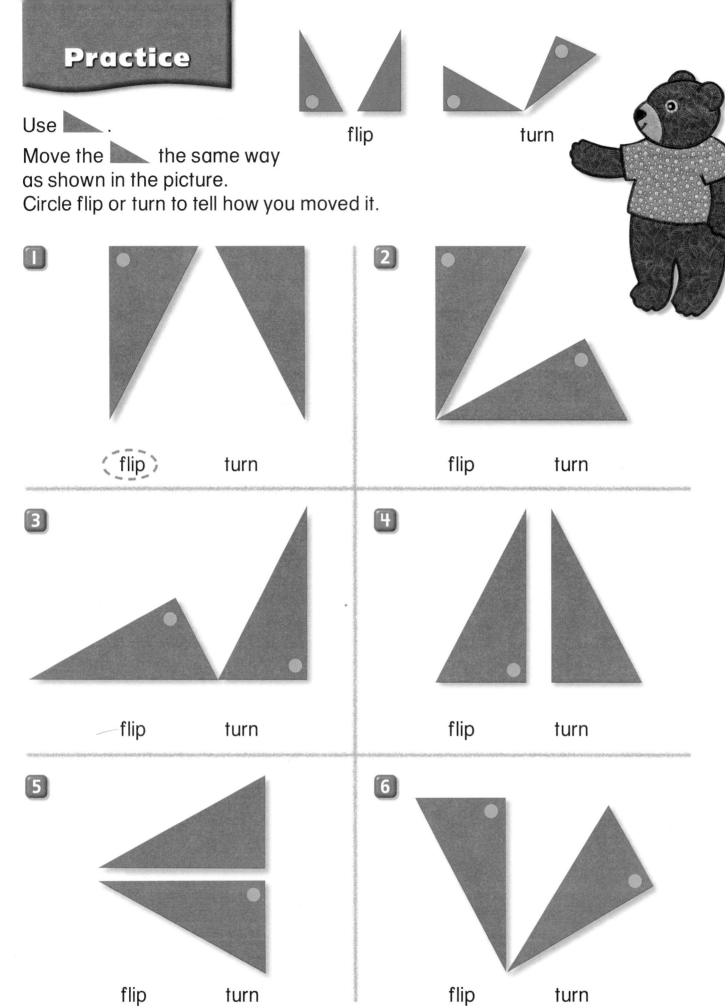.

Move the ◣ the same way
as shown in the picture.
Circle flip or turn to tell how you moved it.

flip

turn

1

(flip)   turn

2

flip   turn

3

flip   turn

4

flip   turn

5

flip   turn

6

flip   turn

🔷 **HOME ACTIVITY** • Ask your child to draw and cut out a shape. Have him or her show how to flip and turn the shape.

Name ______________________________

More About Moving Shapes

Hands On

CRAYONS
CRAYONS

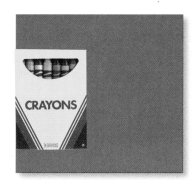

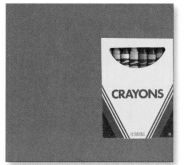

You can move your box of crayons by sliding it.

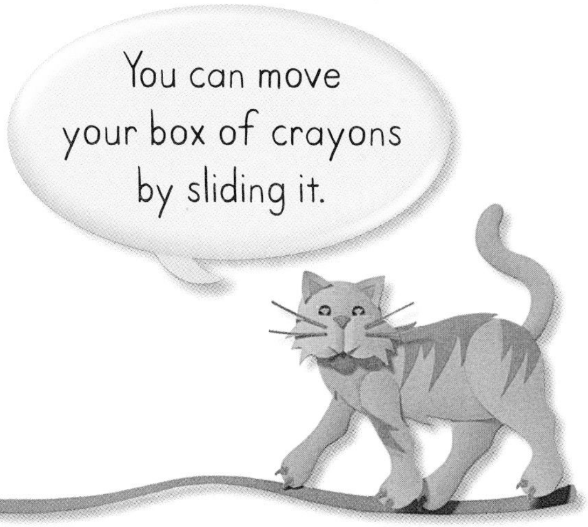

You can **slide**.

Use plane shapes. Put your plane shape on top of the one shown. Slide it to a different place. Trace to show the new place. Draw the dot.

1

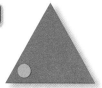

2

3

4

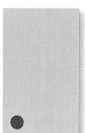

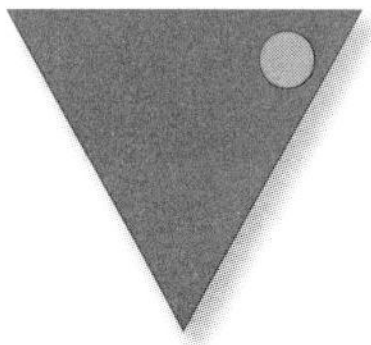

5

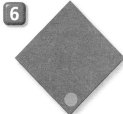

6

Talk About It ▪ Reasoning

How is a slide different from a turn?
How is it the same?

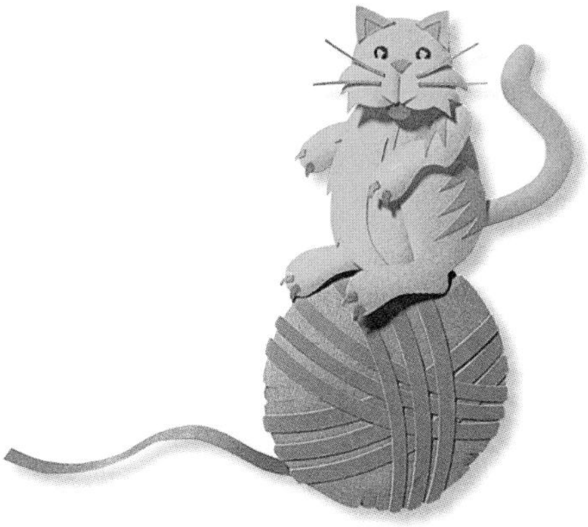

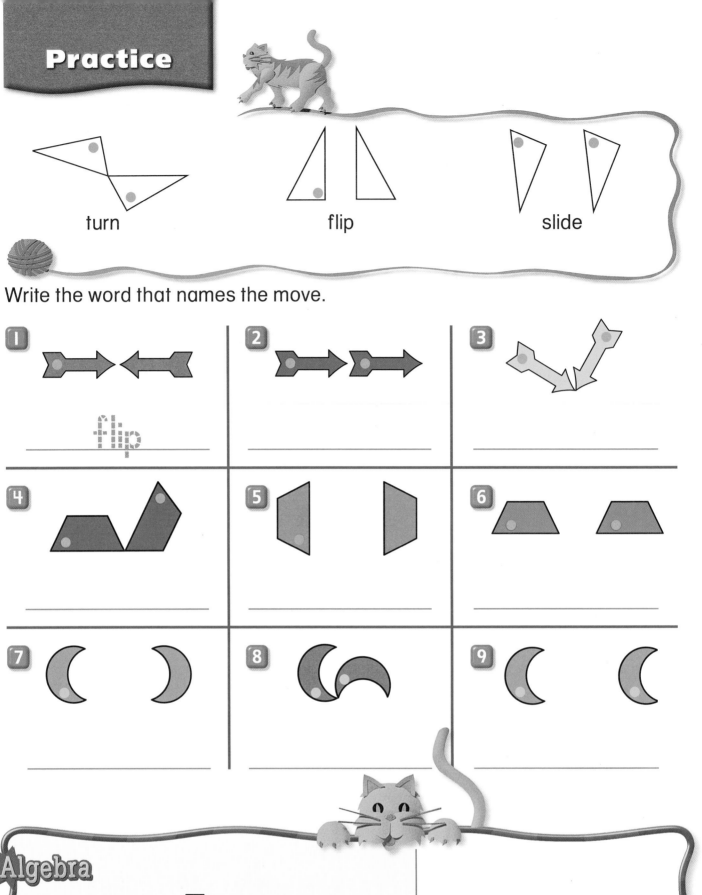

Practice

turn   flip   slide

Write the word that names the move.

1 flip

2

3

4

5

6

7

8

9

Algebra

Draw two more ⬠ to continue the most likely pattern.

10

HOME ACTIVITY • Put together a jigsaw puzzle with your child. Have him or her tell you which kind of move made each piece fit.

© Harcourt

Name _____

CHECK ▪ Concepts and Skills

Color the triangles. Cross out the shapes that are not triangles.

1

Write how many sides and corners.

2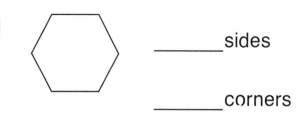

_____ sides

_____ corners

Draw a line of symmetry. The two parts will be congruent.

3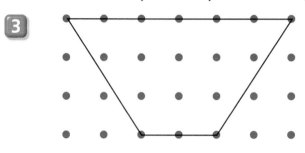

4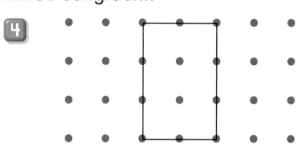

Circle the word that names the move.

5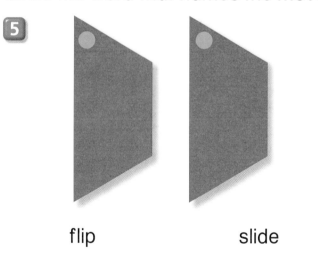

flip   slide

6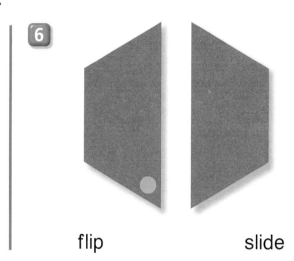

flip   slide

CHECK ▪ Problem Solving

Use plane shapes. Put them together to make a new shape. Draw it. Write the name of the shape you made.

7

_____

_ _ _ _ _ _ _ _ _ _ _ _ _

_____

two triangles

Name _____

Choose the best answer for questions 1–4.

1 Which is a rectangle?

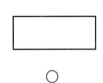 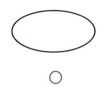

○   ○   ○   ○

2 Which shows a line of symmetry?

 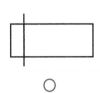 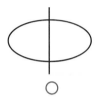

○   ○   ○   ○

3 Which shape can be made from two triangles?

○   ○   ○   ○

4 Which shows a flip?

○   ○   ○   ○

Show What You Know

5 Draw two different shapes that each have 3 sides and 3 corners.

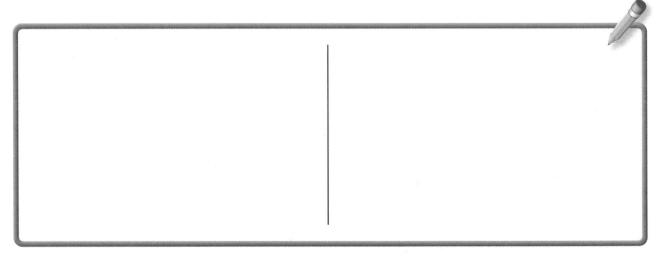

© Harcourt

CHAPTER 18 Solid Figures

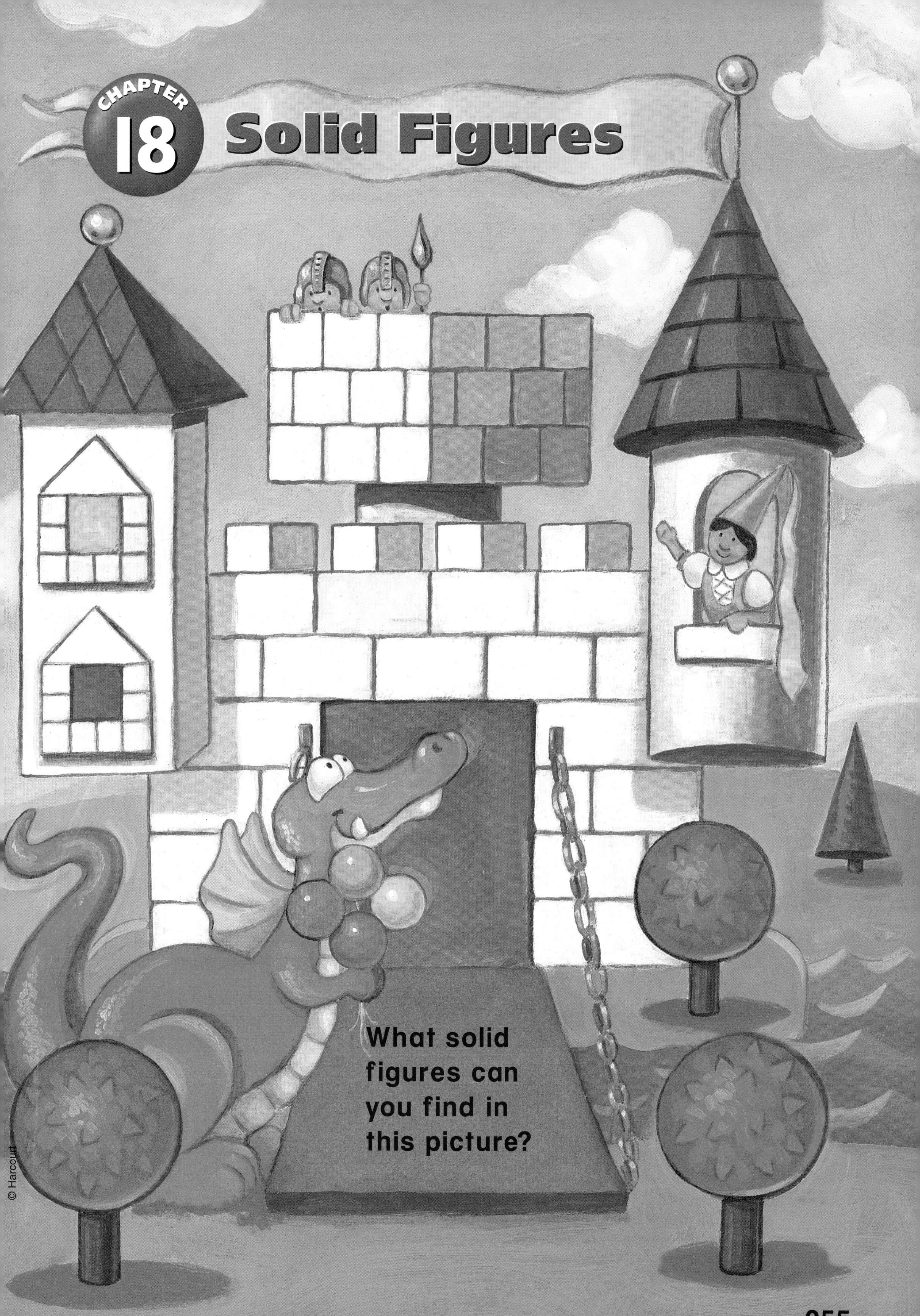

What solid figures can you find in this picture?

SCHOOL HOME CONNECTION

Dear Family,
   Today we started Chapter 18. We will identify and use solid figures. Here is the math vocabulary and an activity for us to do at home.

                    Love,

_____

My Math Words
rectangular prism
sphere
cone
cylinder
pyramid
cube

Vocabulary

rectangular prism   **sphere**

cone   **cylinder**

pyramid   **cube**

ACTIVITY

Play a game of I Spy with your child. Look around the room for an object that is shaped like a solid figure. Give your child clues about the object you have in mind. Your child should name the object and tell you what solid figure it is, using the correct math word.

Books to Share

To read about geometry with your child, look for these books in your local library.

The Goat in the Rug,
by Charles L. Blood and Martin Link, Simon and Schuster, 1990.

Shapes,
by Philip Yenawine, Delacorte, 1991.

Visit *The Learning Site* for additional ideas and activities.
www.harcourtschool.com

© Harcourt

Name _____

Problem Solving
Make a Model

You want to make this model. About how many do you think you will need?

Estimate: about _____ cubes

Build the model. How many did you use?

Count: 10 cubes

Estimate the number of . Then build the model. Write how many  you used.

1

Estimate: about _____ cubes

Count: _____ cubes

2

Estimate: about _____ cubes

Count: _____ cubes

3

Estimate: about _____ cubes

Count: _____ cubes

4

Estimate: about _____ cubes

Count: _____ cubes

© Harcourt

Estimate the number of . Then build the model. Write how many  you used.

1

Estimate: about _____ cubes

Count: _____ 12 cubes

2

Estimate: about _____ cubes

Count: _____ cubes

3

Estimate: about _____ cubes

Count: _____ cubes

4

Estimate: about _____ cubes

Count: _____ cubes

5

Estimate: about _____ cubes

Count: _____ cubes

6

Estimate: about _____ cubes

Count: _____ cubes

Write About It

Look at the model in exercise 3. Explain how you estimated how many cubes you needed to build the model.

HOME ACTIVITY • Ask your child to make a model from blocks or toy bricks at home. Have your child estimate and then count the number of items in each model.

Name _____

CHECK ▪ Concepts and Skills

Color the objects that are close to the shape of the solid figure. Cross out the objects that are not shaped like the solid figure.

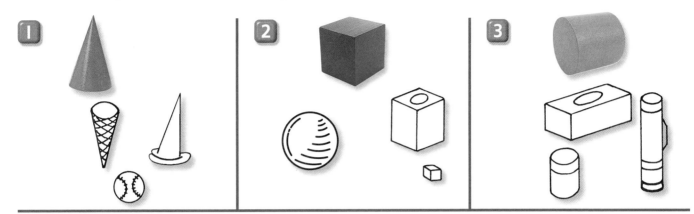

Circle the plane shape you can trace from the solid figure.

4 △ ⬡ ▭

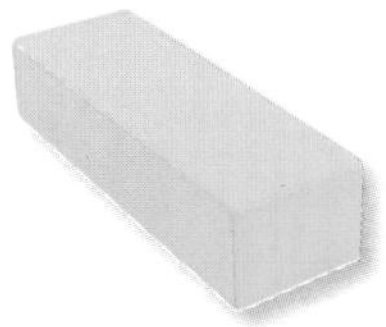

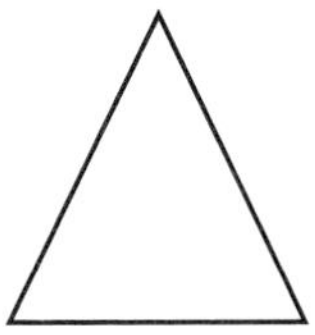

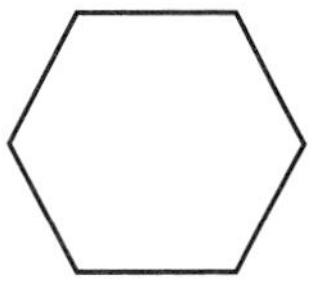

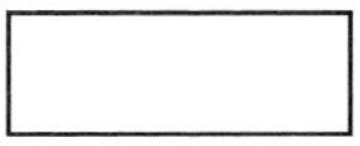

Use solid figures.
Sort them by the number of faces, edges, and corners.
Color the correct figures.

5 0 faces, 0 edges, 0 corners

6 5 faces, 8 edges, 5 corners

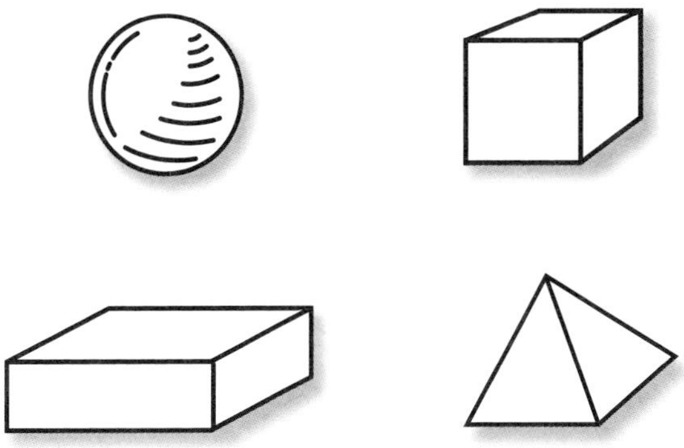

CHECK ▪ Problem Solving

7 Estimate the number of .
Then build the model.
Write how many 🎲 you used.

Estimate: about _____ cubes

Count: _____ cubes

© Harcourt

Name ______________________________

Choose the best answer for questions 1–4.

Standardized Test Prep
Chapters 1–18

1 Which object is close to the shape of this solid figure?

 ○   ○   ○

○

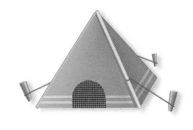

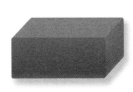

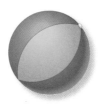

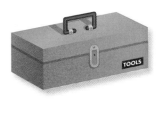

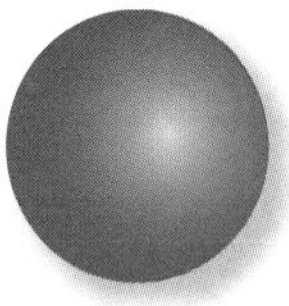

2 Which is the same shape as a face of this solid figure?

 ○   ○   ○   ○

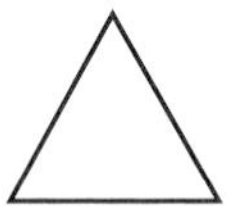

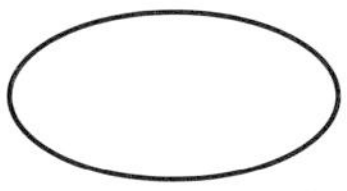

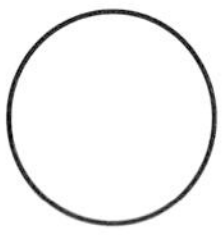

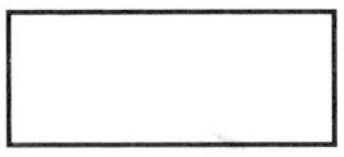

3 How many will you need to make this model?

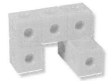

5	6	8	9
○	○	○	○

4 Which number is odd?

4	8	12	15
○	○	○	○

Show What You Know

5 Choose a solid figure. Write its name.

____

Trace one face.

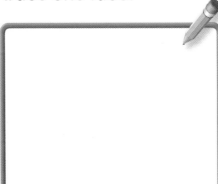

Write how many faces, edges, and corners it has.

________ faces

________ edges

________ corners

Length

How long are the dinosaurs
in this picture? Use string
and a ruler to find out.

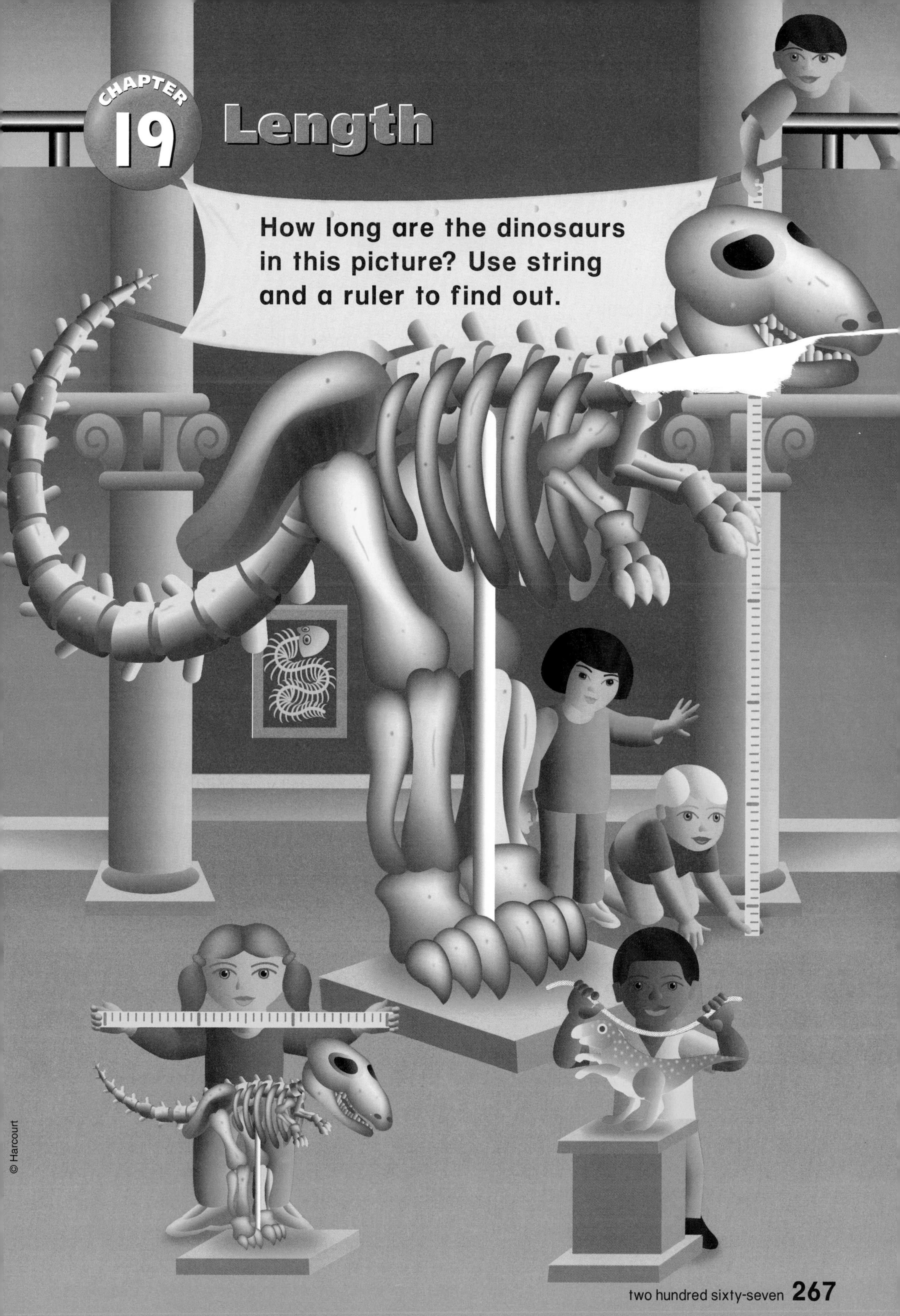

© Harcourt

SCHOOL HOME CONNECTION

Dear Family,
    Today we started Chapter 19. We will look at ways to measure length. Here is the math vocabulary and an activity for us to do together at home.

                    Love,

                    _____

My Math Words

inch
foot
centimeter
meter

Vocabulary

inch A unit to measure short lengths. A paper clip is about 1 inch long.

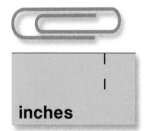

inches

foot A unit to measure longer lengths. A sheet of notebook paper is about 1 foot long.

centimeter A unit to measure short lengths. Your finger is about 1 centimeter wide.

meter A unit to measure longer lengths. Your arms can spread about 1 meter wide.

Visit *The Learning Site* for additional ideas and activities. www.harcourtschool.com

ACTIVITY

Have your child practice measuring length by finding the height of each family member. First, use a ruler, a yardstick, or a tape measure to measure how tall your child is in inches. Write the measurement. Next, help your child measure and write how tall you are. Together, measure other family members and pets and write their heights.

Books to Share

To read about measurement with your child, look for these books in your local library.

Measuring Penny, by Loreen Leedy, Henry Holt, 1998.

Inch by Inch, by Leo Lioni, William Morrow & Company, 1995.

© Harcourt

Name ______________________________

Nonstandard Units

Hands On

Measure the bone with a large clip.
About how many clips long is it?
Measure again with a small clip.
About how many clips long is it?

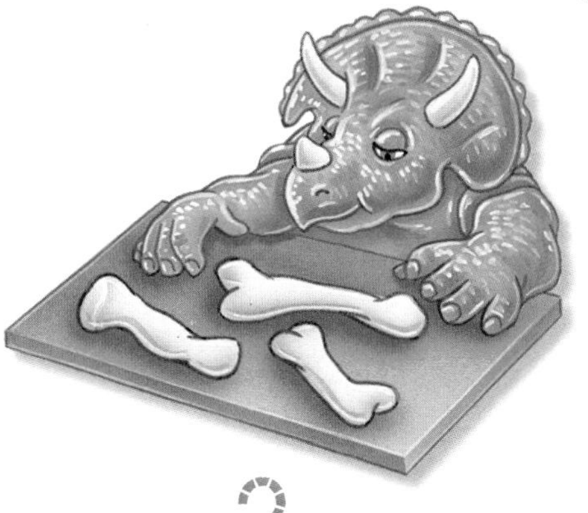

1

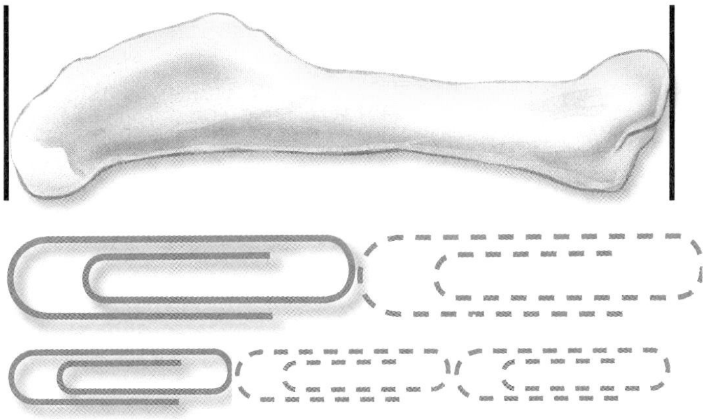

about 2 large clips

about 3 small clips

2

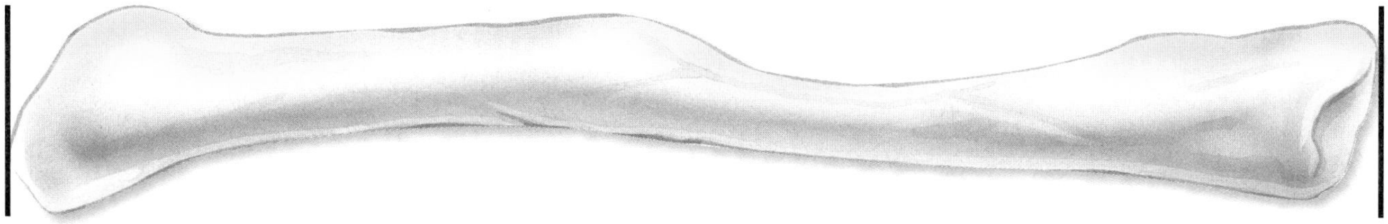

about ______ large clips

about ______ small clips

3

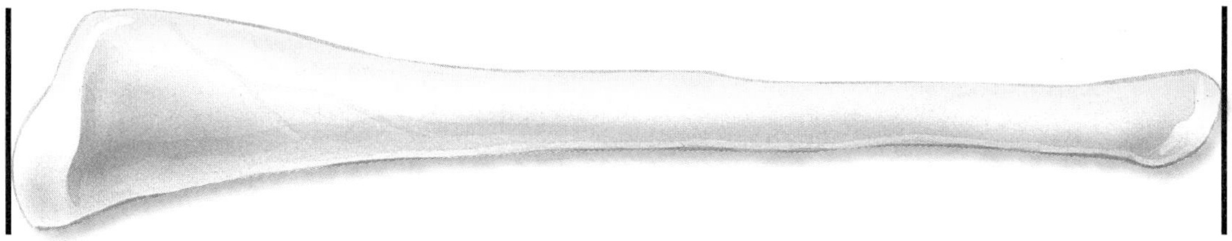

about ______ large clips

about ______ small clips

4

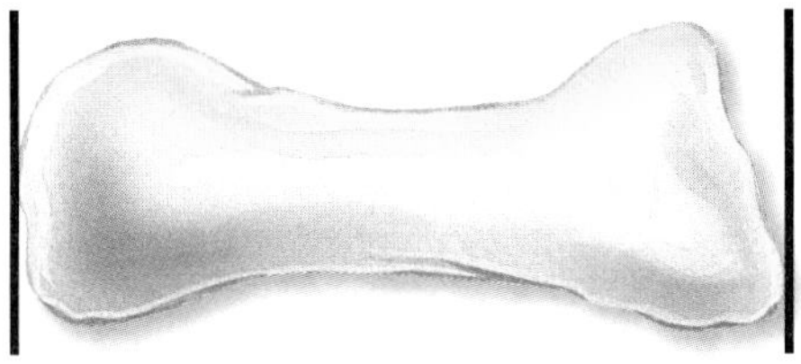

about ______ large clip

about ______ small clips

Talk About It ■ Reasoning

Why do you get a greater number when you measure with small paper clips?

Practice

About how many small clips long is the bone?
Predict. Then measure with a small clip to check.

1

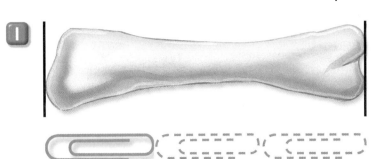

Predict: about ___3___ small clips

Check: about ___3___ small clips

2

Predict: about _____ small clips

Check: about _____ small clips

3

Predict: about _____ small clips

Check: about _____ small clips

4

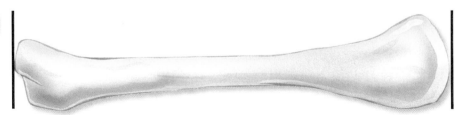

Predict: about _____ small clips

Check: about _____ small clips

© Harcourt

 HOME ACTIVITY • Have your child use other small items that are all alike to measure each dinosaur bone.

Measure short lengths in inches.

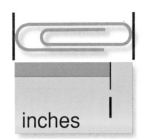

inches

A small paper clip is about 1 inch long.

Measure longer lengths in **feet**.

inches 1 2 3 4 5 6 7 8 9 10 11 12

A hammer is about 1 foot long.
1 foot is 12 inches long.

About how long or high is the real object?
Estimate. Then measure with an inch ruler.

object	estimate	measurement
1	about _____ inches	about _2_ inches
2	about _____ feet	about _____ feet
3	about _____ feet	about _____ feet
4	about _____ inches	about _____ inches

Talk About It ▪ Reasoning

How do you use the inch ruler to measure in feet? Explain.

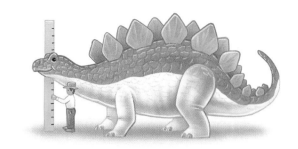

About how long or high is the real object?
Circle the closer estimate.

1

(about 9 inches)

about 9 feet

2

about 2 inches

about 2 feet

3

about 1 inch

about 1 foot

4

about 4 inches

about 4 feet

5

about 5 inches

about 5 feet

6

about 4 inches

about 4 feet

7

about 6 inches

about 6 feet

8

about 6 inches

about 6 feet

Mixed Review

Write the amount.

9

_____ ¢

 HOME ACTIVITY • Have your child estimate the length of items around your home.

Name _____

Centimeters and Meters

Measure short lengths in **centimeters**.

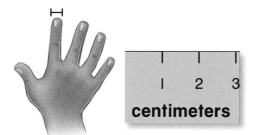

Your finger is about 1 centimeter wide.

Measure long lengths in **meters**.

Your arms can spread about 1 meter wide. 1 meter is 100 centimeters.

About how long or high is the real object?
Estimate. Then measure.

object	estimate	measurement
1 ▭▭▭▭▭▭ ⊢———⊣	about _____ centimeters	about _10_ centimeters
2 🚪	about _____ meters	about _____ meters
3 📄	about _____ centimeters	about _____ centimeters

Talk About It ▪ Reasoning

How would your measurements change if you measured with an inch ruler? Explain.

Practice

Which unit would you use to measure the object?
Circle the better unit of measure.

 1

(centimeters)

meters

 2

centimeters

meters

 3

centimeters

meters

 4

centimeters

meters

5

centimeters

meters

 6

centimeters

meters

Problem Solving ▪ Application

Use a centimeter ruler. Draw a line.
Start your line at the dot.

7 5 centimeters   ●

8 10 centimeters   ●

9 3 centimeters   ●

© Harcourt

HOME ACTIVITY • Have your child find things around your home that can be measured in centimeters. Have him or her find the length or height of each object with a centimeter ruler.

276 two hundred seventy-six

Chapter 19

Name ______________________________

UNDERSTAND > PLAN > SOLVE > CHECK

Problem Solving
Make Reasonable Estimates

Dee has this toy dinosaur.
About how long is it?
Circle the most reasonable estimate.

inches

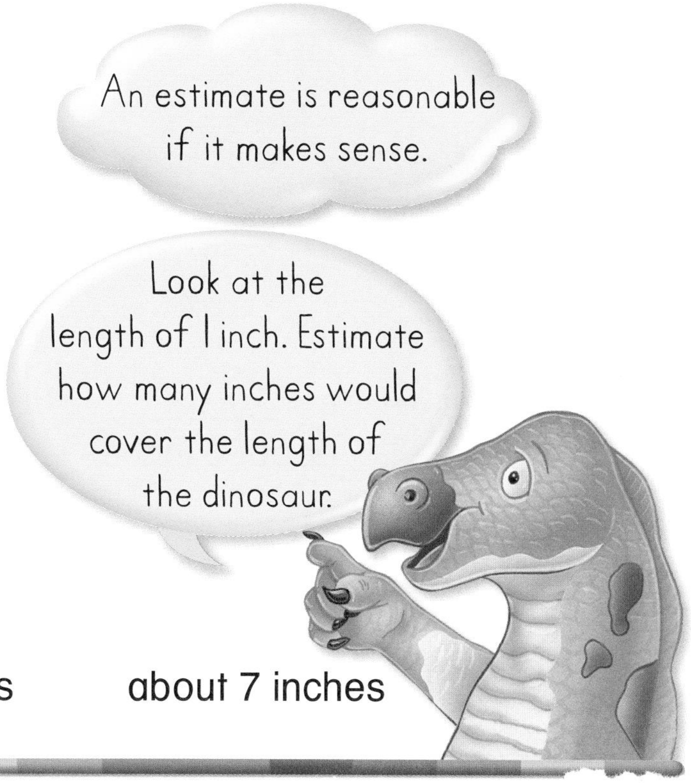

An estimate is reasonable if it makes sense.
Look at the length of 1 inch. Estimate how many inches would cover the length of the dinosaur.

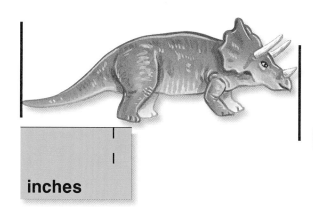

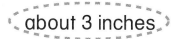

(about 3 inches) about 5 inches about 7 inches

About how long is the toy dinosaur?
Circle the most reasonable estimat

1

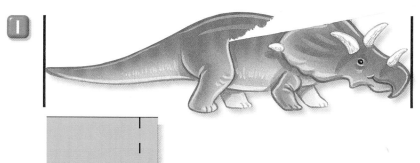

inches

about 2 inches about 4 inches about 6 inches

2

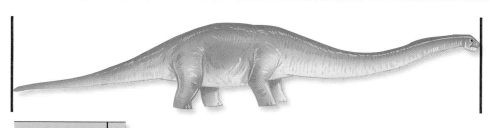

inches

about 2 inches about 3 inches about 5 inches

About how long is the toy dinosaur?
Circle the most reasonable estimate.

1

inches   (about 3 inches)   about 6 inches   about 10 inches

2

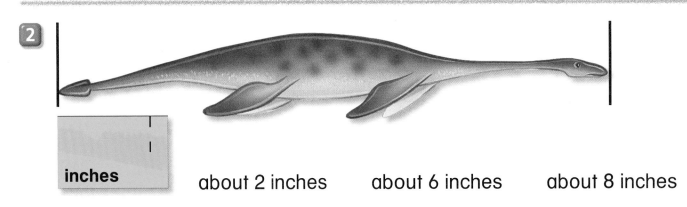

inches   about 2 inches   about 6 inches   about 8 inches

3

inches   about 2 inches   about 4 inches   about 7 inches

Write About It

When might you need to estimate length?
Write a story about such a time.

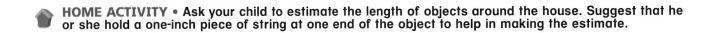

HOME ACTIVITY • Ask your child to estimate the length of objects around the house. Suggest that he or she hold a one-inch piece of string at one end of the object to help in making the estimate.

© Harcourt

Name _____

CHECK ▪ Concepts and Skills

About how many clips long is the bone?

1

about _____ large clips   about _____ small clips

Use an inch ruler. Write the length.

2

about _____ inches

3

about _____ inches

Circle the better unit to measure the real object.

4

centimeters

meters

5

centimeters

meters

Use a centimeter ruler to measure each side. Write how many centimeters.
Add to find the perimeter.

6

_____ + _____ + _____ = _____ centimeters

CHECK ▪ Problem Solving

About how long is the ribbon?
Circle the most reasonable estimate.

inches

7 about 3 inches   about 5 inches   about 9 inches

Name _____

Choose the best answer for questions 1–3.

1 About how many clips long is the shoelace?

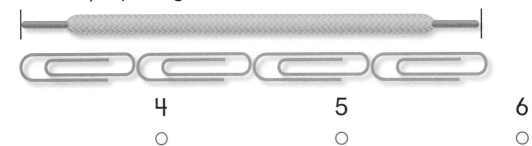

3   4   5   6
○   ○   ○   ○

2 About how long is the caterpillar?

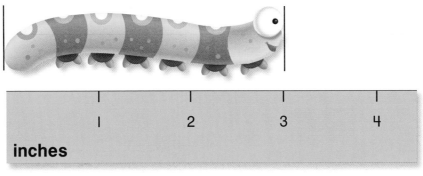

1 inch   2 inches   3 inches   4 inches
○   ○   ○   ○

3 Which object might be 7 feet high?

○   ○   ○   ○

Show What You Know

4 Draw a shape that has 4 sides. Use a centimeter ruler
to measure the sides. Add to find the perimeter.

_____ + _____ + _____ + _____ = _____ centimeters

© Harcourt

CHAPTER

20

Capacity, Weight, and Temperature

FAHRENHEIT

110
100
90
80
70
60
50
40
30
20
10
0
-10

1 CUP

1 PINT 1 PINT

What measurement tools do you see? What would you measure with each tool?

1 QUART

SUGAR 1 POUND

8 OUNCES 8 OUNCES

1 KILOGRAM

© Harcourt

SCHOOL HOME CONNECTION

Dear Family,
 Today we started Chapter 20. We will begin to measure how much things hold, how much things weigh, and how hot or cold the weather is. Here is the math vocabulary and an activity for us to do together at home.

 Love,

 _____

My Math Words

cup
pint
quart
liter
mass
weight

Vocabulary

Units to measure how much a container holds:	
cup	2 cups fill 1 pint
pint	2 pints fill 1 quart
quart	1 quart fills 4 cups or 2 pints
liter	1 liter is a little more than 1 quart

mass   the amount of matter an object has

weight   the measure of the pull of gravity on an object

 Visit *The Learning Site* for additional ideas and activities. www.harcourtschool.com

ACTIVITY

At the grocery store, look for an item that weighs one pound. Let your child hold the item to get an idea of how that amount of weight feels. Then have him or her choose 10 other grocery items and estimate each weight in pounds. Check your child's estimates by reading the weights on the packages.

Books to Share

To read about measurement with your child, look for these books in your local library.

How Big Were the Dinosaurs?, by Bernard Most, Harcourt, Brace & Company, 1994.

Everybody Cooks Rice, by Norah Dooley, Houghton Mifflin, 1995.

Name _____

I **cup**   I **pint**   I **quart**

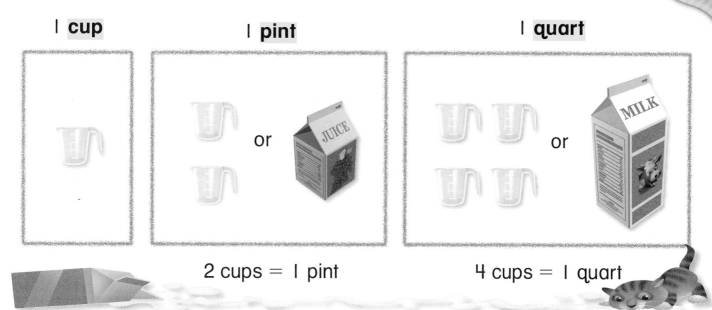

2 cups = I pint   4 cups = I quart

How many cups will fill the container?
Measure with water.

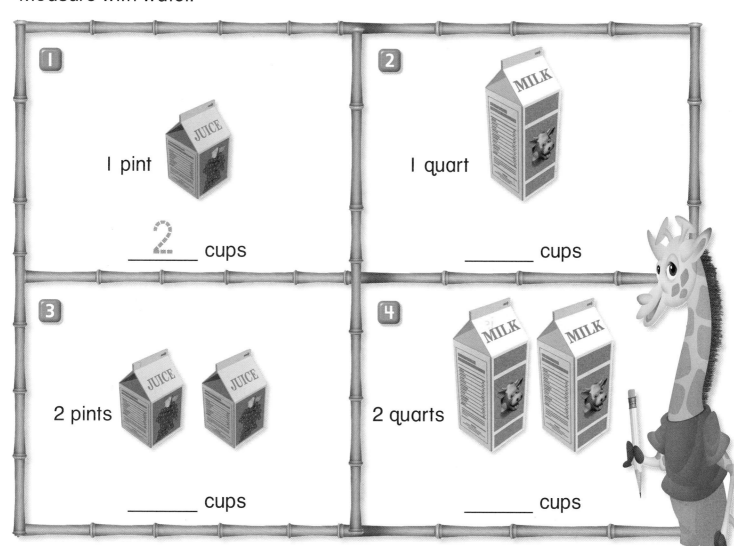

1 I pint   _**2**_ cups

2 I quart   _____ cups

3 2 pints   _____ cups

4 2 quarts   _____ cups

Talk About It ▪ Reasoning
Is I quart equal to 2 pints? How can you tell?

About how much does the container hold?
Circle the reasonable estimate.

 cup   **pint**  **quart**

1
(about 8 quarts)

about 50 quarts

2
about 2 pints

about 30 pints

3
about 5 cups

about 60 cups

4
about 5 quarts

about 80 quarts

5
about 3 quarts

about 13 quarts

6
about 4 pints

about 40 pints

Problem Solving ▪ Application

Circle the correct sentence.

7 Mrs. Green buys 2 quarts of juice. Mrs. Little buys 4 pints of juice.

a. Mrs. Little has more juice.

b. Mrs. Little and Mrs. Green have the same amount of juice.

🔺 **HOME ACTIVITY** • Have your child use a measuring cup to find containers that hold the same amounts of water.

A **liter** is a little more than a quart.

less than 1 liter   **1 liter**   **more than 1 liter**

About how much does the container hold?
Estimate more than, less than, or the same as 1 liter.
Write more than, less than, or same as.

1
_____
more than 1 liter

2
_____
_____ 1 liter

3
_____
_____ 1 liter

4
_____
_____ 1 liter

Talk About It ▪ Reasoning

How could you use a liter container and sand to find out
if another container holds more or less than 1 liter?

Practice

About how much does the container hold?
Circle the reasonable estimate.

1    *(about 2 liters)*

about 20 liters

2    about 1 liter

about 10 liters

3    about 10 liters

about 60 liters

4    about 1 liter

about 10 liters

5    about 5 liters

about 20 liters

6    about 9 liters

about 90 liters

Mixed Review

7 Trace the lines.
Circle the name of the
figures you made.

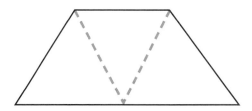

squares

triangles

rectangles

HOME ACTIVITY • Have your child find containers that he or she estimates will hold more than 1 liter, less than 1 liter, and 1 liter. Then have your child check his or her estimates by filling a liter container with water, and pouring that water into the other containers.

Name _____

about 1 **ounce**

about 1 **pound**

Estimate how much the real object weighs.

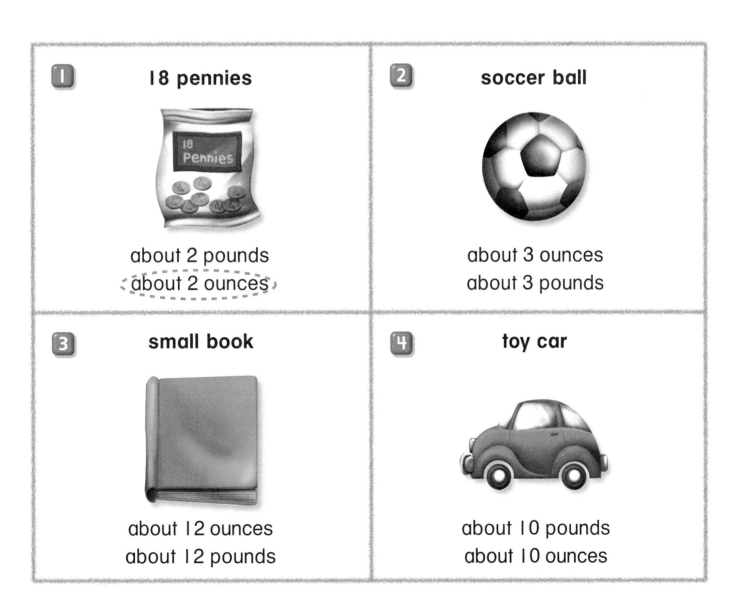

1 18 pennies

about 2 pounds
about 2 ounces

2 soccer ball

about 3 ounces
about 3 pounds

3 small book

about 12 ounces
about 12 pounds

4 toy car

about 10 pounds
about 10 ounces

Talk About It ■ Reasoning

Is a large object always heavy? Explain.

© Harcourt

Estimate how much the real object weighs.

1

about 50 pounds

about 5 ounces

2

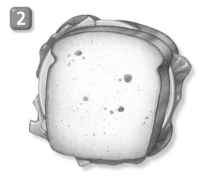

about 9 ounces

about 9 pounds

3

about 10 pounds

about 10 ounces

4

about 8 ounces

about 8 pounds

5

about 1 pound

about 1 ounce

6

about 2 ounces

about 2 pounds

Problem Solving ▪ Mental Math

Solve.

7 Latrice has a 12-pound dog. Her friend's dog weighs 20 pounds more. How many pounds do their two dogs weigh together?

_____ pounds

⬟ **HOME ACTIVITY** • Have your child compare the weights of three objects and put them in order from lightest to heaviest.

Grams and Kilograms

I **gram**

I **kilogram**

What is the mass of the real object?
Estimate. Then measure with a balance.

objects	estimate	measurement
1  pen	about _____ grams	about _____ grams
2  backpack	about _____ kilograms	about _____ kilograms
3 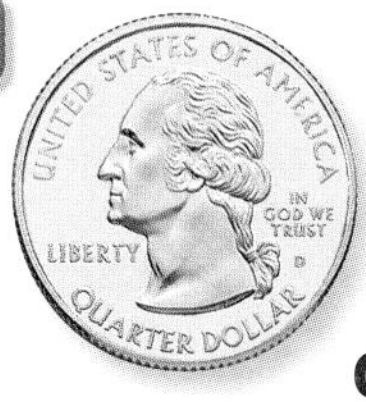 quarter	about _____ grams	about _____ grams
4  wooden blocks	about _____ kilograms	about _____ kilograms

Talk About It ▪ Reasoning

About how many paper clips would
have a mass of I kilogram? Explain.

Which unit would you use to measure the mass?
Circle that unit of measurement.

1

(grams)

liters

centimeters

2

centimeters

kilograms

grams

3

liters

meters

grams

4

centimeters

grams

kilograms

5

grams

kilograms

meters

6

grams

meters

liters

Problem Solving ▪ Reasoning

Circle the reasonable answer.

7 A beagle puppy has a mass of about 1 kilogram. What might be the mass of an adult beagle?

100 kilograms   20 kilograms

8 A baby robin has a mass of about 7 grams. What might be the mass of an adult robin?

20 grams   800 grams

🏠 **HOME ACTIVITY** • On a trip to the supermarket, have your child find items with a mass shown in grams or kilograms. Point out that most grocery items list the mass in parentheses after the weight.

© Harcourt

Problem Solving
Choose a Measuring Tool

UNDERSTAND 〉 PLAN 〉 SOLVE 〉 CHECK

I can use a ruler!

I can use a cup!

I can use a thermometer!

I can use a scale!

Write the name of the tool you would use

1 to find out how long a piece of string is.		~~ruler~~
2 to find out how much water is in a bottle.		_____
3 to find out the temperature on a sunny day.		_____
4 to find out how much milk is in a pitcher.		_____
5 to find out how much a rock weighs.		_____

© Harcourt

scale	cup
ruler	thermometer

Write the name of the tool you would use

1 to find out how much your pet weighs.		scale
2 to find out how much juice is in a glass.		
3 to find out how long a piece of ribbon is.		
4 to find out the temperature of the classroom.		

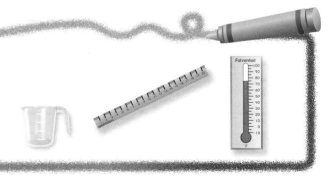

Write About It

Write a sentence about each tool.
Tell what it measures.

HOME ACTIVITY • Make up some stories in which a tool is needed to measure. Have your child tell you which tool he or she would use and why.

© Harcourt

CHECK ▪ Concepts and Skills

About how much does the container hold? Circle the reasonable estimate.

1

about 1 pint

about 10 pints

2

about 1 quart

about 10 quarts

About how much does the container hold? Circle the reasonable estimate.

3

2 liters

12 liters

Estimate how much the real object weighs.

4

about 3 ounces

about 3 pounds

Which unit would you use to measure the mass? Circle that unit of measurement.

5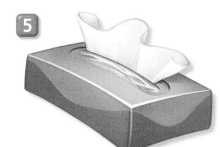

grams

kilograms

Read the thermometer. Write the temperature.

6 _____ °F

CHECK ▪ Problem Solving

scale   **ruler**

cup   **thermometer**

7 Write the name of the tool you would use to find out how much milk is in a bottle.

_____

© Harcourt

Name ________________________________

Choose the best answer for questions 1–4.

Standardized Test Prep
Chapters 1–20

1

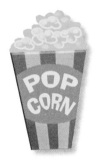

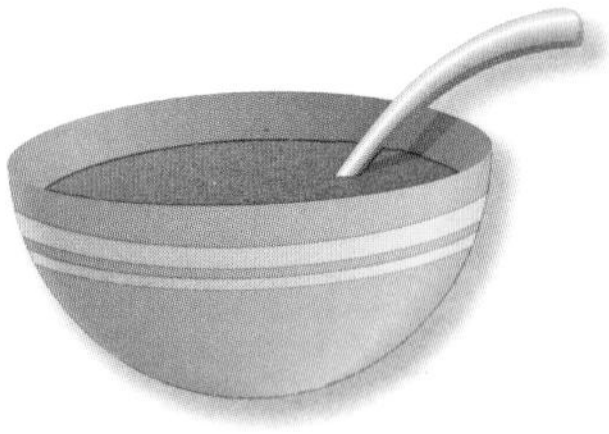

How much soup does the bowl hold?

about 2 pints	about 2 quarts	about 2 cups	about 2 gallons
○	○	○	○

2

Which unit would be used to measure the mass of a small bag of popcorn?

grams	kilograms	liters	meters
○	○	○	○

3

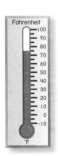

Which shows the temperature on the thermometer?

64°	65°	74°	95°
○	○	○	○

4

What would you use to find out how long the pencil is?

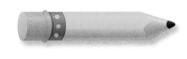

yardstick	scale	thermometer	ruler
○	○	○	○

Show What You Know

5 Use a container. Draw it. Estimate how many cups you think it will hold. Measure to check.

Estimate: ______ cups

Measure: ______ cups

Mrs. Quigley's Quilt

written by Lucy Floyd

illustrated by Christine Mau

This book will help me review plane shapes.

This book belongs to _____.

The winter was very cold. Mrs. Quigley decided
to make a nice quilt to keep her piglets warm.
First, she cut cloth squares. Then she laid out
some squares on the table.

"Too many squares," said Mrs. Quigley. She put some squares together to make rectangles for her quilt.

Tell about the shapes you see in Mrs. Quigley's quilt.

C

"Very nice," said Mrs. Quigley. "I need another shape." She cut some squares in half to make triangles for her quilt. Then she finished sewing the shapes together.

How many triangles does she have?

————

"Perfect!" said Mrs. Quigley.
"It's big enough for all of us!"

Name _____

Groovy Shapes

Look at each design and write how many shapes you see.

How many ovals? _____

How many circles? _____

How many triangles? _____

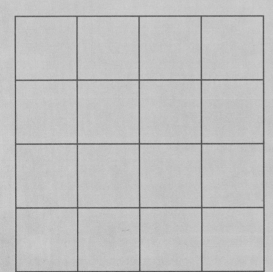

How many squares? _____

How many rectangles? _____

Stretch Your Thinking ▢ Create a design made from a plane shape. See if a classmate can tell how many of that shape you used.

© Harcourt

Name _____

You will need:
9 ■, 3 ■, 3 ■, 1 bag.

1 Put all the ■, ■, and ■ tiles in the bag. Pull out 1 tile. Make a tally mark to show which color you pulled out.

2 Put the tile back. Shake the bag.

3 Repeat 9 times.

4 If you do this 10 more times, which color do you think you will pull out most often?

Write your prediction.

Color	Tally Marks
yellow	
blue	
red	

_____

_____

5 Repeat 10 more times. Make a tally mark each time.

6 Which color tile did you pull out most often?

_____

7 Why do you think this happened?

_____

_____

_____

_____

© Harcourt

Name _____

Skills and Concepts

1 Draw a square.

2 Draw the shape.

3 sides   3 corners

3 Draw a line of symmetry.

4 Draw lines to divide the shape into 4 triangles.

5 Circle turn or flip to tell how the shape was moved.

turn   flip

6 Circle the figures that have the same shape.

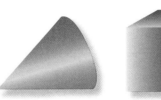

7 Circle the solid figure you can use to trace the shape.

8 Write how many.

_____ faces   _____ edges

_____ corners

9 Use ⬭. Write the length.

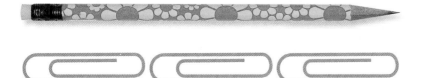

_____ clips

Study Guide and Review • Unit 4

© Harcourt

10 Write how many centimeters. Then write the perimeter.

 2 cm

_____ + _____ + _____ + _____ = _____

Circle the reasonable estimates.

11

about 2 liters   about 20 liters

12

about 30 quarts   about 3 quarts

13

about 1 ounce   about 1 pound

Which unit would you use to measure?
Circle the better unit of measure.

14

grams   kilograms   liters

15

centimeters   meters

Problem Solving

16 About how long is the object? Circle the most reasonable estimate.

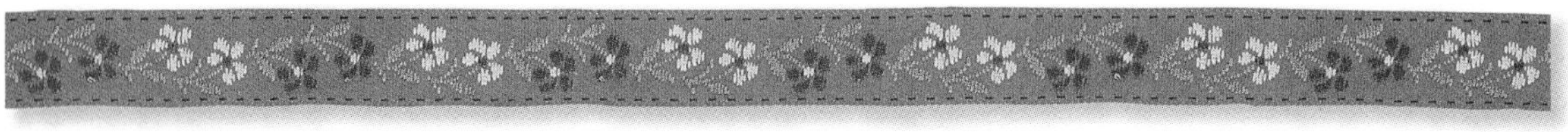

about 6 inches   about 1 inch   about 3 inches

Study Guide and Review • Unit 4

© Harcourt

Ant Farm

Amy wanted to place colored
tape around an ant farm.

- She had 20 inches of colored tape.

- Amy made a 4-cornered shape
  using all of the tape to outline
  the perimeter.

Draw one way the shape could look.
Measure and label each
side in inches.

Show your work.

Technology

Name _____

Mighty Math Zoo Zillions • Solid Figures and Plane Shapes

1 Click .

2 Click 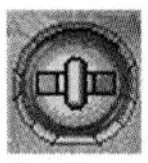 .

3 Click N.

4 Play 5 times.

Practice and Problem Solving

How many of each solid figure do you see?

1 sphere _____   cone _____

cylinder _____   cube _____

pyramid _____

rectangular prism _____

2 **Reasoning**

Which solid figure above has only 1 plane shape that can be traced? _____

PROBLEM SOLVING ON LOCATION

At the Museum

The Illinois State Museum has beautiful Amish quilts. They are taken from town to town so that people all around the state can see them.

This quilt has 4 small squares that make up 1 larger square. There are 5 squares in all.

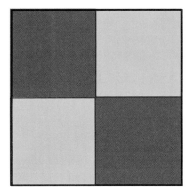

Draw and color this quilt to make 14 squares in all.

This quilt has 4 small triangles that make up 2 larger triangles. There are 8 triangles in all.

Draw and color this quilt to make 16 triangles in all.

© Harcourt

Name _____

PROBLEM SOLVING ON LOCATION

At the Restaurant

People from all over the world come to New York City. They bring their recipes for great food with them.

What different kinds of pizzas can you make with these toppings?

MUSHROOMS   SAUSAGE   PEPPERONI   ONIONS

Draw two or more toppings on each pizza. Write the name of each topping.

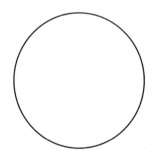 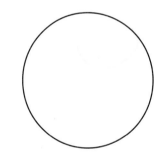 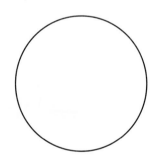

_____
_____
_____

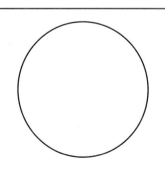 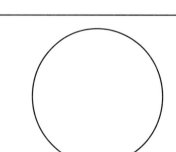 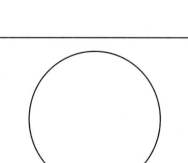

_____
_____
_____

© Harcourt

CHAPTER 21 Numbers to 1,000

ANIMAL COUNT

Animals	How many?
antelopes	475
buffaloes	100
flamingos	250
zebras	325

Make up a question about the numbers on the chart.

SCHOOL HOME CONNECTION

Dear Family,
 Today we started Chapter 21. We will read, write, and use numbers to 1,000. Here is the math vocabulary and an activity for us to do together at home.

 Love,

 _____

My Math Words

hundreds
tens
ones
one thousand

Vocabulary

hundreds, tens, and ones The value of the digits in 3-digit numbers.

247

hundreds	tens	ones
2	4	7

200　　40　　7

one thousand

1,000　ones
　100　tens
　 10　hundreds

ACTIVITY

Have your child count out small objects such as paper clips into groups of 10. Have him or her form hundreds by putting ten groups of 10 into sandwich bags. When not enough groups of 10 are left to make another hundred, have your child put the remaining groups of 10 together and any extra paper clips in a third group. Have your child tell how many hundreds, tens, and ones there are and write the number.

Books to Share

To read about numbers with your child, look for this book in your local library.

Betcha!
by Stuart J. Murphy. HarperCollins, 1997.

Visit *The Learning Site* for additional ideas and activities. www.harcourtschool.com

© Harcourt

Name _Leah_

What is the value of each digit in 258?

hundreds	tens	ones

2	5	8

2 hundreds   5 tens   8 ones
200   50   8

Circle the value of the blue digit.

1   6̲34

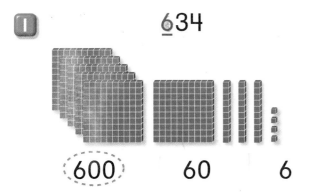

(600)   60   6

2   903̲

300   30   (3)

3   42̲7

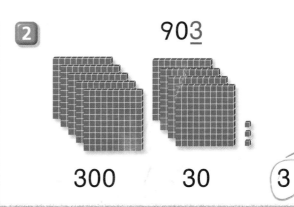

200   (20)   2

4   5̲55

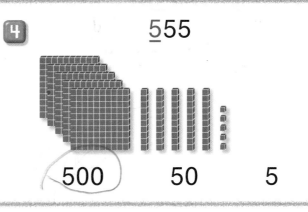

(500)   50   5

5   26̲6

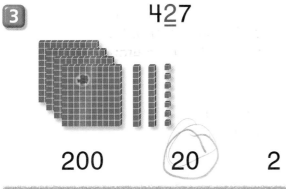

600   (60)   6

6   878̲

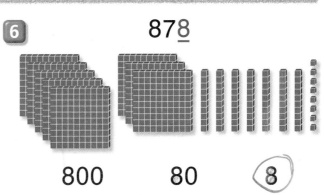

800   80   (8)

Talk About It ■ Reasoning

Ralph says 598 is larger than 621 because 598 has larger digits.
What do you say?

hundreds	tens	ones
1	4	7

Circle the value of the blue digit.

1   1 4̲7

400   (40)   4

2   9̲40

(900)   90   9

3   318̲

800   80   (8)

4   462̲

200   20   (2)

5   5̲23

(500)   50   5

6   646̲

600   60   (6)

7   75̲4

500   (50)   5

8   29̲5

900   (90)   9

9   8̲39

(800)   80   8

10   2̲86

(200)   20   2

11   98̲8

800   (80)   8

12   379̲

900   90   (9)

Problem Solving ▪ Estimation

Circle the reasonable estimate.

13 There are _____ children in my class.

200   (20)   2,000

14 Andy has _____ sisters.

3,000   30   3

15 The phone book has _____ pages.

500   50   5,000

16 Wing hit _____ home runs in the baseball game.

4,000   40   4

© Harcourt

 HOME ACTIVITY • Using a large book such as the phone book, pick any page and point out the page number. Ask your child to tell the value of the hundreds, tens, and ones digits.

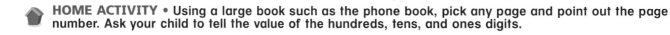

Name _____

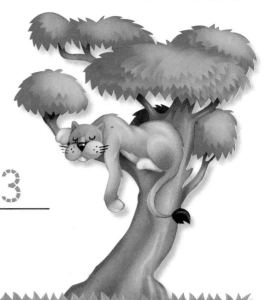

hundreds	tens	ones
2	4	3

Numbers can be written in different ways.

two hundred forty-three

200 + 40 + 3

243

Read the number. Write it in different ways.

1 one hundred eighty-five

hundreds	tens	ones
1	8	5

100 + 80 + 5

185

2 five hundred nine

hundreds	tens	ones
5	0	9

500 + 0 + 9

509

3 three hundred sixty-seven

hundreds	tens	ones
3	0	7

300 + 0 + 7

307

4 eight hundred forty-six

hundreds	tens	ones
8	4	6

800 + 40 + 6

846

Talk About It ▪ Reasoning

How do you know that 400 + 20 + 3 is the same as 423? Prove your answer.

© Harcourt

Practice

Read the number.
Write it in different ways.

1 three hundred fifty-one

hundreds	tens	ones
3	5	1

300 + 50 + 1

351

2 six hundred eighty

hundreds	tens	ones
600	80	0

600 + 80 + 0

680

3 four hundred thirty-nine

hundreds	tens	ones
400	30 9	

400 + 30 + 9

439

4 seven hundred twelve

hundreds	tens	ones
700	10 2	

700 + 10 + 2

712

Problem Solving ▪ Application

Write the number to solve.

5 Pat has 6 bags with 100 marbles in each bag. He also has 4 loose marbles. How many marbles does he have altogether? Write an addition sentence to show the number.

_____ + _____ + _____ = _____

🔺 **HOME ACTIVITY** • Name any number up to 1,000, such as six hundred fifty-eight. Have your child write that number with hundreds, tens, and ones (6 hundreds, 5 tens, 8 ones), in expanded notation (600+50+8), and as a number in standard form (658).

© Harcourt

Name _____Leah Lupa_____

This table tells the weight of some animals in the zoo.

Animal	Weight
zebra	765 pounds
bear	972 pounds
seal	217 pounds
tiger	455 pounds
chimpanzee	81 pounds

Use the table to answer the questions.

1. Which animal weighs 7 hundreds, 6 tens, and 5 ones?

zebra

2. How much does the bear weigh?

972 pounds

3. Which animal has a weight of four hundred fifty-five pounds?

tiger

4. How much does a chimpanzee weigh?

81 pounds

5. Which animal weighs 200 + 10 + 7 pounds?

seal

6. Name two animals which would weigh close to 1,000 pounds together.

bear

zebra

© Harcourt

This table tells how many kinds of animals and plants are endangered in the world.

273

Group	Number of Endangered Species
mammals	333
birds	273
reptiles	115
fish	122
plants	719

Use the table to answer the questions.

1 Which group has 3 hundreds, 3 tens, and 3 ones?

mammals

2 How many kinds of fish are endangered?

122

3 Which group has one hundred fifteen endangered species?

reptiles

4 How many kinds of plants are endangered?

719

5 Which group has 200 + 70 + 3 endangered species?

birds

Write About It

Write some problems using the information in the table. Ask a classmate to solve your problems.

HOME ACTIVITY • With your child, find tables in the newspaper or in magazines. Talk about the information given in the tables.

© Harcourt

The number just before 540 is 539.

The number between 539 and 541 is 540.

The number just after 540 is 541.

Write the number that is just before, between, or just after.

before	between	after
1 _299_ , 300	299, _300_ , 301	234, _235_
2 _____ , 825	519, _____ , 521	100, _____
3 _____ , 601	333, _____ , 335	969, _____
4 _____ , 150	698, _____ , 700	609, _____
5 _____ , 777	997, _____ , 999	499, _____
6 _____ , 568	448, _____ , 450	327, _____

Talk About It ■ **Reasoning**

How is finding numbers before, after, and between other numbers like counting? What number is just after 999?

Write the number that is just before, between, or just after.

1 __788__, 789

2 449, _____, 451

3 299, _____

4 _____, 501

5 99, _____, 101

6 698, _____

7 89, _____

8 _____, 350

9 _____, 400

10 209, _____, 211

11 767, _____

12 _____, 888

13 329, _____

14 89, _____, 91

Problem Solving ▪ Reasoning

Choose your own way to solve this problem.

15 Emma has 537 stickers. Juan has 538 stickers. Chen has 539 stickers. Which number is closest to 639?

_____

HOME ACTIVITY • Say any 3-digit number, and have your child tell you which number comes just before and just after.

326 three hundred twenty-six

Chapter 22

© Harcourt

Order Numbers on a Number Line ★Algebra

Put the numbers in order from least to greatest. A number line can help you find the order.

For order from least to greatest, go from left to right.

| 311 | 301 | 308 |

←———•———————————•———————————•———————→
300 301 302 303 304 305 306 307 308 309 310 311 312 313 314

_301_, _308_, _311_

Write the numbers in order from least to greatest.
Use the number line to help you.

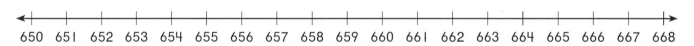
650 651 652 653 654 655 656 657 658 659 660 661 662 663 664 665 666 667 668

1 | 657 651 661 | _____, _____, _____

2 | 656 665 663 | _____, _____, _____

3 | 659 650 654 | _____, _____, _____

4 | 658 655 667 | _____, _____, _____

Talk About It ▪ Reasoning

How could you use the symbols > or < in the problems above?

Write the numbers in order from least to greatest.
Use the number line to help you.

← 420 421 422 423 424 425 426 427 428 429 430 431 432 433 434 435 436 437 438 →

1 | 427 422 435 431 | 422, 427, 431, 435

2 | 420 425 422 432 | _____, _____, _____, _____

3 | 420 423 430 432 | _____, _____, _____, _____

4 | 436 421 424 430 | _____, _____, _____, _____

5 | 425 433 437 429 | _____, _____, _____, _____

6 | 431 426 438 422 | _____, _____, _____, _____

Mixed Review

Write the total amount.

7 _____¢

8 _____¢

HOME ACTIVITY • Name any three numbers up to 999. Have your child write the numbers and then order them from least to greatest. Repeat with three different numbers.

Problem Solving
Find a Pattern

Pedro sees a pattern in the numbers 345, 445, 545.
He is going to write the next four numbers.
Can you guess Pedro's rule? What numbers will he write?

The rule could be count ___on by 100___.

345, 445, 545, __645__, __745__, __845__, __945__

345   445   545   ?

Find the pattern. Write the rule.
Continue the pattern.

1 Ann sees a pattern in the numbers 813, 823, 833.

The rule could be count __10_____.

813, 823, 833, __843__, __853__, __863__, __873__

2 Meg sees a pattern in the numbers 224, 222, 220.

The rule could be count __subtract 2__.

224, 222, 220, __218__, __216__, __214__, __212__

3 Alvin sees a pattern in the numbers 705, 605, 505.

The rule could be count __subtract 100__

705, 605, 505, __405__, __305__, __205__, __105__

Find the pattern. Write the rule.
Continue the pattern.

1 Steffie sees a pattern in the numbers 364, 354, 344.

The rule could be count ___back by 10___.

364, 354, 344, __334__, __324__, __314__, __304__

2 Ramesh sees a pattern in the numbers 441, 444, 447.

The rule could be count ___add 3___.

441, 444, 447, __750__, __453__, __456__, __459__

3 Linda sees a pattern in the numbers 525, 530, 535.

The rule could be count ___Count by 5___.

525, 530, 535, __540__, __545__, __450__, __455__

4 Bob sees a pattern in the numbers 973, 975, 977.

The rule could be count ___add 3___.

973, 975, 977, __980__, __983__, __986__, __989__

Write About It

Al had $2.25, but he wanted to earn more money.
Mom said she would pay Al to brush the cat.
Al had $2.35 on Monday, $2.45 on Tuesday, and $2.55 on
Wednesday. How much is Mom paying Al each day?

HOME ACTIVITY • With your child, look at the exercises in this lesson. Ask your child to explain how he or she decided what the rule was for each pattern.

Unit Fractions

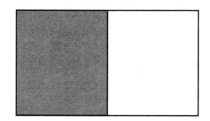

1 of 2 equal parts.
One-half is red.

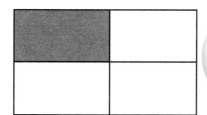

1 of 4 equal parts.
One-fourth is red.

The top number tells how many parts you are talking about.

The bottom number tells how many equal parts are in the whole.

$\frac{1}{2}$ 1 red part
2 equal parts

$\frac{1}{4}$ 1 red part
4 equal parts

Color one part red.
Circle the fraction for the red part.

1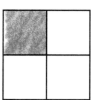

$\frac{1}{2}$ $\frac{1}{4}$ $\frac{1}{6}$

2

$\frac{1}{3}$ $\frac{1}{9}$ $\frac{1}{12}$

3

$\frac{1}{3}$ $\frac{1}{4}$ $\frac{1}{5}$

4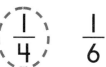

$\frac{1}{3}$ $\frac{1}{6}$ $\frac{1}{7}$

5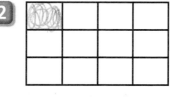

$\frac{1}{4}$ $\frac{1}{8}$ $\frac{1}{10}$

6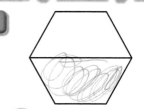

$\frac{1}{2}$ $\frac{1}{3}$ $\frac{1}{4}$

Talk About It ▪ Reasoning

Larinda has $\frac{1}{2}$ of a red apple. Sarah has $\frac{1}{2}$ of a green apple.
Larinda says she has more than Sarah.
Could this be true? Explain.

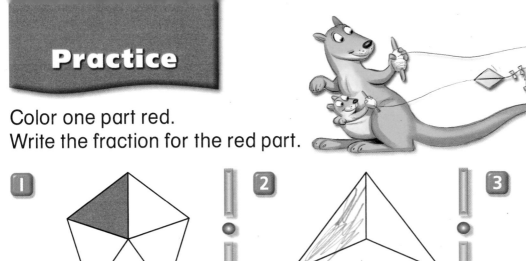

Practice

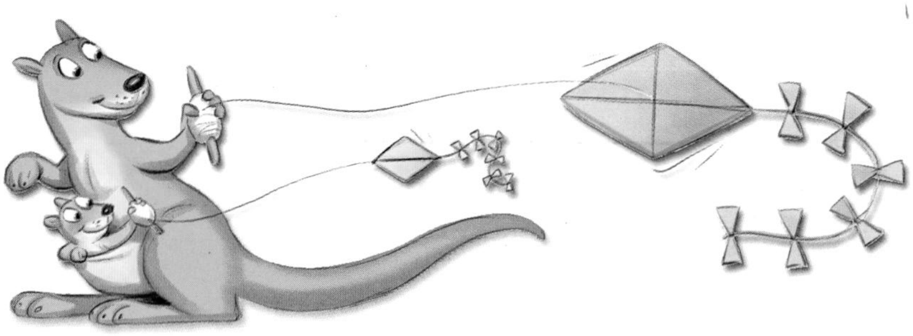

Color one part red.
Write the fraction for the red part.

1 $\dfrac{1}{5}$

2 $\dfrac{1}{3}$

3 $\dfrac{1}{4}$

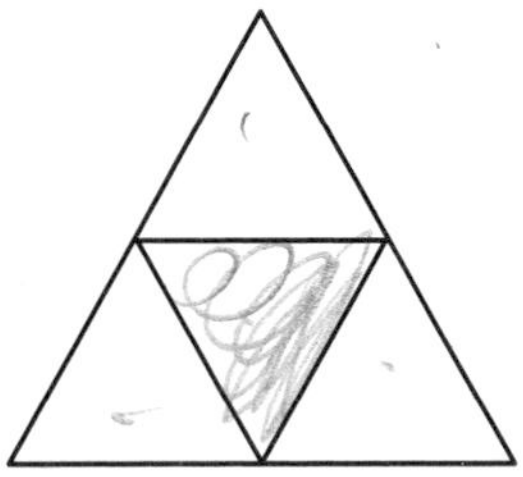

4 $\dfrac{1}{10}$

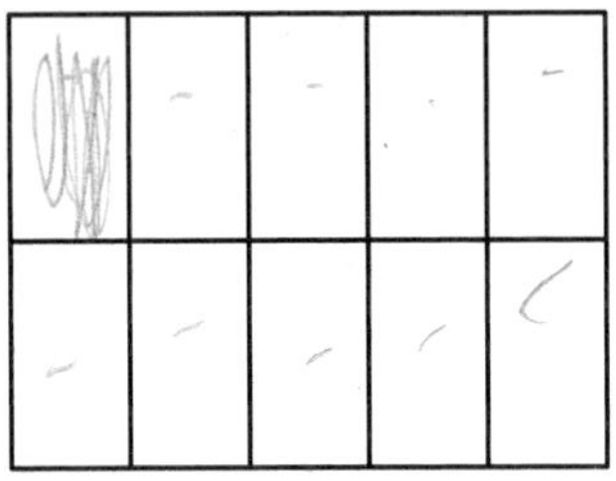

5 $\dfrac{1}{2}$

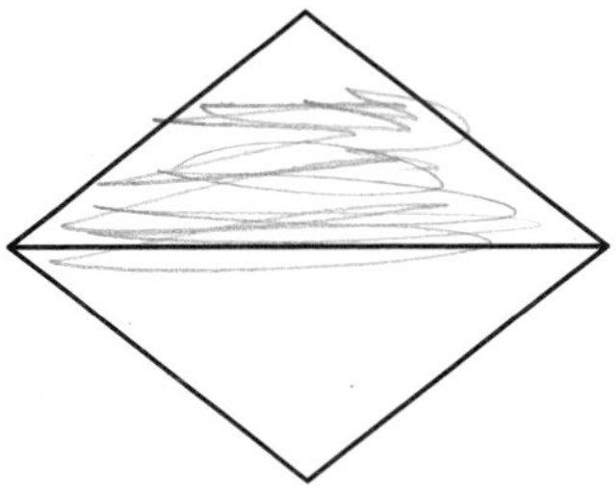

6 $\dfrac{1}{10}$

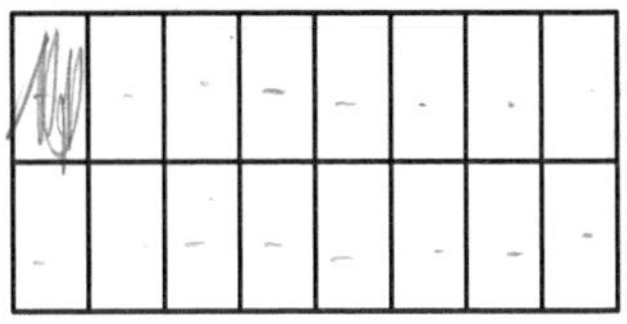

7 $\dfrac{1}{8}$

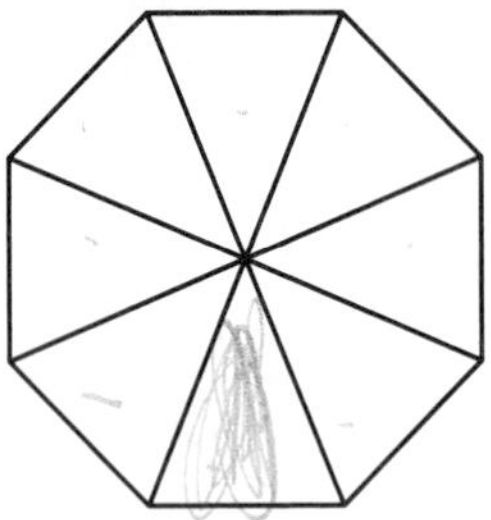

8 $\dfrac{1}{4}$

9 $\dfrac{1}{6}$

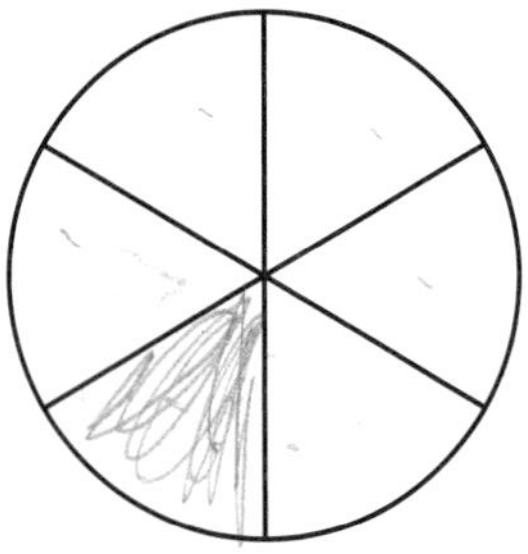

Problem Solving ▪ Visual Thinking

Circle the correct picture.

10 Which pizza has $\dfrac{1}{10}$ missing?

🔷 **HOME ACTIVITY** • With your child, draw pictures of shapes and divide them into equal parts. Ask your child to color one part and tell you the fraction.

Name _____

Which fraction is greater, $\frac{1}{3}$ or $\frac{1}{5}$?

UNDERSTAND

What do you want to find out?

PLAN

You can make a model to solve the problem.

SOLVE

$\frac{1}{5}$	$\frac{1}{5}$	$\frac{1}{5}$	$\frac{1}{5}$	$\frac{1}{5}$

$\frac{1}{3}$	$\frac{1}{3}$	$\frac{1}{3}$

$\frac{1}{3}$ is greater than $\frac{1}{5}$.

You can compare fractions by using fraction bars.

CHECK

Does your answer make sense?
Explain.

Use fraction bars. Color one part of each whole.
Circle the fraction that is greater.

1

$\frac{1}{2}$	$\frac{1}{2}$

$\frac{1}{4}$	$\frac{1}{4}$	$\frac{1}{4}$	$\frac{1}{4}$

($\frac{1}{2}$) $\frac{1}{4}$

2

$\frac{1}{10}$	$\frac{1}{10}$	$\frac{1}{10}$	$\frac{1}{10}$	$\frac{1}{10}$	$\frac{1}{10}$	$\frac{1}{10}$	$\frac{1}{10}$	$\frac{1}{10}$	$\frac{1}{10}$

$\frac{1}{6}$	$\frac{1}{6}$	$\frac{1}{6}$	$\frac{1}{6}$	$\frac{1}{6}$	$\frac{1}{6}$

$\frac{1}{10}$ $\frac{1}{6}$

Practice

Use fraction bars.
Color one part of each whole.
Circle the fraction that is less.

1

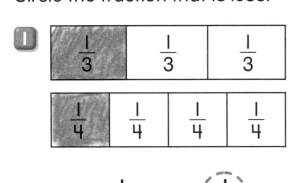

$\dfrac{1}{3}$ $\left(\dfrac{1}{4}\right)$

2

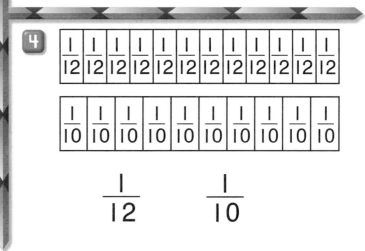

$\dfrac{1}{12}$ $\dfrac{1}{6}$

3

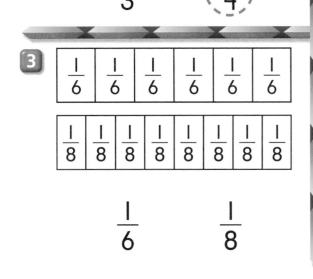

$\dfrac{1}{6}$ $\dfrac{1}{8}$

4

$\dfrac{1}{12}$ $\dfrac{1}{10}$

Problem Solving ▪ Reasoning

Circle true or false.
Explain your thinking.

5

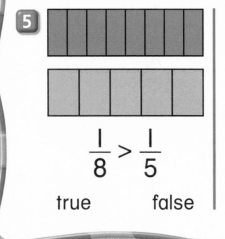

$\dfrac{1}{8} > \dfrac{1}{5}$

true false

6

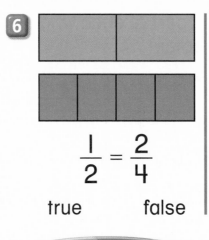

$\dfrac{1}{2} = \dfrac{2}{4}$

true false

7

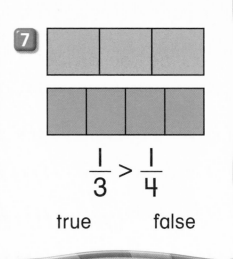

$\dfrac{1}{3} > \dfrac{1}{4}$

true false

© Harcourt

HOME ACTIVITY • Cut the same food (for example, a slice of bread) into different numbers of equal parts. Ask your child to name each fractional part and tell which part is greater and which is less.

Chapter 23

Each part is $\frac{1}{4}$ of the whole.

What is the fraction for the whole?

 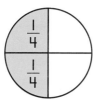 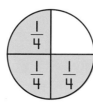

Remember, look at the bottom number of the fraction. It tells how many equal parts are in the whole.

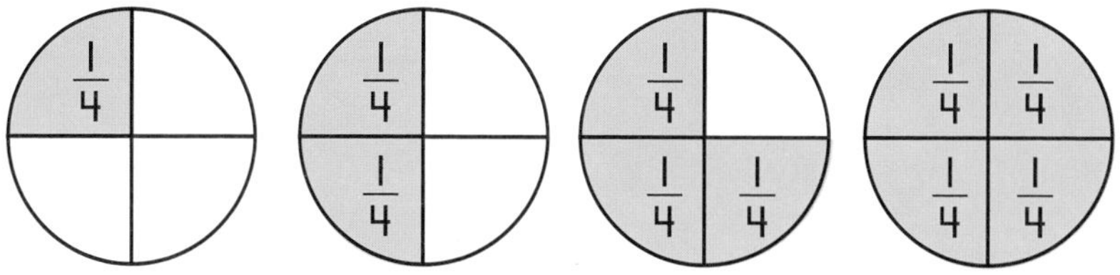

Count.

$\frac{1}{4}$ $\frac{2}{4}$ $\frac{3}{4}$ $\frac{4}{4}$

$\frac{4}{4}$

_____ = 1 whole

The fraction for the whole always equals one.

Count the parts. Write each fraction.
Write the fraction for the whole.

1

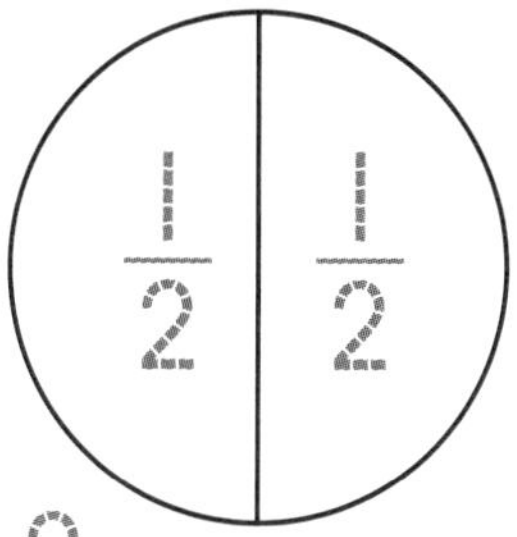

$\frac{1}{2}$ $\frac{1}{2}$

$\frac{2}{2}$

_____ = 1 whole

2

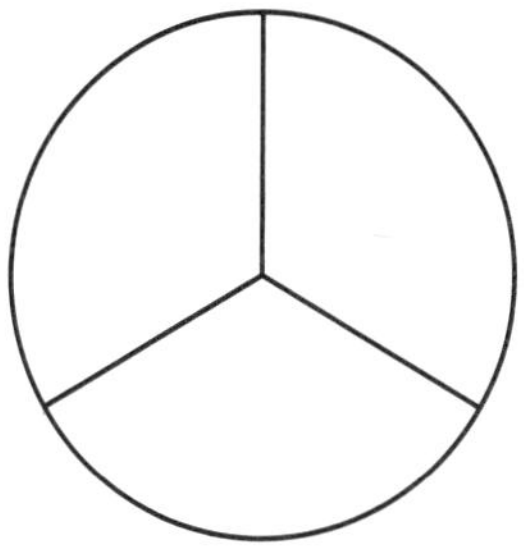

_____ = 1 whole

3

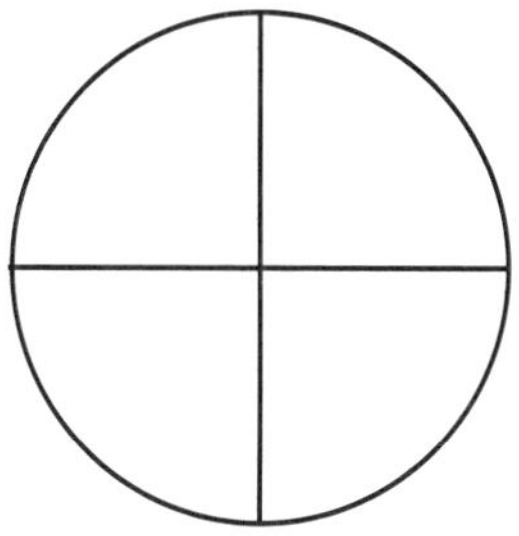

_____ = 1 whole

4

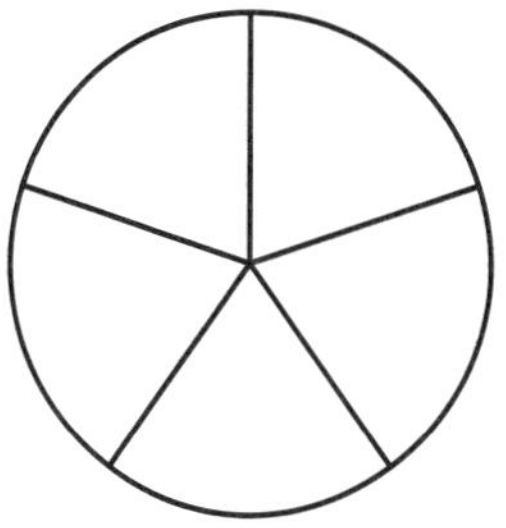

_____ = 1 whole

Talk About It ▪ Reasoning

If $\frac{2}{2}$ equals 1 whole, what does $\frac{4}{2}$ equal?

$\frac{2}{2}=1$ $\frac{4}{2}=?$

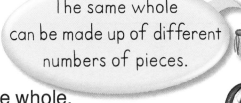

The same whole can be made up of different numbers of pieces.

Count the parts. Write each fraction. Write the fraction for the whole.

1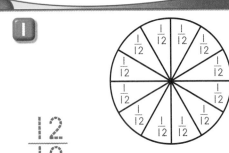

$\dfrac{12}{12}$ _____ = 1 whole

2

_____ = 1 whole

3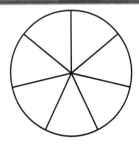

_____ = 1 whole

4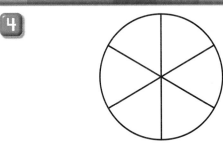

_____ = 1 whole

5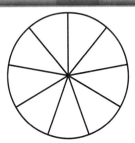

_____ = 1 whole

6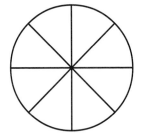

_____ = 1 whole

Problem Solving ▪ Application

Show how to solve this problem.

7 There are 12 children at a party. Each child has $\dfrac{1}{6}$ of a pizza. How many whole pizzas will the children eat? _____ pizzas

🏠 **HOME ACTIVITY** • After you cut a sandwich or a pizza, ask your child to name the fraction for the whole.

Name _____

CHECK ▪ Concepts and Skills

Write the number of parts.
Are the parts equal? Circle yes or no.

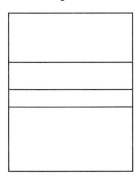

yes

no

_____ parts

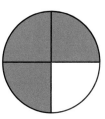

yes

no

_____ parts

Color one part red.
Write the fraction for the red part.

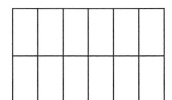

_____

Write the fraction for the
green part.

4

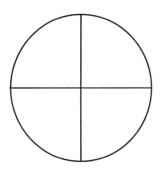

_____

Count the parts. Write each fraction.
Write the fraction for the whole.

_____ = 1 whole

CHECK ▪ Problem Solving

Use fraction bars. Color one part of each whole.
Circle the fraction that is greater.

6

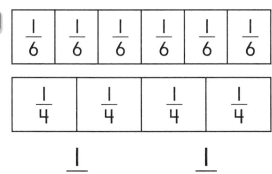

| $\frac{1}{6}$ | $\frac{1}{6}$ | $\frac{1}{6}$ | $\frac{1}{6}$ | $\frac{1}{6}$ | $\frac{1}{6}$ |

| $\frac{1}{4}$ | $\frac{1}{4}$ | $\frac{1}{4}$ | $\frac{1}{4}$ |

$\frac{1}{4}$ $\frac{1}{6}$

7

| $\frac{1}{8}$ | $\frac{1}{8}$ | $\frac{1}{8}$ | $\frac{1}{8}$ | $\frac{1}{8}$ | $\frac{1}{8}$ | $\frac{1}{8}$ | $\frac{1}{8}$ |

| $\frac{1}{10}$ | $\frac{1}{10}$ | $\frac{1}{10}$ | $\frac{1}{10}$ | $\frac{1}{10}$ | $\frac{1}{10}$ | $\frac{1}{10}$ | $\frac{1}{10}$ | $\frac{1}{10}$ | $\frac{1}{10}$ |

$\frac{1}{8}$ $\frac{1}{10}$

Name _____

Choose the best answer for questions 1–4.

1 Which picture shows 3 equal parts?

○   ○   ○   ○

---

2 Which fraction tells what part is shaded?

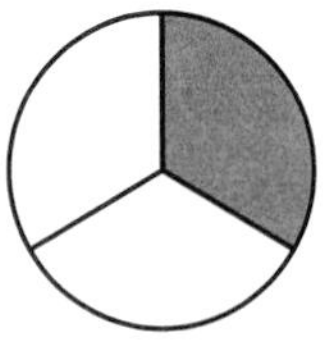

$\dfrac{1}{2}$ $\dfrac{1}{3}$ $\dfrac{1}{4}$ $\dfrac{1}{5}$

○   ○   ○   ○

3 Which fraction tells what part is shaded?

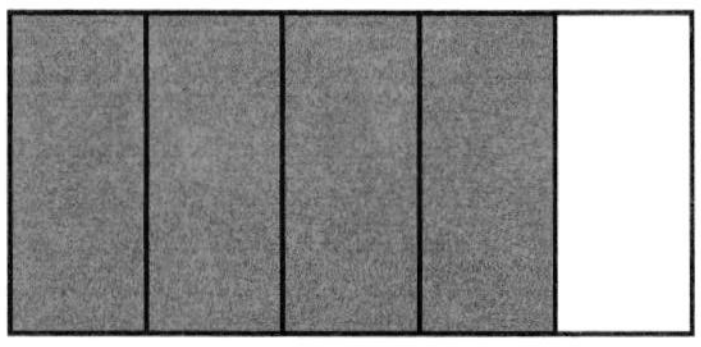

$\dfrac{1}{5}$ $\dfrac{1}{4}$ $\dfrac{5}{4}$ $\dfrac{4}{5}$

○   ○   ○   ○

---

4 Which fraction names the whole circle?

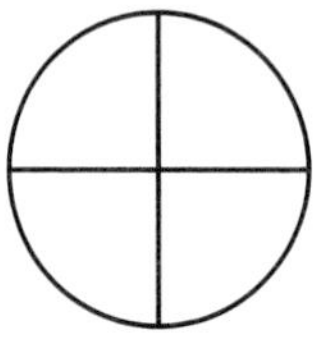

$\dfrac{1}{4}$ $\dfrac{2}{4}$ $\dfrac{3}{4}$ $\dfrac{4}{4}$

○   ○   ○   ○

Show What You Know

5 Draw a rectangle.
Draw 4 equal parts.

Color some parts blue.
What fraction is blue?

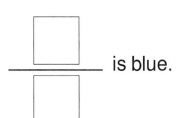

_____ is blue.

© Harcourt

Name _____

Compare parts of a group. Look at > or <.
Circle true or false.

$\frac{1}{3}$

$\frac{2}{3}$

$\frac{1}{3} < \frac{2}{3}$

(true)   false

$\frac{1}{4}$

$\frac{2}{4}$

$\frac{2}{4} < \frac{1}{4}$

true   (false)

1 $\frac{2}{4}$

$\frac{3}{4}$

$\frac{2}{4} > \frac{3}{4}$

true   false

2 $\frac{1}{5}$

$\frac{4}{5}$

$\frac{1}{5} < \frac{4}{5}$

true   false

3 $\frac{4}{6}$

$\frac{3}{6}$

$\frac{4}{6} > \frac{3}{6}$

true   false

4 $\frac{2}{3}$

$\frac{3}{3}$

$\frac{2}{3} < \frac{3}{3}$

true   false

Talk About It ▪ **Reasoning**

How do you know that $\frac{1}{3}$ of a group of 6 is less than $\frac{2}{3}$ of a group of 6?

Compare the red parts. Write > or <.

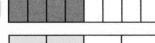 $\dfrac{1}{3}$

 $\dfrac{2}{3}$

$\dfrac{1}{3}$ is less than $\dfrac{2}{3}$.

$\dfrac{1}{3}$ $\boxed{<}$ $\dfrac{2}{3}$

 $\dfrac{1}{4}$

$\dfrac{2}{4}$

$\dfrac{2}{4}$ is greater than $\dfrac{1}{4}$.

$\dfrac{2}{4}$ $\boxed{>}$ $\dfrac{1}{4}$

Compare the red parts .
Write > or <.

1 $\dfrac{4}{6}$

$\dfrac{1}{6}$

$\dfrac{4}{6}$ $\bigcirc$ $\dfrac{1}{6}$

2  $\dfrac{2}{4}$

 $\dfrac{3}{4}$

$\bigcirc$

Problem Solving ▪ Reasoning

Circle true or false. Explain your thinking.

3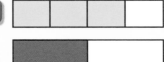

$\dfrac{4}{8} = \dfrac{2}{4}$

true   false

4

$\dfrac{3}{4} < \dfrac{1}{2}$

true   false

5

$\dfrac{1}{7} < \dfrac{1}{9}$

true   false

HOME ACTIVITY • During mealtime, set out a group of 5 peas, chicken nuggets, or other foods. Eat 1 part and have your child eat 2 parts. Ask your child to name the fractional part each of you ate and tell who ate the greater part.

© Harcourt

Name _____

Cheryl ate $\frac{1}{3}$ of a small pizza.

Mike ate $\frac{1}{8}$ of the same size pizza.

Who ate more pizza?

_____

UNDERSTAND

You need to find out who ate more pizza.

PLAN

Choose a way to solve the problem.

SOLVE

Make a model.

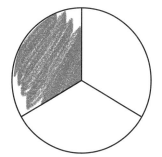

Cheryl's Pizza   Mike's Pizza

CHECK

How did your model help you
know who ate more pizza? Explain.

_____

Make a model to solve these problems.

1. Caryn ate $\frac{1}{4}$ of a grapefruit.

   Beth ate $\frac{1}{2}$ of a grapefruit.

   Who ate more grapefruit? _____

2. Kevin cut an apple into 6 equal pieces.
   Then he ate 2 pieces.
   What part did Kevin eat?

   _____

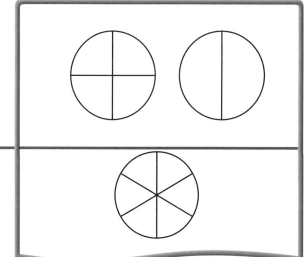

Use ●. Make and draw a model to solve.

1. Tim has 3 apples. $\frac{1}{3}$ of the apples are green.

   $\frac{2}{3}$ of the apples are red.

   Are there more red or green apples?

   red

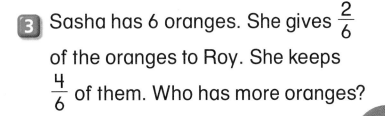

2. Frank has 4 marbles. 3 marbles are blue and 1 marble is red. What fraction of the marbles are blue?

   _____

3. Sasha has 6 oranges. She gives $\frac{2}{6}$ of the oranges to Roy. She keeps $\frac{4}{6}$ of them. Who has more oranges?

   _____

4. Toni has 2 corn muffins and 3 bran muffins. What fraction of the muffins are bran?

   _____

Write About It

Write a story about two friends sharing food.
Use fractions to tell how much each friend eats.

HOME ACTIVITY • Make up problems similar to the ones on this page. Have your child use objects to model and solve them.

© Harcourt

Name _____

CHECK ■ Concepts and Skills

Write the fraction for the yellow part.

     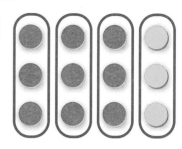

_____   _____   _____

Write the fraction for the blue part.

_____   _____   _____

Compare the blue parts. Look at > or <. Circle true or false.

  $\dfrac{2}{4}$   $\dfrac{4}{5}$

$\dfrac{3}{4}$ $\dfrac{2}{5}$

 $\dfrac{2}{4} < \dfrac{3}{4}$ $\dfrac{4}{5} < \dfrac{2}{5}$

true   false   true   false

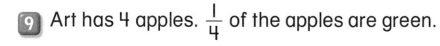

CHECK ■ Problem Solving

Use 4 ⬤. Make and draw a model to solve.

9 Art has 4 apples. $\dfrac{1}{4}$ of the apples are green.

$\dfrac{3}{4}$ of the apples are red. Are there more _____

red or green apples? — — — — — — —

_____

© Harcourt

Name _____

Choose the best answer for questions 1–5.

1 Which fraction tells what part of the group is yellow?

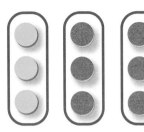

$\frac{1}{2}$ ○ $\frac{1}{8}$ ○ $\frac{1}{3}$ ○ $\frac{1}{4}$ ○

2 Which is true?

$\frac{4}{5}$

$\frac{2}{5}$

$\frac{4}{5} < \frac{2}{5}$ ○

$\frac{4}{5} = \frac{2}{5}$ ○

$\frac{4}{5} > \frac{2}{5}$ ○

$\frac{2}{5} > \frac{4}{5}$ ○

3 Jonathan has 3 blue beads and 2 yellow beads.
What part of the group of beads is yellow?

$\frac{1}{5}$ ○ $\frac{5}{5}$ ○ $\frac{3}{5}$ ○ $\frac{2}{5}$ ○

4
$$\begin{array}{r} 51 \\ +\ 40 \\ \hline \end{array}$$

11 ○   81 ○   90 ○   91 ○

5
$$\begin{array}{r} 21 \\ -\ 18 \\ \hline \end{array}$$

3 ○   4 ○   17 ○   39 ○

Show What You Know

6 Draw 8 circles. Color $\frac{1}{4}$ green.

Draw 12 circles. Color $\frac{1}{4}$ blue.

Hannah Hen's Kitchen

By Linda Cave   Illustrated by Lisa Campbell Ernst

This book will help me review fractions.

This book belongs to _____.

A

Hannah Hen liked to bake.
She made some cornbread.

"That smells good," said Danny Dog.

"Very good," said Cassie Cat.
"May we have some?"

B

"Yes, I love to share!

You can have —————————, Danny Dog.

You can have —————————, Cassie Cat.

And I can have —————————.
Then all the cornbread will be gone."

**Draw lines to show how Hannah Hen
will cut the cornbread.**

"That smells good," said Danny Dog and
Cassie Cat.
"Very good," said Paulie Pig.
"May we have some?"

"Yes, I love to share!" said Hannah Hen.

"We can each have _____.
Then all the cornbread will be gone."

**Draw lines to show how Hannah Hen
will cut the cornbread.**

D

"That smells good," said Danny Dog and Cassie Cat.
"Very good," said Paulie Pig.
"Mmm, good," said Gary Goat and Kathy Kid.
"May we have some?"
"Yes, I love to share!" said Hannah Hen.

"We can each have _____.

Then all the cornbread will be gone."

**Draw lines to show how Hannah Hen
will cut the cornbread.**

E

"That smells good," said Danny Dog and Cassie Cat.
"Very good," said Paulie Pig.
"Mmm, good," said Gary Goat and Kathy Kid.
"Tasty," said Sally Sheep and Martin Mule.
"May we have some?"

"Yes, I love to share!" said Hannah Hen.

"We can each have _____.
Then all the cornbread will be gone."

**Draw lines to show how Hannah Hen
will cut the cornbread.**

F

"Oh, no," said Danny Dog.
"Harry Horse and Cora Crow are coming."
"If we give them cornbread, we will

each have _____," said Hannah Hen.
"That is too little," the animals said.
"We don't want a part of one.
We each want a whole one."

G

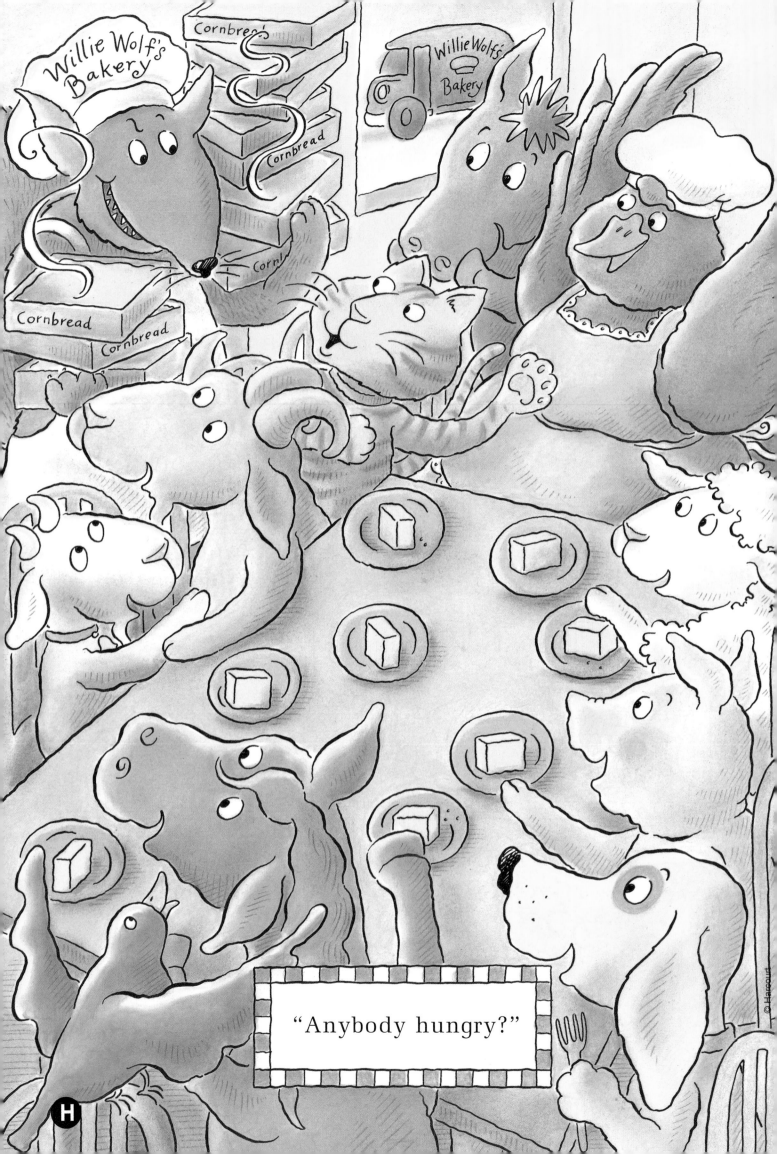

"Anybody hungry?"

Name _____

Mysterious Message

Use your reasoning skills to solve the message below. Shade the fractional parts of words to figure out the mystery message. Write the letters you shade in order on the lines below. Good luck!

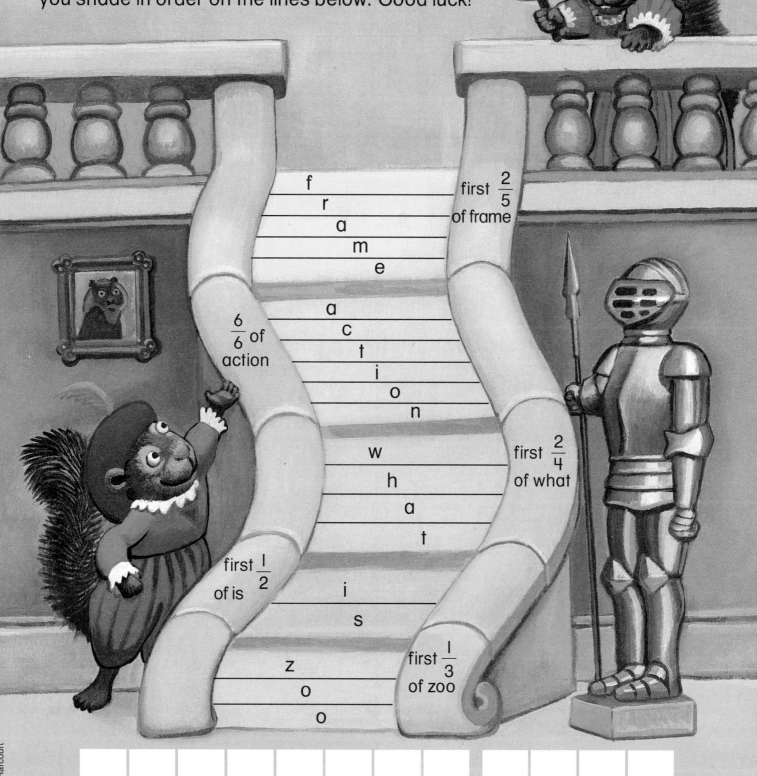

first $\frac{2}{5}$ of frame

$\frac{6}{6}$ of action

first $\frac{2}{4}$ of what

first $\frac{1}{2}$ of is

first $\frac{1}{3}$ of zoo

f
r
a
m
e
a
c
t
i
o
n
w
h
a
t
i
s
z
o
o

Stretch Your Thinking ▪ Give directions that use
fractional parts of words to spell your name.

© Harcourt

Name _____

1 How many sixths should be shaded to show the same amount as $\frac{1}{3}$?

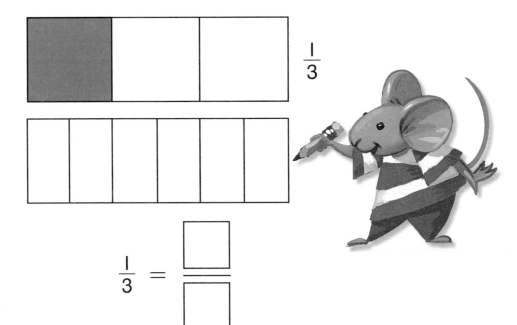

$\frac{1}{3}$

$\frac{1}{3} = \frac{\boxed{}}{\boxed{}}$

2 How many fourths should be shaded to show the same amount as $\frac{1}{2}$?

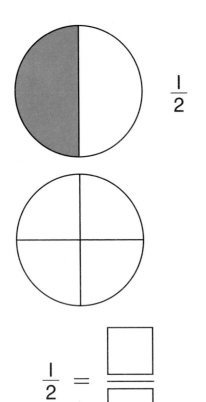

$\frac{1}{2}$

$\frac{1}{2} = \frac{\boxed{}}{\boxed{}}$

3 How many eighths should be shaded to show the same amount as $\frac{1}{4}$?

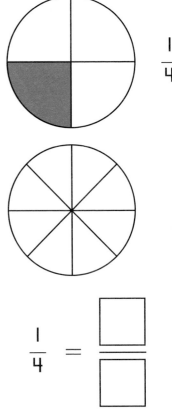

$\frac{1}{4}$

$\frac{1}{4} = \frac{\boxed{}}{\boxed{}}$

Challenge • Chapters 21–24

Name ____________________

Study Guide and Review

Skills and Concepts

1 Write how many hundreds, tens, and ones. Then write the number.

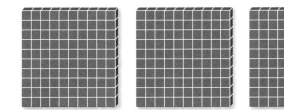

_____ hundreds _____ tens _____ ones _____

2 Write the number in different ways.

two hundred thirty-five

hundreds	tens	ones

_____ + _____ + _____

_____

3 Write the numbers that are 100 less and 100 more than 421.

100 less _____

100 more _____

4 Write greater than, less than, or equal to. Write >, <, or =.

123 is ____________ 45

123 ◯ 45

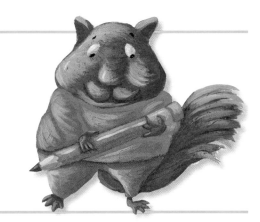

5 Write the numbers in order from least to greatest.

300 301 302 303 304 305 306 307 308 309 310 311 312 313 314 315

306	301	314	310

_____, _____, _____, _____

6 Write the number of parts. Are the parts equal?
Circle yes or no.

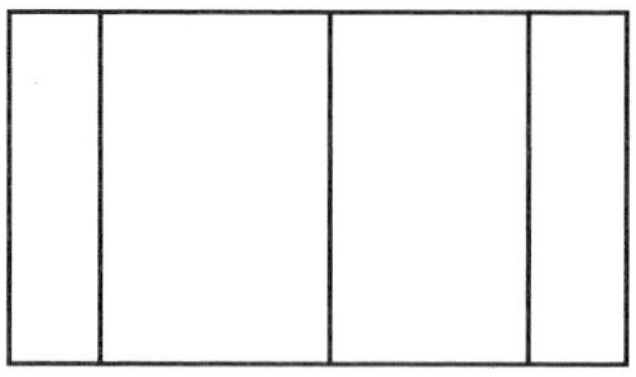

yes

no

_____ parts

---

7 Write the fraction for the shaded part.

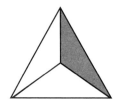

_____

---

8 Write the fraction in each part.
Count. Write the fraction for
the whole.

_____

9 Circle the equal parts.
Color to show the fraction.

$\frac{1}{6}$

---

10 Compare the shaded parts. Circle true or false.

 $\frac{1}{4}$

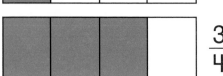 $\frac{3}{4}$

$\frac{1}{4} > \frac{3}{4}$

true   false

Problem Solving

11 Find the pattern. Write the rule. Continue the pattern.

Dion sees a pattern in the numbers 235, 239, 243, 247.

The rule could be count _____.

235, 239, 243, 247, _____, _____, _____, _____

© Harcourt

Name _____

Hats Off!

Wendy saw a group of football players standing on the sideline.

- One-third of the players were wearing helmets.

- There were more than 7 players in the group.

Draw a picture to show the possible number of players in the group. Circle the number of players in the group who were wearing helmets.

Show your work.

Technology

Name _____

Mighty Math Carnival Countdown • Compare and Order

1. Click  .

2. Click  .

3. Click T.

4. Play 5 times.

Practice and Problem Solving

Write >, <, or =.

1 432 ◯ 423

2 299 ◯ 300

3 509 ◯ 509

4 97 ◯ 970

5 There were 350 people at the fair. Then 100 more came. Now how many are at the fair?

_____ people

6 There were 781 cars in the lot. Then 100 cars left. How many cars are left?

_____ cars

---

7 **Reasoning**

Circle the one that is closest to 987.

885   886   887

three hundred sixty-six

365

Name _____

PROBLEM SOLVING ON LOCATION

At the Market

At the farmers' market in Findlay, Ohio, you can buy fresh fruits and vegetables all summer long!

Show different ways to make a fresh fruit salad. Use 12 fruits in all. Write the numbers.

Use more apples than pears.

Apples	+	Grapes	+	Pears	=	12
	+		+		=	12
	+		+		=	12

Use fewer apples than grapes.

Apples	+	Grapes	+	Pears	=	12
	+		+		=	12
	+		+		=	12

Use more grapes than pears.

Apples	+	Grapes	+	Pears	=	12
	+		+		=	12
	+		+		=	12

Name _____

PROBLEM SOLVING ON LOCATION

At the Seashore

People love to collect seashells on
the beach at Cape May, New Jersey.

Some children share their seashells equally.
What fraction of the shells does each child get?

Use ● to solve. Draw to show your work.

2 children share 12 seashells.

Each child gets ⬚/⬚ of the shells.

---

3 children share 12 seashells.

Each child gets ⬚/⬚ of the shells.

---

4 children share 12 seashells.

Each child gets ⬚/⬚ of the shells.

© Harcourt

Write as many addition problems as you can, using the numbers in the picture.

SCHOOL HOME CONNECTION

Dear Family,
   Today we started Chapter 25. We will look at ways to add 3-digit numbers. Here is the math vocabulary and an activity for us to do together at home.

   Love,

   _____

Vocabulary

decimal point The dot in a money amount that separates dollars from cents.

dollar sign The symbol at the beginning of a money amount that shows dollars.

decimal point ⌐
dollar sign ⟶ $ 4.80

ACTIVITY

With your child, look through newspaper ads to find two items priced between $1.00 and $4.99. Have your child use real money, if possible, to find the cost of buying both items. Repeat with other prices.

Books to Share

To read about adding 3-digit numbers with your child, look for these books in your local library.

The 329th Friend,
by Marjorie Weinman Sharmat,
Simon & Schuster, 1992.

The Purse,
by Kathy Caple,
Houghton Mifflin, 1992.

Visit *The Learning Site* for additional ideas and activities. www.harcourtschool.com

© Harcourt

Name _____

What is 300 + 100?

$3 + 1 = \underline{4}$

Knowing your facts can help you add hundreds.

3 hundreds + 1 hundred = _____ hundreds $300 + 100 = \underline{400}$

Add.

1 $5 + 4 = \underline{\hspace{2cm}}$

   5 hundreds + 4 hundreds = _____ hundreds

   $500 + 400 = \underline{\hspace{2cm}}$

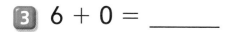

2 $3 + 5 = \underline{\hspace{2cm}}$

   3 hundreds + 5 hundreds = _____ hundreds

   $300 + 500 = \underline{\hspace{2cm}}$

3 $6 + 0 = \underline{\hspace{2cm}}$

   6 hundreds + 0 hundreds = _____ hundreds

   $600 + 0 = \underline{\hspace{2cm}}$

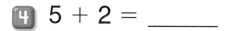

4 $5 + 2 = \underline{\hspace{2cm}}$

   5 hundreds + 2 hundreds = _____ hundreds

   $500 + 200 = \underline{\hspace{2cm}}$

Talk About It ▪ **Reasoning**

How does knowing the sum of 4 + 3 help you add 400 + 300?

© Harcourt

Add.

1
2	2 hundreds	200
+4	+4 hundreds	+400
6	6 hundreds	600

2
4	4 hundreds	400
+5	+5 hundreds	+ 500
	hundreds	

3
1	1 hundred	100
+7	+7 hundreds	+ 700
	hundreds	

4
2	2 hundreds	200
+2	+2 hundreds	+ 200
	hundreds	

5
3	3 hundreds	300
+4	+4 hundreds	+ 400
	hundreds	

6
5	5 hundreds	500
+0	+0 hundreds	+ 0
	hundreds	

7
6	6 hundreds	600
+3	+3 hundreds	+ 300
	hundreds	

8
3	3 hundreds	300
+2	+2 hundreds	+ 200
	hundreds	

Algebra

Use the pattern to help you add.

9
| 4 | 40 | 400 |
| +3 | +30 | + 300 |

10
| 8 | 80 | 800 |
| +1 | +10 | + 100 |

ACTIVITY • Put out 4 dollars and 5 dollars. Remind your child that each dollar is worth 100 ¢. Ask your child to find 4¢ + 5¢ (9¢), then 400¢ + 500¢ (900¢). Repeat with other groups of dollars.

369

three hundred seventy

Chapter 25

© Harcourt

$135 + 147 =$ _____

Step 1

Add the ones.
Regroup 12 ones to
make 1 ten and 2 ones.
Write 1 in the tens column.

hundreds	tens	ones
1	3	5
+ 1	4	7
		2

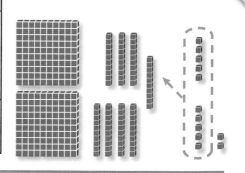

Step 2

Add the tens.
Write the number
of tens.

hundreds	tens	ones
	1	
1	3	5
+ 1	4	7
	8	2

Step 3

Add the hundreds.
Write the number
of hundreds.

hundreds	tens	ones
	1	
1	3	5
+ 1	4	7
2	8	2

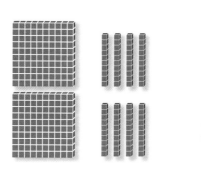

Use ▪▪▪▪▪▪▪▪▪ ▪. Add. Regroup if you need to.

1

hundreds	tens	ones
	□	
6	4	5
+ 1	3	5

2

hundreds	tens	ones
	□	
3	3	6
+ 2	2	7

3

hundreds	tens	ones
	□	
4	6	1
+ 5	1	8

Talk About It ▪ Reasoning

What would happen if you added the hundreds place first, the tens place
second, and the ones place last?

Use ▬▬▬▬▬ ▫. Add. Regroup if you need to.

1

hundreds	tens	ones
	☐	
2	1	9
+ 2	5	4
4	7	3

2

hundreds	tens	ones
	☐	
3	5	8
+ 1	1	2

3

hundreds	tens	ones
	☐	
1	6	5
+ 4	2	9

4

hundreds	tens	ones
	☐	
2	8	4
+ 5	0	7

5

hundreds	tens	ones
	☐	
7	0	5
+ 1	3	4

6

hundreds	tens	ones
	☐	
3	6	8
+	1	6

7

hundreds	tens	ones
	☐	
2	4	9
+ 1	2	3

8

hundreds	tens	ones
	☐	
6	3	9
+ 1	5	6

9

hundreds	tens	ones
	☐	
4	4	7
+ 3	4	3

Problem Solving ▪ Estimation

Estimate. Circle **greater than 500** or **less than 500**.

10 309 + 43

greater than 500
less than 500

11 232 + 693

greater than 500
less than 500

© Harcourt

CTIVITY • Ask your child to tell you how he or she knows when to regroup. Use one of the
on this page.

Name _____

There are 365 books about polar bears and 208 books about penguins. How many books are there altogether?

Step 1

Add the ones. Regroup if you need to. Write the number of ones.

```
   ¦
   365
 +208
    3
```

Step 2

Add the tens. Regroup if you need to. Write the number of tens.

```
    ¦
   365
 +208
   73
```

Step 3

Add the hundreds. Write the number of hundreds.

```
    ¦
   365
 +208
  573
```

There are __573__ books altogether.

Add.

1
```
   ¦
   522
 +185
   707
```

2
```
   907
 +  30
```

3
```
   226
 +457
```

4
```
   544
 +315
```

5
```
   248
 +537
```

6
```
   653
 +  37
```

7
```
   193
 +284
```

8
```
    25
 +492
```

9
```
   709
 +259
```

10
```
   888
 +   9
```

11
```
   282
 +254
```

12
```
   303
 +353
```

Talk About It ▪ Reasoning

Why do you regroup the ones if the sum is ten or more?

Practice

Add.

1
```
  853
+  72
─────
  925
```

2
```
  690
+ 309
─────
```

3
```
  418
+ 479
─────
```

4
```
  184
+ 713
─────
```

5
```
  537
+ 248
─────
```

6
```
  435
+  94
─────
```

7
```
   66
+ 682
─────
```

8
```
  373
+ 107
─────
```

9
```
  255
+ 219
─────
```

10
```
  363
+ 561
─────
```

11
```
  978
+   6
─────
```

12
```
  230
+ 435
─────
```

13
```
  772
+  47
─────
```

14
```
  431
+ 322
─────
```

15
```
   83
+ 385
─────
```

16
```
  151
+ 444
─────
```

Mixed Review
Add or subtract.

17
```
  45        65        94       73¢        82        24
+ 35      − 16      − 53      − 29¢      +  4      + 58
────      ────      ────      ─────      ────      ────
```

© Harcourt

Name _____

CHECK ▪ Concepts and Skills

Add.

 | 1   1 hundred   100
    +7   +7 hundreds   +700
    ──────────────────────────
          hundreds

 | 3   3 hundreds   300
    +3   +3 hundreds   +300
    ──────────────────────────
          hundreds

Use  ▪. Add. Regroup if you need to.

3

hundreds	tens	ones
☐	☐	
6	1	8
+ 2	7	4

4

hundreds	tens	ones
☐	☐	
1	2	0
+ 3	3	8

5

hundreds	tens	ones
☐	☐	
3	8	3
+ 4	4	6

Add.

6

hundreds	tens	ones
☐	☐	
8	1	9
+	7	6

7

hundreds	tens	ones
☐	☐	
1	3	7
+ 6	0	0

8

hundreds	tens	ones
☐	☐	
4	5	2
+ 4	9	0

CHECK ▪ Problem Solving

Choose a method to solve each problem.

9
$8.08
+$1.70

10
859
+   2

11
$2.17
+$3.00

12
55
+574

Name _____

Choose the best answer for questions 1–6.

1
$$200$$
$$+ 700$$

9	90	99	900
○	○	○	◉

2
$$434$$
$$+ 512$$
946

922	940	946	948
○	○	◉	○

3
$$\$1.85$$
$$+ \$5.12$$
6.97

$4.73	$6.73	$6.97	$7.97
○	○	◉	○

4
$$703$$
$$+ 105$$
808

602	608	802	808
○	○	○	◉

5
$$\$4.56$$
$$+ \$3.22$$
7.78

$7.78	$7.84
◉	○
$8.84	$17.84
○	○

6 Michael has 2 football cards and 4 baseball cards. What fraction of the group is football cards?

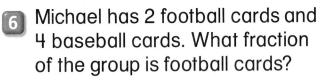

$\frac{2}{4}$	$\frac{2}{6}$	$\frac{4}{6}$	$\frac{6}{6}$
◉	○	○	○

Show What You Know

7 Use   . Make up your own addition problems. Write the numbers.

Regroup once.

hundreds	tens	ones
☐	☐	
	7	1

Regroup twice.

hundreds	tens	ones
☐	☐	
+		
6	3	2

© Harcourt

Subtracting 3-Digit Numbers

Biking Trail 120 miles
Hiking Trail 280 miles
Campsite 150 miles

Mount Snow 365 miles
Mount Sunny 320 miles

Write as many subtraction problems as you can, using the numbers in the picture.

SCHOOL HOME CONNECTION

Dear Family,
    Today we started Chapter 26. We will look at ways to subtract 3-digit numbers. Here is the math vocabulary and an activity for us to do together at home.

    Love,

    _____

Vocabulary

regroup To break 1 hundred into 10 tens or to break 1 ten into 10 ones.

$$
\begin{array}{r}
7\ 14 \\
\not{8}\not{4}5 \\
-\ 375 \\
\hline
470
\end{array}
$$

Regroup 1 hundred as 10 tens. Then you have 7 hundreds and 14 tens.

ACTIVITY

Before you take a trip, discuss the total number of miles you will travel. Then along the way, look at road signs that give the distance in miles to your destination. Ask your child to subtract that distance from the total miles to find out how many miles you have traveled so far.

Books to Share

To read about 3-digit subtraction with your child, look for these books at your local library.

The King's Commissioners, by Aileen Friedman, Scholastic, 1995.

The Hundred Dresses, by Eleanor Estes, Harcourt, 1974.

The Philharmonic Gets Dressed, by Karla Kuskin, HarperCollins, 1986.

© Harcourt

Visit *The Learning Site* for additional ideas and activities. www.harcourtschool.com

383

Name _____

What is **500 – 300**?

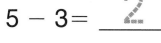

5 – 3 = __2__

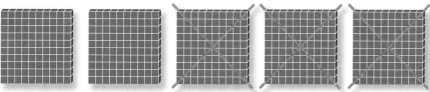

Knowing the subtraction facts can help you subtract hundreds.

5 hundreds – 3 hundreds = __2__ hundreds

500 – 300 = __200__

Subtract.

1 9 – 5 = _____

9 hundreds – 5 hundreds = _____ hundreds

900 – 500 = _____

_____

2 7 – 6 = _____

7 hundreds – 6 hundreds = _____ hundreds

700 – 600 = _____

_____

3 8 – 5 = _____

8 hundreds – 5 hundreds = _____ hundreds

800 – 500 = _____

Talk About It ▪ **Reasoning**

How does knowing 6 – 3 help you find 600 – 300?
Explain your thinking.

Practice

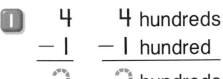

Subtract.

1

4	4 hundreds	400
−1	−1 hundred	−100
3	3 hundreds	300

2

7	7 hundreds	700
−3	−3 hundreds	−300
	hundreds	

3

9	9 hundreds	900
−7	−7 hundreds	−700
	hundreds	

4

8	8 hundreds	800
−4	−4 hundreds	−400
	hundreds	

5

5	5 hundreds	500
−4	−4 hundreds	−400
	hundred	

6

8	8 hundreds	800
−6	−6 hundreds	−600
	hundreds	

7

4	4 hundreds	400
−4	−4 hundreds	−400
	hundreds	

8

9	9 hundreds	900
−6	−6 hundreds	−600
	hundreds	

Algebra

Use addition to subtract.

9 $500 + 300 = 800$, so $800 - \underline{\hspace{1cm}} = 500$

10 $200 + 700 = 900$, so $900 - \underline{\hspace{1cm}} = 200$

11 $400 + 300 = 700$, so $700 - \underline{\hspace{1cm}} = 400$

TIVITY • Put out 5 dollars and take away 1. Remind your child that each dollar is worth 100
your child to find 5 − 1 (4) and then 500 − 100 (400). Repeat with other groups of dollars.

Name _____

236 − 129 = _____

Step 1
Show 236.
Look at the ones.
Should you regroup?

(Yes)   No

hundreds	tens	ones
	□	□
2	3	6
− 1	2	9

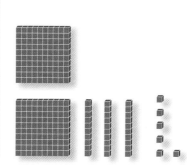

Step 2
Regroup 1 ten as 10 ones. Now there are 16 ones. Subtract 9 from 16.
Write how many ones are left.

hundreds	tens	ones
	2	16
2	3	6
− 1	2	9
		7

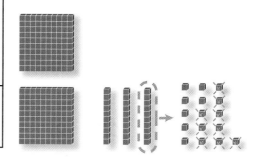

Step 3
Subtract the tens.
Subtract the hundreds.
Write how many tens and hundreds are left.

hundreds	tens	ones
	2	16
2	3	6
− 1	2	9
1	0	7

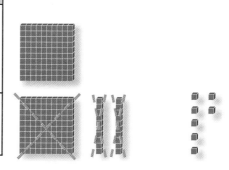

Use   . Subtract.

1

hundreds	tens	ones
	□	□
9	6	3
− 7	5	7

2

hundreds	tens	ones
	□	□
7	8	7
− 2	4	5

3

hundreds	tens	ones
	□	□
6	4	1
− 3	2	5

Talk About It ▪ Reasoning

Why is it easier to subtract ones first?

Practice

Use ▦ ▭ ▫ . Subtract.

1

hundreds	tens	ones
8	⁴5̶	¹⁰0̶
− 6	1	3
2	3	7

2

hundreds	tens	ones
9	□ 8	□ 2
− 9	1	9

3

hundreds	tens	ones
5	□ 9	□ 0
− 2	3	8

4

hundreds	tens	ones
4	□ 2	□ 8
− 1	1	3

5

hundreds	tens	ones
7	□ 9	□ 4
− 2	5	7

6

hundreds	tens	ones
6	□ 4	□ 8
−	3	9

7

hundreds	tens	ones
3	□ 9	□ 1
− 1	0	6

8

hundreds	tens	ones
8	□ 6	□ 5
−	3	8

9

hundreds	tens	ones
7	□ 7	□ 5
− 6	0	7

Problem Solving ▪ Mental Math

Count on to add. Count back to subtract.

10 $428 + 30 =$ _____

11 $157 + 300 =$ _____

12 $563 − 100 =$ _____

13 $296 − 20 =$ _____

CTIVITY • Have your child choose a subtraction problem on this page and tell you the steps
followed to solve it.

Name _____

$329 - 197 =$ _____

Step 1

Show 329.
Subtract the ones.
Write how many
ones are left.

hundreds	tens	ones
□	□	
3	2	9
− 1	9	7
		2

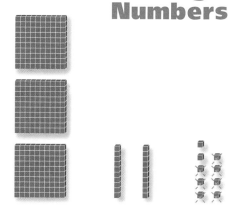

Step 2

Can you subtract 9 tens?
If not, regroup 1 hundred
as 10 tens. Now there are
12 tens. Subtract. Write
how many tens are left.

hundreds	tens	ones
2	12	
3	2	9
− 1	9	7
	3	2

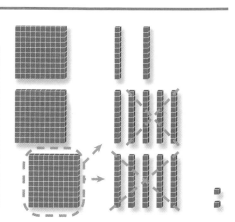

Step 3

Subtract the hundreds.
Write how many
hundreds are left.

hundreds	tens	ones
2	12	
3	2	9
− 1	9	7
1	3	2

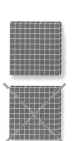

Subtract.

1

hundreds	tens	ones
□	□	
8	4	8
− 4	7	5

2

hundreds	tens	ones
□	□	
9	2	4
− 6	5	3

3

hundreds	tens	ones
□	□	
7	5	9
− 1	9	5

Talk About It ■ Reasoning

What happens if you subtract the hundreds first when you
subtract 3-digit numbers?

Subtract.

1

hundreds	tens	ones
6 7	10 0	7
− 1	6	3
5	4	4

2

hundreds	tens	ones
□ 9 8	□ 4	6
− 5	8	3
3	6	3

3

hundreds	tens	ones
3	□ 8	□ 1
−	4	4
3	3	7

4

hundreds	tens	ones
□ 8	□ 2	8
− 6	7	4
1	5	4

5

hundreds	tens	ones
□ 5	□ 2	7
− 2	4	5
2	8	2

6

hundreds	tens	ones
8	□ 3 4	□ 2
− 3	2	6
5	1	6

7

hundreds	tens	ones
□ 5 6	□ 0	4
− 3	1	0
2	9	4

8

hundreds	tens	ones
9	□ 8	□ 7
− 1	6	9
8	1	8

9

hundreds	tens	ones
7	□ 3	□ 6
− 7	1	7
0	1	9

Mixed Review

Find the pattern. Write the rule. Continue the pattern.

10 Edie sees a pattern in the numbers 819, 719, 619.

The rule could be count ___subsrract by 100___.

___819___, ___719___, ___619___, 519, 419, 319, 219, 119

ACTIVITY • Give your child two 3-digit numbers and have him or her subtract.

dred ninety

Name _____

There are 340 people at the beach.
137 of the people go in the water.
How many people do not go in the water?

Step 1
There are not enough ones to subtract without regrouping. Regroup 1 ten as 10 ones.

$$\begin{array}{r} {\scriptstyle 3\ 10} \\ 3\cancel{4}0 \\ -137 \\ \hline \end{array}$$

Step 2
Subtract the ones.
Subtract the tens.

$$\begin{array}{r} {\scriptstyle 3\ 10} \\ 3\cancel{4}0 \\ -137 \\ \hline 03 \end{array}$$

Step 3
Subtract the hundreds.

$$\begin{array}{r} {\scriptstyle 3\ 10} \\ 3\cancel{4}\cancel{0} \\ -137 \\ \hline 203 \end{array}$$

 203 people do not go in the water.

Subtract.

1	2	3	4
$\begin{array}{r} {\scriptstyle 8\,1\,2} \\ 926 \\ -\ 45 \\ \hline 881 \end{array}$	$\begin{array}{r} 739 \\ -284 \\ \hline 455 \end{array}$	$\begin{array}{r} 409 \\ -206 \\ \hline 203 \end{array}$	$\begin{array}{r} 198 \\ -\ 48 \\ \hline 150 \end{array}$

5	6	7	8
$\begin{array}{r} 542 \\ -226 \\ \hline 316 \end{array}$	$\begin{array}{r} 673 \\ -\ 37 \\ \hline 636 \end{array}$	$\begin{array}{r} 603 \\ -353 \\ \hline 250 \end{array}$	$\begin{array}{r} 258 \\ -142 \\ \hline 116 \end{array}$

9	10	11	12
$\begin{array}{r} 709 \\ -259 \\ \hline 450 \end{array}$	$\begin{array}{r} 888 \\ -\ \ 9 \\ \hline 879 \end{array}$	$\begin{array}{r} 532 \\ -250 \\ \hline 282 \end{array}$	$\begin{array}{r} 190 \\ -\ 84 \\ \hline 106 \end{array}$

Talk About It ▪ Reasoning

How do you know if you need to regroup? Explain with examples.

© Harcourt

Practice

Subtract.

1.
```
  4 10
  506
- 452
   54
```

2.
```
  5
  675
-  94
  581
```

3.
```
  864
- 123
  747
```

4.
```
    4
  458
-  29
  429
```

5.
```
  8
  903
- 250
  653
```

6.
```
  7
  784
-   7
  777
```

7.
```
  8
  965
- 781
  187
```

8.
```
  6
  175
-  57
  118
```

9.
```
  688
- 347
  371
```

10.
```
  8
  393
-  78
  315
```

11.
```
  8
  950
- 370
  580
```

12.
```
  566
- 425
  141
```

13.
```
  7
  837
- 263
  574
```

14.
```
  698
-  68
  630
```

15.
```
  759
- 555
  204
```

16.
```
  8
  390
- 147
  283
```

Problem Solving ▪ Reasoning

Write the two numbers that make each difference.
Use the numbers in the box.

897	653
543	252

17. Difference of 645 _____ and _____

18. Difference of 110 _____ and _____

HOME ACTIVITY • Make up a subtraction problem using two 3-digit numbers. Ask your child to find the difference on a sheet of paper. Repeat with other problems.

© Harcourt

Problem Solving
Too Much Information

Draw a line through the sentence that is not needed. Then solve.

1 While on a trip, the Rodriguez family sees 156 trucks and 138 vans. ~~They see 65 station wagons.~~ How many more trucks than vans do they see?

_18_ more trucks.

$$\begin{array}{r} {}^{4}\ {}^{16} \\ 1\,\cancel{5}\,\cancel{6} \\ -\ 1\,3\,8 \\ \hline 1\,8 \end{array}$$

2 They drive 507 miles on Monday. They drive 245 miles on Tuesday. They drive 428 miles on Wednesday. How many more miles do they drive on Monday than on Tuesday?

_____ more miles.

$$\begin{array}{r} \cancel{5}10\,7 \\ -\ 2\,4\,5 \\ \hline 2\,6\,2 \end{array}$$

3 Mr. Rodriguez buys juice for $2.25. Juan buys snacks for $1.49. Juan gets trail mix. How much money do they spend altogether?

_____

$$\begin{array}{r} {}^{1}\qquad{}^{1} \\ \$2.25 \\ +\ 1.49 \\ \hline 3.74 \end{array}$$

4 Susie has 140 postcards. The postcards cost 18¢ each. She sends 32 postcards. How many postcards does Susie have left?

_____ postcards

$$\begin{array}{r} 1\,\cancel{4}\,{}^{1}0 \\ -\ 3\,2 \\ \hline 1\,0\,8 \end{array}$$

© Harcourt

Draw a line through the sentence that is not needed. Then solve.

1 Mr. Rodriguez drives 335 miles. ~~They stop to eat lunch for 1 hour.~~ Then they drive 238 miles more. How many miles do they drive in all?

_573_ miles

$$\begin{array}{r} 1 \\ 335 \\ +238 \\ \hline 573 \end{array}$$

2 Juan counts 235 cars. Susie counts 247 cars. Mrs. Rodriguez counts 303 cars. How many fewer cars does Juan count than Suzie?

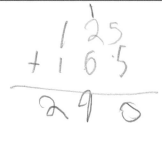

_____ fewer cars

$$\begin{array}{r} 247 \\ -235 \\ \hline 12 \end{array}$$

3 Nevada Falls is 594 feet high. Smith Falls is 320 feet high. It is 100 feet wide at the top. How much higher is Nevada Falls than Smith Falls?

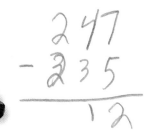

_____ feet

$$\begin{array}{r} 594 \\ -320 \\ \hline 274 \end{array}$$

4 The family hikes on a trail for 5 hours. They see 125 sparrows. They see 165 ravens. How many sparrows and ravens do they see altogether?

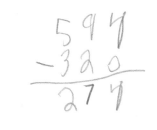

_____ sparrows and ravens

$$\begin{array}{r} 1 \\ 125 \\ +165 \\ \hline 290 \end{array}$$

Write About It

Write a word problem for a classmate to solve.
Put in one sentence that is not needed to solve the problem.

© Harcourt

🏠 **HOME ACTIVITY** • Have your child explain to you how he or she solved the problems in this lesson.

Name _____

CHECK ▪ Concepts and Skills

Subtract.

 1.

9	9 hundreds	900
−6	−6 hundreds	−600
	_____ hundreds	

 2.

5	5 hundreds	500
−3	−3 hundreds	−300
	_____ hundreds	

Use ▦ ▭▭▭ ▪ . Subtract.

3.

hundreds	tens	ones
☐	☐	☐
7	1	8
− 4	4	5

4.

hundreds	tens	ones
☐	☐	☐
4	6	9
− 3	7	2

5.

hundreds	tens	ones
☐	☐	☐
5	5	0
−	2	4

Subtract.

6.
```
 633
−170
```

7.
```
 743
− 26
```

8.
```
 956
−592
```

9.
```
 244
−226
```

CHECK ▪ Problem Solving

Draw a line through the sentence that is not needed. Then solve.

10. Dad has a beehive with 634 bees. He gets a new hive with 529 bees. The bees make 60 pounds of honey. How many fewer bees are in the new hive?

_____ fewer bees

Name _____

Choose the best answer for questions 1–7.

1
$$\begin{array}{r} 800 \\ -\ 600 \\ \hline \end{array}$$

2   200   300   2000
○   ◉   ○   ○

2
$$\begin{array}{r} 726 \\ -\ 302 \\ \hline 424 \end{array}$$

416   424   428   1028
○   ◉   ○   ○

3
$$\begin{array}{r} 532 \\ -\ 520 \\ \hline 012 \end{array}$$

6   11   12   46
○   ○   ◉   ○

4
$$\begin{array}{r} 356 \\ -\ 145 \\ \hline 211 \end{array}$$

211   389   400   401
◉   ○   ○   ○

5
$$\begin{array}{r} \$4.56 \\ +\ \$3.48 \\ \hline 08 \end{array}$$

$1.08 $1.09 $8.09 $8.04
◉   ○   ○   ○

6 What number is just after 326?

327   328   427   527
◉   ○   ○   ○

7 Together, Matt and Ann have 145 stickers.
23 of the stickers have flowers. 45 of the stickers
belong to Matt. How many belong to Ann?

100   213   190   290
◉   ○   ○   ○

Show What You Know

8 Use ▦ ▬ ▪. Make up your own
subtraction problems. Write the numbers.

Regroup once.

hundreds	tens	ones
□	□	
□	□	□
2	4	8

Regroup twice.

hundreds	tens	ones
□	□	□
□	□	□
1	8	7

© Harcourt

SCHOOL HOME CONNECTION

Dear Family,
    Today we started Chapter 27. We will use addition and subtraction of 3-digit numbers in new ways. Here is the math vocabulary and an activity for us to do together at home.

                    Love,

    _____

Vocabulary

estimate sums To find *about* how many in all. One way to do this is to round each number to the closer hundred and add the hundreds.

Estimate   179   is about   200
             +493   is about   +500
                                  700

So, 179 + 493 is about 700.

estimate differences To find *about* how many are left. One way to do this is to round each number to the closer hundred and subtract the hundreds.

Estimate   775   is about   800
             −318   is about   −300
                                  500

So, 775 − 318 is about 500.

Visit *The Learning Site* for additional ideas and activities. www.harcourtschool.com

ACTIVITY

When shopping at the supermarket, help your child compare prices. Choose two similar items that weigh the same amount. The items should cost between $1.00 and $4.99. Have your child estimate the difference in price between the two items and tell which is the better buy.

Books to Share

To read about 3-digit addition and subtraction with your child, look for these books in your local library.

Pigs Will Be Pigs, by Amy Axelrod, Simon & Schuster, 1994.

Easy Math Puzzles, by David A. Adler, Holiday House, 1997.

© Harcourt

Name _____

Tim wants a train that costs $3.98 and a ball that costs $2.95. About how much money does Tim need? First use rounding to estimate the sum. Then solve. Was your answer reasonable?

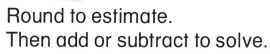

For 50¢ or more, round to the next dollar.

$3.98 is about $4.00.
$2.95 is about $3.00.

Estimate	Solve
$4.00 + $3.00 $7.00	$3.98 + $2.95 $6.93

$6.93 is about $7.00, so the answer is reasonable.

Round to estimate.
Then add or subtract to solve.

1 Ei has $8.72. Julia has $4.63. How much more money does Ei have than Julia?

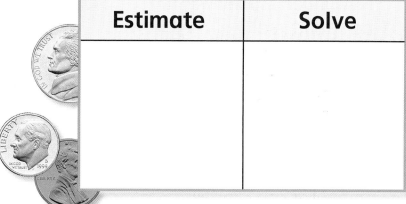

Estimate	Solve

_____

2 Lynnette has $2.89. She gets $2.80 more. How much money does she have altogether?

Estimate	Solve

_____

Talk About It ▪ Reasoning
Why might you estimate to add and subtract 3-digit numbers?

Does your answer make sense?

Round to estimate.
Then add or subtract to solve.

	Estimate	Solve
1 Tonio has $8.99. Earl has $5.85. How much more money does Tonio have than Earl? $3.14	$9.00 − $6.00 $3.00	$8.99 − $5.85 $3.14
2 Tonio takes all of his money to the pet store. He buys a cat toy for $4.68. How much money does he have left? _____		
3 Earl wants to buy cat food for $3.75 and a cat collar for $.98. How much money will he spend in all? _____		
4 How much of Earl's $5.85 will he have left after he buys the cat food and the cat collar? _____		

Problem Solving ▪ Reasoning

5 Janine wants a book for $2.49 and some markers for $1.25. She estimates she will need about $3.00. Is she correct? Why or why not?

© Harcourt

🏠 **HOME ACTIVITY** • Have your child tell you why he or she estimated the way he or she did on this page.

Add or subtract.

1
```
  5 10
  6̶0̶5̶
- 443
─────
  162
```

2
```
  $8.75
- $0.59
──────
```

3
```
  646
+ 100
─────
```

4
```
  555
- 381
─────
```

5
```
  $5.45
+ $4.25
──────
```

6
```
  752
- 339
─────
```

7
```
  685
- 302
─────
```

8
```
  467
+ 450
─────
```

9
```
   63
+ 631
─────
```

10
```
  $7.82
- $2.10
──────
```

11
```
  956
- 595
─────
```

12
```
  $1.57
+ $4.23
──────
```

13
```
  469
- 408
─────
```

14
```
  333
- 153
─────
```

$7.00

15
```
  846
- 839
─────
```

16
```
  675
- 564
─────
```

Talk About It ▪ Reasoning

How can estimating help you find out if your answer makes sense?

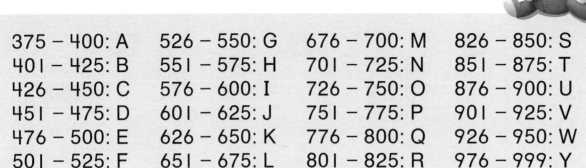

Add or subtract. Use the code to answer the riddle.

375 – 400: A	526 – 550: G	676 – 700: M	826 – 850: S
401 – 425: B	551 – 575: H	701 – 725: N	851 – 875: T
426 – 450: C	576 – 600: I	726 – 750: O	876 – 900: U
451 – 475: D	601 – 625: J	751 – 775: P	901 – 925: V
476 – 500: E	626 – 650: K	776 – 800: Q	926 – 950: W
501 – 525: F	651 – 675: L	801 – 825: R	976 – 999: Y

Why can't you feed a teddy bear?

```
  400      988      342      781      899      325      250
+  23    - 503    +  84    - 400    -  23    + 524    + 250
```

423   485   ___   ___   ___   ___   ___

B   E

```
  608      473      425
-  10    + 396    + 425
```

___   ___   ___

,

___   ___

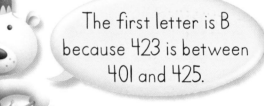

The first letter is B because 423 is between 401 and 425.

```
  425      860      446      219      590      532      371
+ 415    -   5    + 430    + 302    -  80    -  42    +  93
```

___   ___   ___   ___   ___   ___   ___

!

___   ___   ___   ___   ___   ___   ___

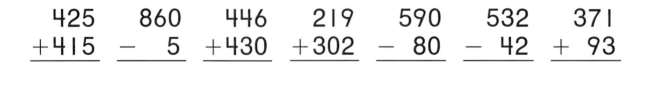

🏠 **HOME ACTIVITY** • You and your child can have fun using the code on this page. Make up addition and subtraction problems with answers that spell out "I love you." Have your child solve the problems, write the letters, and read the message.

Name _____

Mary has $6.50. She buys a sandwich for $2.35 and milk for $1.15. How much money does Mary have left?

Mary has
$3.00 left.

Step 1	Step 2
Add the amounts Mary spent.	Subtract the sum from the amount Mary had to start with.
$2.35 + $1.15 $3.50	$6.50 − $3.50 $3.00

Add or subtract.
Do one step at a time.

	Step 1	Step 2
1 Sho has 481 trading cards. He sells 218 of his cards. Then he buys 156 more. How many cards does Sho have now? _____ cards		
2 Liz has 222 stamps in one book and 349 stamps in another book. If she gives 107 stamps to a friend, how many stamps will she have left? _____ stamps		
3 Steve weighs 172 pounds. Jan weighs 65 pounds. The ramp they are standing on holds up to 350 pounds. How many more pounds can the ramp hold? _____ pounds		

© Harcourt

Add or subtract.
Do one step at a time.

	Step 1	Step 2
	¹ 380 +259 ‾‾‾‾‾ 639	4 15 7̶5̶5̶ −639 ‾‾‾‾‾ 116

1 The school has 755 books to sell. First grade sells 380 books. Second grade sells 259 books. How many books are left?

116 books

2 Steve has saved 115 pennies. He gives 65 to his little sister. Steve saves 132 more pennies. Now how many pennies does Steve have?

_____ pennies

3 Jenny has $8.48 in her bank. She takes out $2.45. Then she takes out $6.00 more. How much money is left in the bank?

_____

4 Greg has 309 blue blocks and 483 red blocks in a box. He uses 287 blocks for a building. How many blocks are still in the box?

_____ blocks

Write About It

Make up your own multiple step problem.
Ask a friend to solve it.

HOME ACTIVITY • Together with your child, look at the exercises in this lesson. Ask your child to explain how he or she decided when to add or subtract. There may be more than one way to solve the problems.

Chapter 27

Name _____

CHECK ▪ Concepts and Skills

Add or subtract.

1
$6.60
$^5$
−$3.57
3.03

2
$5.95
+$0.24
5.71

3
$9.48
−$2.15
7.33

4
$7.46
−$1.74
5.12

Round to estimate.
Then add or subtract to solve.

5 Edie has $3.80 in her bank. She gets $4.75 for her birthday. How much money does Edie have now?

_____

Estimate	Solve
5$	3.80 +4.75 8.55

Add or subtract.

6
112
+549
661

7
$4.86
−$2.01
2.85

8
762
+ 42
720

9
955
−595
360

CHECK ▪ Problem Solving

Add or subtract.
Do one step at a time.

10 Harry has $8.57. He buys a toy for $4.00. Then his grandpa gives him $2.25. How much money does Harry have now?

_____

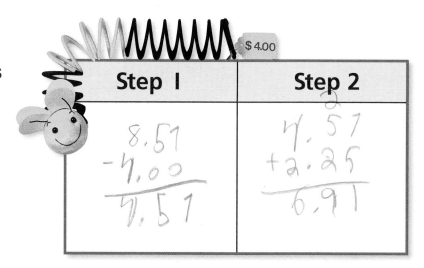

Step 1	Step 2
8.57 −4.00 4.57	4.57 +2.25 6.91

© Harcourt

Name _____

Choose the best answer for questions 1–5.

1
$$
\begin{array}{r}
56\!\!/1 \\
+\ 238 \\
\hline
\end{array}
$$

231   337   798   799
◉   ○   ○   ◉

2
$$
\begin{array}{r}
987 \\
-\ 659 \\
\hline
328
\end{array}
$$

228   328   329   332
○   ◉   ○   ○

3 André has $7.23. Amy has $8.93. About how much more money does Amy have than André?

About $1.50   About $2.00   About $15.96   About $16.00
○   ○   ○   ◉

4 Which number tells how many?

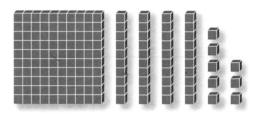

13   147   148   418
○   ○   ◉   ○

5 Demario had 275 basketball cards. He gave 98 of the cards to James. Then Demario got 104 more basketball cards. How many basketball cards did he have then?

171   177   281   477
○   ◉   ○   ○

Show What You Know

6 Write a price between $2.00 and $3.00 on each tag. Find the cost of both toys together. Write the addition problem.

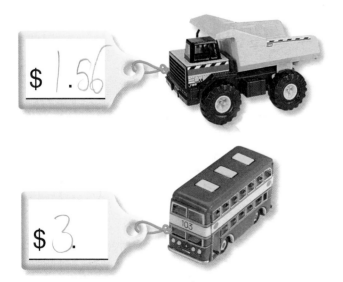

$ 1.56

$ 3.

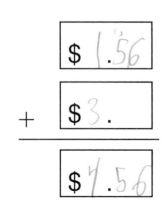

$ 1.56
+ $ 3.
_____
$ 4.56

Multiplication Concepts

What equal groups do you see in this picture?

SCHOOL HOME CONNECTION

Dear Family,
  Today we started Chapter 28. We will learn how to multiply. Here is the math vocabulary and an activity for us to do together at home.

  Love,

  _____

Vocabulary

multiplication sentence A number sentence that gives the total for a number of equal groups and the number in each group.

$5 \times 10 = 50$ is a multiplication sentence.

product The answer in a multiplication problem.

$$4 \times 5 = 20$$
product

Visit *The Learning Site* for additional ideas and activities.
www.harcourtschool.com

ACTIVITY

With your child, look for equal groups of 2, 3, 4, and 5. Groups of 2 and 4 might be the ears and legs on neighborhood animals. Groups of 3 and 5 might be flowers in a garden. Have your child draw pictures of the groups and write multiplication sentences to tell about the pictures.

Books to Share

To read about multiplication with your child, look for these books in your local library.

Each Orange Had 8 Slices,
by Paul Giganti, Jr., Greenwillow, 1992.

Amanda Bean's Amazing Dream,
by Cindy Neuschwander, Scholastic, 1998.

© Harcourt

Multiplication Facts 2, 5, and 10

Look for equal groups. Write multiplication facts about them.

SCHOOL HOME CONNECTION

Dear Family,
    Today we started Chapter 29. We will recall the multiplication facts with 2, 5, and 10. Here is the math vocabulary and an activity for us to do together at home.

        Love,

_____

My Math Word

multiply

Vocabulary

multiply To find out how many in all when you know the number of groups and the number in each group.

These objects are in equal groups.

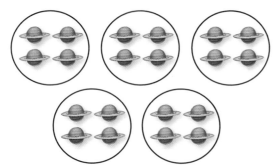

How many are in 5 groups of 4?

$$\begin{array}{r} 4 \text{ in each group} \\ \times 5 \text{ groups} \\ \hline 20 \end{array}$$

Visit *The Learning Site* for additional ideas and activities. www.harcourtschool.com

ACTIVITY

When in the supermarket, pick up an item that has 10 items in one package. For example, if 10 bars come in a box, ask your child to use multiplication to tell how many bars would be in three boxes. Do the same with other items.

Books to Share

To read about multiplication with your child, look for these books in your local library.

Anno's Mysterious Multiplying Jar, by Masaichiro and Mitsumasa Anno, Putnam & Grosset Group, 1983.

Shoes, Shoes, Shoes, by Anne Morris, William Morrow & Company, 1998.

Can You Count Ten Toes?, by Lezlie Evans, Houghton Mifflin, 1998.

© Harcourt

There are 7 groups of 2 wheels.
How many wheels are there in all?
Skip-count.

You can skip-count by twos to find the product.

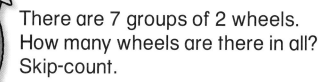

$\underline{2}$, $\underline{4}$, $\underline{6}$, $\underline{8}$, $\underline{10}$, $\underline{12}$, $\underline{14}$

$7 \times 2 = \underline{14}$ wheels

You can multiply to find the product.

How many wheels are there in all?
Write the product.

1

$1 \times 2 = \underline{\quad}$

$2 \times 2 = \underline{\quad}$

$3 \times 2 = \underline{\quad}$

2

$4 \times 2 = \underline{\quad}$

$5 \times 2 = \underline{\quad}$

$6 \times 2 = \underline{\quad}$

Talk About It ▪ Reasoning

Why could you use doubles to solve these problems?

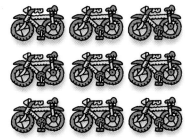

Write the product.

1

$7 \times 2 =$ __14__ $8 \times 2 =$ _____ $9 \times 2 =$ _____

2
$\begin{array}{r} 2 \\ \times 1 \\ \hline 2 \end{array}$
$\begin{array}{r} 1 \\ \times 2 \\ \hline \end{array}$
$\begin{array}{r} 2 \\ \times 2 \\ \hline \end{array}$
$\begin{array}{r} 2 \\ \times 3 \\ \hline \end{array}$
$\begin{array}{r} 3 \\ \times 2 \\ \hline \end{array}$
$\begin{array}{r} 2 \\ \times 4 \\ \hline \end{array}$
$\begin{array}{r} 4 \\ \times 2 \\ \hline \end{array}$

3
$\begin{array}{r} 2 \\ \times 5 \\ \hline \end{array}$
$\begin{array}{r} 5 \\ \times 2 \\ \hline \end{array}$
$\begin{array}{r} 2 \\ \times 6 \\ \hline \end{array}$
$\begin{array}{r} 6 \\ \times 2 \\ \hline \end{array}$
$\begin{array}{r} 2 \\ \times 7 \\ \hline \end{array}$
$\begin{array}{r} 7 \\ \times 2 \\ \hline \end{array}$

4
$\begin{array}{r} 2 \\ \times 8 \\ \hline \end{array}$
$\begin{array}{r} 8 \\ \times 2 \\ \hline \end{array}$
$\begin{array}{r} 2 \\ \times 9 \\ \hline \end{array}$
$\begin{array}{r} 9 \\ \times 2 \\ \hline \end{array}$
$\begin{array}{r} 2 \\ \times 10 \\ \hline \end{array}$
$\begin{array}{r} 10 \\ \times 2 \\ \hline \end{array}$

Problem Solving ▪ Visual Thinking

5 Write the multiplication sentence that this number line shows.

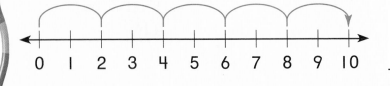

_____ $\times$ _____ $=$ _____

🔺 **HOME ACTIVITY** • Give your child a multiplication problem with 2, for example, 6×2. Ask your child to name the product. Repeat with different problems with 2 until your child has memorized the facts.

Name _____

There are 8 groups of 5 fingers.
How many fingers are there in all?
Skip-count.

You can skip-count by fives
to find the product.

____5____, __10__, __15__, __20__, __25__, __30__, __35__, __40__

$8 \times 5 =$ __40__ fingers

You can multiply to
find the product.

How many fingers are there in all?
Write the product.

1

  $1 \times 5 =$ _____

  $2 \times 5 =$ _____

$3 \times 5 =$ _____

2

 $4 \times 5 =$ _____

 $5 \times 5 =$ _____

$6 \times 5 =$ _____

Talk About It ▪ Reasoning
What patterns do you see when you multiply with 5?

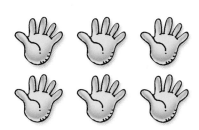

© Harcourt

How many fingers are there in all?
Write the product.

1

$7 \times 5 = \underline{35}$ $8 \times 5 = \underline{\hspace{1cm}}$ $9 \times 5 = \underline{\hspace{1cm}}$

Write the product.

2

$\begin{array}{r} 5 \\ \times 1 \\ \hline 5 \end{array}$ $\begin{array}{r} 1 \\ \times 5 \\ \hline \end{array}$ $\begin{array}{r} 5 \\ \times 2 \\ \hline \end{array}$ $\begin{array}{r} 2 \\ \times 5 \\ \hline \end{array}$ $\begin{array}{r} 5 \\ \times 3 \\ \hline \end{array}$ $\begin{array}{r} 3 \\ \times 5 \\ \hline \end{array}$

3

$\begin{array}{r} 5 \\ \times 4 \\ \hline \end{array}$ $\begin{array}{r} 4 \\ \times 5 \\ \hline \end{array}$ $\begin{array}{r} 5 \\ \times 6 \\ \hline \end{array}$ $\begin{array}{r} 6 \\ \times 5 \\ \hline \end{array}$ $\begin{array}{r} 7 \\ \times 5 \\ \hline \end{array}$ $\begin{array}{r} 5 \\ \times 7 \\ \hline \end{array}$

Algebra

Look for a pattern. Write the missing numbers.

4

$\begin{array}{r} 5 \\ \times 1 \\ \hline \square \end{array}$ $\begin{array}{r} 5 \\ \times \square \\ \hline 10 \end{array}$ $\begin{array}{r} 5 \\ \times 3 \\ \hline \square \end{array}$ $\begin{array}{r} 5 \\ \times \square \\ \hline 20 \end{array}$ $\begin{array}{r} \square \\ \times 5 \\ \hline 25 \end{array}$ $\begin{array}{r} 5 \\ \times \square \\ \hline 30 \end{array}$

HOME ACTIVITY • Give your child a multiplication problem with 5, for example, 8 × 5. Ask your child to name the product. Repeat with different problems with 5 until your child has memorized the facts.

Name _____

There are 3 groups of 10 counters.
How many counters are there in all?
Skip-count.

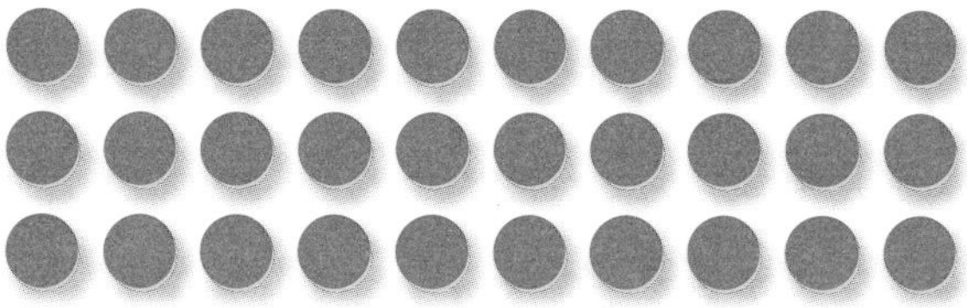

You can skip-count by tens to find the product.

You can multiply to find the product.

$3 \times 10 =$ _____ counters

How many counters are there in all?
Write the product.

1 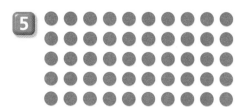 $1 \times 10 =$ _____	**2** $2 \times 10 =$ _____
3  $3 \times 10 =$ _____	**4** $4 \times 10 =$ _____
5 $5 \times 10 =$ _____	**6** $6 \times 10 =$ _____

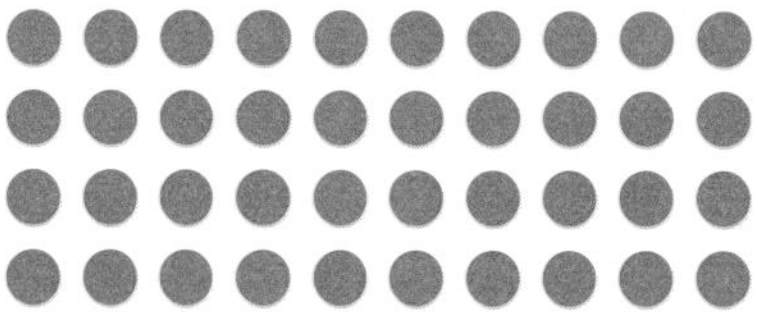

Talk About It ■ **Reasoning**

What patterns do you see when you multiply with 10?

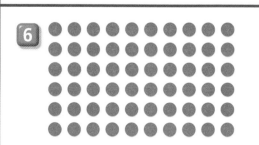

© Harcourt

How many counters are there in all?
Write the product.

1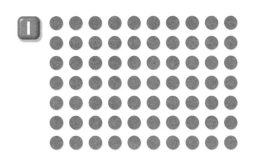

$7 \times 10 =$ ___70___

2

$8 \times 10 =$ _____

3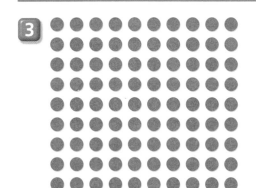

$9 \times 10 =$ _____

4

$10 \times 10 =$ _____

Write the product.

5
$$\begin{array}{r} 10 \\ \times 8 \\ \hline \end{array}$$
$$\begin{array}{r} 10 \\ \times 2 \\ \hline \end{array}$$
$$\begin{array}{r} 10 \\ \times 1 \\ \hline \end{array}$$
$$\begin{array}{r} 10 \\ \times 5 \\ \hline \end{array}$$
$$\begin{array}{r} 4 \\ \times 10 \\ \hline \end{array}$$
$$\begin{array}{r} 6 \\ \times 10 \\ \hline \end{array}$$

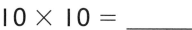

6
$$\begin{array}{r} 10 \\ \times 9 \\ \hline \end{array}$$
$$\begin{array}{r} 5 \\ \times 10 \\ \hline \end{array}$$
$$\begin{array}{r} 10 \\ \times 7 \\ \hline \end{array}$$
$$\begin{array}{r} 3 \\ \times 10 \\ \hline \end{array}$$
$$\begin{array}{r} 1 \\ \times 10 \\ \hline \end{array}$$
$$\begin{array}{r} 10 \\ \times 10 \\ \hline \end{array}$$

© Harcourt

 HOME ACTIVITY • Give your child a multiplication problem with 10, for example, 5 × 10. Ask your child to name the product. Repeat with different problems with 10 until your child has memorized the facts.

Name _____

Problem Solving
Use Logical Reasoning

?	
2	4
3	6
4	8

The rule could be 2. Multiply each number by 2.

UNDERSTAND

What do you want to find out?

PLAN

You can use logical reasoning to find the pattern and write a rule.

SOLVE

Multiply 2	
2	4
3	6
4	8

CHECK

Does your answer make sense? Explain.

Write the rule.

1

0	0
1	5
2	10

2

5	50
6	60
7	70

© Harcourt

Write the rule.

1

1	2
2	4
3	6
4	8
5	10

2

5	50
6	60
7	70
8	80
9	90

3

6	30
7	35
8	40
9	45
10	50

4 Complete the table.

×	1	2	3	4	5	6	7	8	9	10
2	2									
5										
10										

Problem Solving ▪ Reasoning

5 Jorge drinks 5 glasses of milk a day.
How much milk does he
drink in a week?

_____ glasses

🏠 **HOME ACTIVITY** • Each day, work with your child for a short time on multiplication facts. For example, find the value for groups of nickels or dimes by using multiplication. 5 nickels is 5 × 5 = 25.

© Harcourt

CHECK ▪ Concepts and Skills

How many fingers are there in all?
Write the product.

  |  |

$3 \times 5 =$ _____ | $5 \times 5 =$ _____ | $7 \times 5 =$ _____

Write the product.

2.
$$\begin{array}{r} 5 \\ \times 5 \\ \hline \end{array} \quad \begin{array}{r} 5 \\ \times 2 \\ \hline \end{array} \quad \begin{array}{r} 10 \\ \times 5 \\ \hline \end{array} \quad \begin{array}{r} 3 \\ \times 5 \\ \hline \end{array} \quad \begin{array}{r} 5 \\ \times 9 \\ \hline \end{array} \quad \begin{array}{r} 4 \\ \times 5 \\ \hline \end{array}$$

3.
$$\begin{array}{r} 1 \\ \times 10 \\ \hline \end{array} \quad \begin{array}{r} 10 \\ \times 9 \\ \hline \end{array} \quad \begin{array}{r} 4 \\ \times 10 \\ \hline \end{array} \quad \begin{array}{r} 10 \\ \times 4 \\ \hline \end{array} \quad \begin{array}{r} 3 \\ \times 10 \\ \hline \end{array} \quad \begin{array}{r} 10 \\ \times 10 \\ \hline \end{array}$$

Multiply.

4.
$$\begin{array}{r} 9 \\ \times 5 \\ \hline \end{array} \quad \begin{array}{r} 10 \\ \times 8 \\ \hline \end{array} \quad \begin{array}{r} 7 \\ \times 5 \\ \hline \end{array} \quad \begin{array}{r} 2 \\ \times 5 \\ \hline \end{array} \quad \begin{array}{r} 5 \\ \times 6 \\ \hline \end{array} \quad \begin{array}{r} 2 \\ \times 10 \\ \hline \end{array}$$

CHECK ▪ Problem Solving

Write the rule.

5.

1	10
2	20
3	30

6.

6	12
7	14
8	16

Name _____

Choose the best answer for questions 1–7.

1
$$\begin{array}{r} 2 \\ \times 9 \\ \hline \end{array}$$

14 ○   16 ○   18 ○   19 ○

2
$$\begin{array}{r} 5 \\ \times 4 \\ \hline \end{array}$$

16 ○   20 ○   22 ○   25 ○

3
$$\begin{array}{r} 10 \\ \times 1 \\ \hline \end{array}$$

10 ○   11 ○   20 ○   100 ○

4
$$\begin{array}{r} 6 \\ \times 2 \\ \hline \end{array}$$

0 ○   12 ○   35 ○   36 ○

5
$$\begin{array}{r} 5 \\ \times 8 \\ \hline \end{array}$$

13 ○   35 ○   40 ○   45 ○

6
$$\begin{array}{r} 10 \\ \times 2 \\ \hline \end{array}$$

2 ○   12 ○   20 ○   30 ○

7 A collie weighs 100 pounds. A beagle weighs 35 pounds.
A bloodhound weighs 180 pounds. How much do the collie
and the beagle weigh together?

45 pounds ○   135 pounds ○   280 pounds ○   315 pounds ○

Show What You Know

8 Finish the table.
Write a rule.
Write numbers that
follow the rule.

Multiply _____	
2	
5	
10	

© Harcourt

CHAPTER 30 Division Concepts

Share the party items equally among the children. How many will each child get?

SCHOOL HOME CONNECTION

Dear Family,
   Today we started Chapter 30. We will begin to learn about division. Here is the math vocabulary and an activity for us to do together at home.

   Love,

_____

My Math Words

divide
quotient

Vocabulary

divide To separate a group of objects into equal smaller groups.

$$6 \div 3 = 2$$

↑

division symbol

Read as *six divided by three equals two.*

quotient The answer in a division problem.

$$20 \div 5 = 4$$

↑

quotient

Visit *The Learning Site* for additional ideas and activities.
www.harcourtschool.com

ACTIVITY

Give your child dried beans to divide into equal groups. Cut egg cartons into 3-cup, 4-cup, and 5-cup sections. Have your child count out 15 beans into the 3-cup section, forming 3 equal groups. Ask how many beans are in each cup. Repeat, using different numbers of beans and cups.

Books to Share

To read about division with your child, look for these books in your local library.

Divide and Ride,
by Stuart J. Murphy, HarperCollins, 1997.

Madeline,
by Ludwig Bemelmans, Penguin, 2000.

© Harcourt

Name ____________________

Make Equal Groups

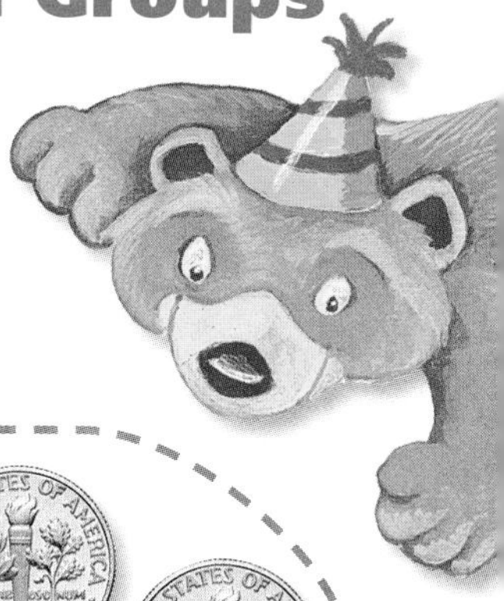

Circle equal groups.
How many groups are there?
How many are left over?

1 Divide 10 coins into groups of 5.

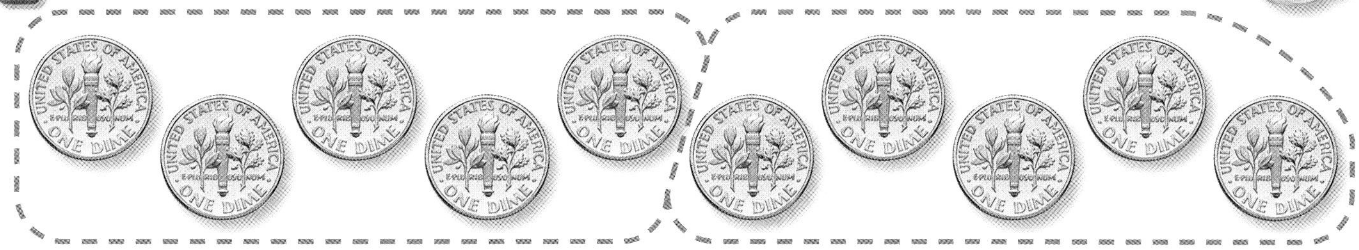

2 groups   0 left over

2 Divide 14 apples into groups of 6.

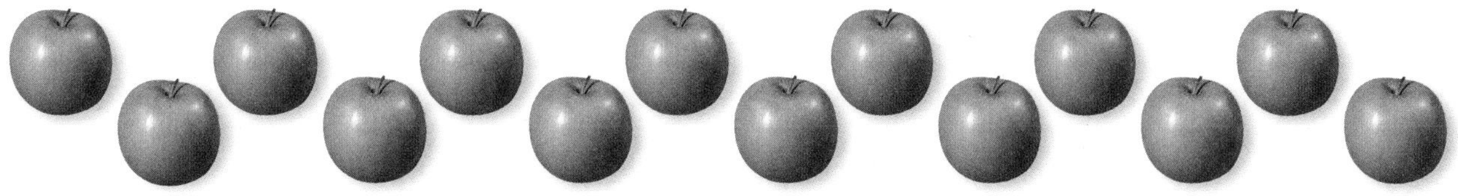

_______ groups   _______ left over

3 Divide 13 balloons into groups of 3.

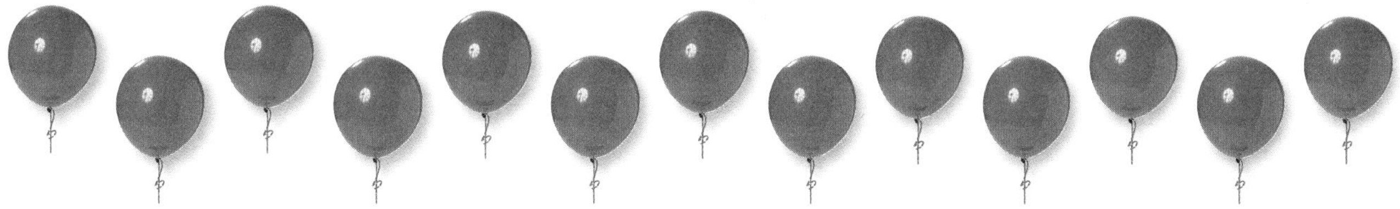

_______ groups   _______ left over

4 Divide 10 peanuts into groups of 2.

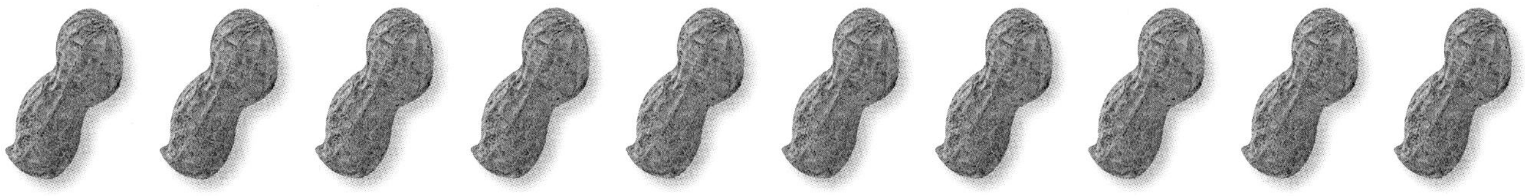

_______ groups   _______ left over

Talk About It ■ Reasoning

You have 12 plums. How many ways can you make equal groups with no plums left over?

Practice

Circle equal groups.
How many groups are there?
How many are left over?

1 Divide 16 cups into groups of 4.

_____4_____ groups   _____0_____ left over

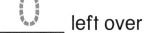

2 Divide 11 napkins into groups of 3.

_____ groups   _____ left over

3 Divide 15 forks into groups of 4.

_____ groups   _____ left over

Problem Solving ■ Visual Thinking

4 There are 15 pencils. Each child gets 2 pencils.

How many children are there?   _____ children

How many pencils are left over?   _____ left over

© Harcourt

🏠 **HOME ACTIVITY** • Have your child use small items, such as paper clips, to make equal groups.

Name _____

There are 8 counters.
How many groups of 2 counters can you make?

The ÷ sign tells you to divide.

$$8 \div 2 = ?$$

number of counters   number in each group   number of groups

Start with 8.
Take away groups of 2 until you get 0.

8	6	4	2
− 2	− 2	− 2	− 2
6	4	2	0

You can subtract 2 from 8 four times,
since there are 4 groups of 2 in 8.

The answer is the **quotient**.

$$8 \div 2 = \underline{4}$$

Show the total with ⚫. Subtract the number in each group.
Write the differences and the quotient.

1 You have 20 ⚫. Make groups of 5.

20	15	10	5
− 5	− 5	− 5	− 5

$$20 \div 5 = \underline{\hspace{1cm}}$$

2 You have 9 ⚫. Make groups of 3.

9	6	3
− 3	− 3	− 3

$$9 \div 3 = \underline{\hspace{1cm}}$$

Talk About It ▪ Reasoning
How is subtracting over and over like division?

Use subtraction to find the quotient.

1 You have 12 ⬤. Make groups of 2.

12	10	8	6	4	2
− 2	− 2	− 2	− 2	− 2	− 2
10	8	6	4	2	0

$12 \div 2 = \underline{6}$

---

2 You have 15 ⬤. Make groups of 5.

15	10	5
− 5	− 5	− 5

$15 \div 5 = \underline{\quad}$

---

3 You have 20 ⬤. Make groups of 10.

20	10
−10	−10

$20 \div 10 = \underline{\quad}$

---

4 You have 18 ⬤. Make groups of 3.

18	15	12	9	6	3
− 3	− 3	− 3	− 3	− 3	− 3

$18 \div 3 = \underline{\quad}$

Mixed Review
Add or subtract.

5

tens	ones
☐	☐
9	4
−3	7

6

tens	ones
☐	
3	2
+3	8

7

tens	ones
☐	
1	6
+3	7

8

tens	ones
☐	☐
4	1
−1	6

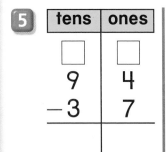

HOME ACTIVITY • Give your child 12 pennies, and ask how many groups of 6 pennies he or she can make. Help your child make 2 groups of 6 and write 12 − 6 = 6, 6 − 6 = 0, so 12 ÷ 6 = 2.

Name _____

Problem Solving
Choose the Operation

Circle the number sentence that makes sense for the problem. Then solve.

1 Jana has 6 hens. On Monday, each hen laid 4 eggs. How many eggs were laid on Monday?

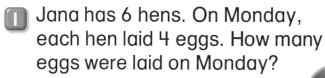

___24___ eggs

$6 + 4 =$ _____

$6 \times 4 = 24$

2 Mr. Jones has 853 cows. Mr. Peters has 539 cows. How many more cows does Mr. Jones have than Mr. Peters?

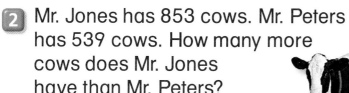

_____ more cows

$853 - 539 =$ _____

$853 + 539 =$ _____

3 Craig planted 15 seeds in 5 minutes. How many seeds can he plant in 1 minute?

_____ seeds

$15 - 5 =$ _____

$15 \div 5 =$ _____

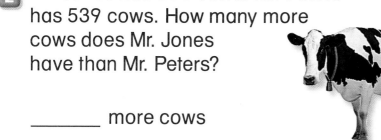

NET WT.
500 mg.

$1.49

NET WT.
100 mg.

Popular
Cutting
Flower

ANNUAL

4 Arial has $4.67. She buys seeds for $2.80. How much money does she have left?

_____

$\$4.67 \times \$2.80 =$ _____

$\$4.67 - \$2.80 =$ _____

5 There are 24 hours in a day. Each class is 4 hours long. How many classes could you take in a day?

_____ classes

$24 \times 4 =$ _____

$24 \div 4 =$ _____

© Harcourt

Circle the number sentence that makes sense for the problem. Then solve.

1 Ali has put stamps in a book. The book has 10 pages. Each page holds 2 stamps. How many stamps are in the book?

_20_ stamps

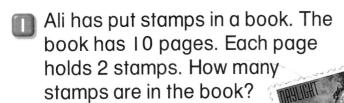

$(10 \times 2 = \underline{20})$

$10 \div 2 = \underline{5}$

2 Mr. Lucky has 46 big boxes and 21 small boxes on the shelf. How many more big boxes are there than little boxes?

_____ more big boxes

$46 + 21 = \underline{67}$

$46 - 21 = \underline{25}$

3 There are 16 cookies. Four friends share the cookies equally. How many cookies does each friend get?

_____ cookies

$16 - 4 = \underline{18}$

$16 \div 4 = \underline{12}$

4 Maria has 15 pictures. If she gives 3 pictures to each friend, how many friends get pictures?

_____ friends

$15 \div 3 = \underline{5}$

$15 \times 4 = \underline{60}$

Write About It

Make up your own math story problem. You can add, subtract, multiply, or divide. Ask a classmate to solve it.

HOME ACTIVITY • With your child, look at the exercises in this lesson. Ask your child to explain how he or she decided whether to add, subtract, multiply, or divide.

Name _____

Problem Solving
Choose a Strategy

Mrs. Bear has 12 plums.
She gives 2 to each of her cubs.
How many cubs does she have?

UNDERSTAND

You need to find out how many cubs
there are in Mrs. Bear's family.

Strategies
Draw a Picture
Make a Model
Make a List

PLAN

Choose a way to solve the problem.
You could draw a picture.

SOLVE

There are ___6___ cubs in Mrs. Bear's
family.

CHECK

Does your answer make sense? Explain.

Choose a strategy to solve the problem.

1. Juan has 20¢. He finds 15¢ more.
   If one peach costs 5¢, how many
   peaches can Juan buy?

   ___1___ peaches

2. There are 32 plants. If Craig plants
   them in 4 equal rows, how many
   plants will be in each row?

   ___2___ plants

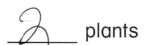

© Harcourt

Choose a strategy to solve the problem.

1 Liz has $9.00.
Tickets cost $3.00 each.
How many tickets can Liz buy?

_____3_____ tickets

2 Kathy has 30 coins in her collection.
She stacks her coins in 3 equal piles.
How many coins are in each pile?

_____ coins

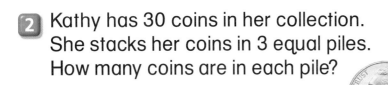

3 Leroy has 5 red apples and 5 green apples. He gives 2 apples to each of his friends.
How many friends get apples?

_____ friends

4 Mary has 10 red flowers and 2 pink flowers. She puts her flowers in 4 vases. How many flowers are in each vase?

_____ flowers

Write About It

Make up your own math story problem. Ask a classmate to solve it. He or she can choose any strategy to solve the problem.

© Harcourt

HOME ACTIVITY • Make up addition, subtraction, multiplication, and division problems for your child to solve.

Name _____

CHECK ■ Concepts and Skills

1 Divide 14 counters into 3 equal groups. Circle the groups.

How many counters in each group? _____ counters

How many left over? _____

Circle equal groups. How many groups are there? How many are left over?

2 Divide 10 pennies into groups of 2.

_____ groups   _____ left over

Use subtraction to find the quotient.
Write the differences and the quotient.

3 You have 10 ●. Make groups of 2.

$10 \div 2 = $ _____

CHECK ■ Problem Solving

Choose a strategy to solve the problem.

4 There are 9 raisins and 3 boys. Each boy gets an equal number of raisins. How many raisins does each boy get?

Strategies
Draw a Picture
Make a Model
Make a List

_____ raisins

© Harcourt

Name _____

Choose the best answer for questions 1–4.

1 Which tells about 17 ⬤ divided into 4 equal groups?

⚫⚫⚫⚫⚫   ⚫⚫⚫⚫   ⚫⚫⚫⚫   ⚫⚫⚫⚫   ⚫

3 in each group   4 in each group   4 in each group   4 in each group
   5 left over   2 left over   0 left over   1 left over
      ○   ○   ○   ◉

2 Which tells about 6 ⬤ divided into 3 equal groups?

⚫⚫   ⚫⚫   ⚫⚫

3 in each group   1 in each group   2 in each group   2 in each group
   2 left over   2 left over   0 left over   1 left over
      ○   ○   ⬤   ○

3 Corey has 12 muffins. He gives them equally to 6 friends.
Which tells how many muffins each friend can have?

   12 × 6   12 + 6   12 ÷ 6   12 − 6
      ○   ○   ⬤   ○

4 Patricia has 24 puzzle pieces. She puts 16 of
them in the puzzle. How many pieces are left?

      4   8   18   40
      ○   ○   ○   ○

Show What You Know

5 Draw 20 stars. Show two ways to put them in equal groups.
Write the numbers.

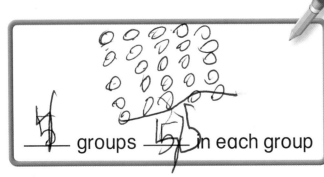

____ groups ____ in each group

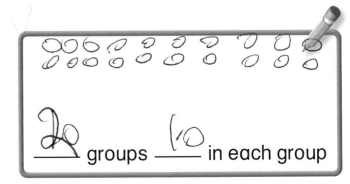

____ groups ____ in each group

© Harcourt

Can I Play?

written by Ann Lee Earnshaw

illustrated by Ed Martinez

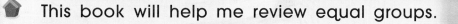

This book will help me review equal groups.

This book belongs to _____.

Rebecca has 12 marbles.

She wants to share them equally with John.

"Here are _____ marbles for you

and _____ marbles for me," said Rebecca.

"That's fair," said John. "Now can we play?"

They were just about to
start the game when Melissa and Jeff
came over. "Can we play?" asked Melissa.
"Yes, you can play," said Rebecca.

"Here are ____ marbles for you, Jeff,

and ____ marbles for you, Melissa,

and ____ marbles for you, John,

and ____ marbles for me," said Rebecca.

D

They were just about to start the game
when Tom and Susan came over.
"Can we play?" they asked.
"Yes, you can play," said Rebecca.
"Now how many marbles will we get?"
asked Jeff.
"Each of us will get _____
marbles," said Rebecca.

"That's fair," said John. "Let's play!"

Name _____

Watch Your Step!

Use your skills to find your way home. Write the missing addition, subtraction, multiplication and division signs as you follow the path.

Start

$2 \boxed{} 3 = 6$

$4 \boxed{} 1 = 5$

$5 \boxed{} 5 = 10$

$50 \boxed{} 40 = 10$

$2 \boxed{} 1 = 2$

$8 \boxed{} 2 = 4$

$38 \boxed{} 26 = 12$

$5 \boxed{} 4 = 20$

$$\boxed{} \begin{array}{r} 10 \\ 8 \\ \hline 80 \end{array}$$

$$\boxed{} \begin{array}{r} 98 \\ 7 \\ \hline 91 \end{array}$$

$10 \boxed{} 5 = 2$

$24 \boxed{} 12 = 12$

$400 \boxed{} 300 = 700$

$2 \boxed{} 6 = 12$

$15 \boxed{} 3 = 5$

$5 \boxed{} 5 = 25$

$76 \boxed{} 77 = 153$

Home

Talk about It □ Explain how you found your way home.

Name _____

14 + 6 = 21
This statement is false.
14 + 6 = 20
Now this statement is true.

Mark each number sentence as true or false.
If the statement is false, correct it so that it is true.

		True	False
1	$3 \times 2 = 6$	True	False
2	$14 + 16 = 110$	True	False
3	$10 \div 5 = 2$	True	False
4	$8 + 3 = 10$	True	False
5	$15 < 18$	True	False
6	2 quarters $=$ 5 dimes	True	False
7	$128 + 134 = 261$	True	False
8	$96 - 56 = 40$	True	False
9	$8 \times 4 = 24$	True	False
10	$100 > 200$	True	False

Skills and Concepts

Add.

1

    4   4 hundreds   400
   +3   +3 hundreds   +300

2

hundreds	tens	ones
	☐	
3	5	6
+2	1	8

3 $916 + 16 =$ _____

Subtract.

4

    6   6 hundred   600
   −1   −1 hundred   −100

5

hundreds	tens	ones
☐	☐	☐
8	2	2
−2	0	6

6

hundreds	tens	ones
☐	☐	☐
1	6	8
−1	4	9

Add or subtract.

7

   $5.90
  −$2.89

8

   $1.45
  +$1.00

9

    52
  +189

10

   492
  −385

11 Write the sum. Then write the product.

   $4 + 4 + 4 =$ _____ $3 \times 4 =$ _____

12 Write how many rows and how many in each row. Then write the product.

_____ rows   _____ in each row

_____ × _____ = _____

---

13 5 × 3 = _____

3
×5
—

14   2
×8
—

15   6
×5
—

16   10
×4
—

---

17 Circle equal groups. How many groups are there? How many are left over?

_____ groups   _____ left over

Problem Solving

18 Mr. Porter has 45 pieces of wood. He stacks the wood in 5 equal piles. How many pieces of wood are in each pile?

_____ pieces

Here Kitty, Kitty

Allan saw some kittens at the pet store. He decided to find out how many there were in all.

- The kittens were in groups of 5.
- There were more than 18 kittens in the store.

Use both addition and multiplication to show how many kittens could have been in the store.

Show your work.

Technology

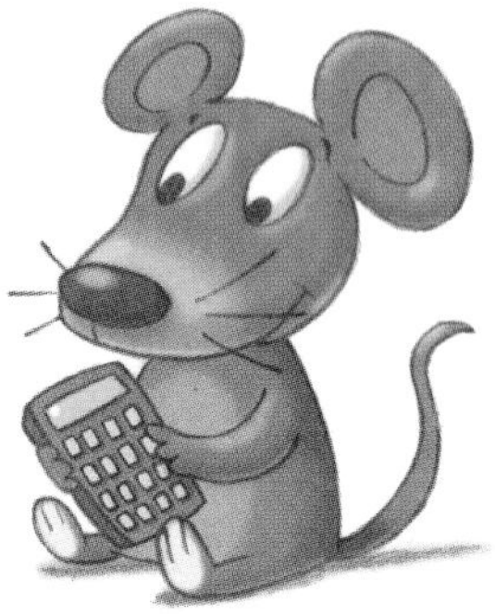

Name ________________________________

Calculator • Addition, Subtraction, and Place Value

Start with 435.

Which numbers can you add and still have 4 hundreds?

45	**55**	**65**

Use a .

Press AC 4 3 5 + 4 5 = .

Write the answer 480

Press AC 4 3 5 + 5 5 = .

Write the answer ______

Press AC 4 3 5 + 6 5 = .

Write the answer ______

So, you can add 45 and 55 and still have 4 hundreds.

Practice and Problem Solving

Use a . Circle the numbers.

1. Which can you *add* to 347 and still have 3 hundreds?

   23 81 48 39 65 92 52 19 70

2. Which can you *subtract* from 568 and still have 5 hundreds?

   19 25 45 82 68 30 96 73 57

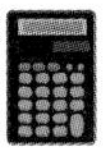

PROBLEM SOLVING ON LOCATION

At the Fair

At the Kansas State Fair, you can go on exciting rides, enjoy special foods, and see many interesting things.

You have $7.00 to spend at the fair. How do you spend it?

State Fair Prices		
 Entrance Fee	$2.00
Ferris Wheel	$.50
Petting Zoo	$1.00
Pony Ride	$1.00
Lunch	$1.50

Complete the chart.

Activity	Price	Total Spent
Entrance Fee	$2.00	$2.00

PROBLEM SOLVING ON LOCATION

On the Farm

Iowa is the "corn capital" of our country. More corn is grown in Iowa than in any other state.

How many different ways can you put 12 corn plants into more than one row?

Use 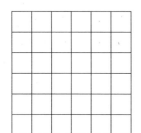 .

Draw to show each way you find.
Write the numbers.

_____ rows

_____ in each row

_____ rows

_____ in each row

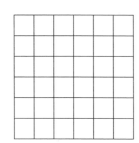

_____ rows

_____ in each row

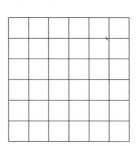

_____ rows

_____ in each row

© Harcourt

PICTURE GLOSSARY

A.M. (page 137)
The time between midnight and noon.

add (page 3)

$$2 + 4 = 6$$

addend (page 3)

$$5 + 2 = 7$$

after (page 63)

30 comes **after** 29.

29, **30**

bar graph (page 77)

Hours of Playing Sports Each Week										
Suzy										
Carl										
Ben										
Beth										
Ari										
	0	1	2	3	4	5	6	7	8	9	10

before (page 63)

39, 40

39 comes **before** 40.

between (page 63)

19, **20**, 21

20 comes **between** 19 and 21.

calendar (page 141)

November						
S	M	Tu	W	Th	F	S
		1	2	3	4	5
6	7	8	9	10	11	12
13	14	15	16	17	18	19
20	21	22	23	24	25	26
27	28	29	30			

centimeter (page 275)

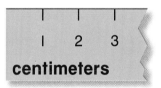

circle (page 241)

cone (page 257)

congruent figures (page 245)

Figures with the same size and shape are **congruent**.

© Harcourt

455

corner (page 243)

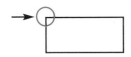

a **corner** of a plane shape

a **corner** of a solid figure

count back (page 21)

$$7 - 3 = \underline{?}$$

Start at 7. Count back 3.

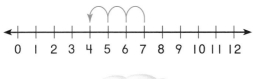

6, 5, **4**

$$7 - 3 = 4$$

count on (page 5)

$$3 + 2 = \underline{?}$$

Start at 3. Count on 2.

4, **5**

$$3 + 2 = 5$$

cube (page 257)

cup (page 285)

cylinder (page 257)

difference (page 21)

$$6 - 4 = \mathbf{2}$$

difference

digit (page 49)

digit

51

digit

51 has two **digits.**

dime (page 97)

10¢   10 cents

© Harcourt

divide (page 436)

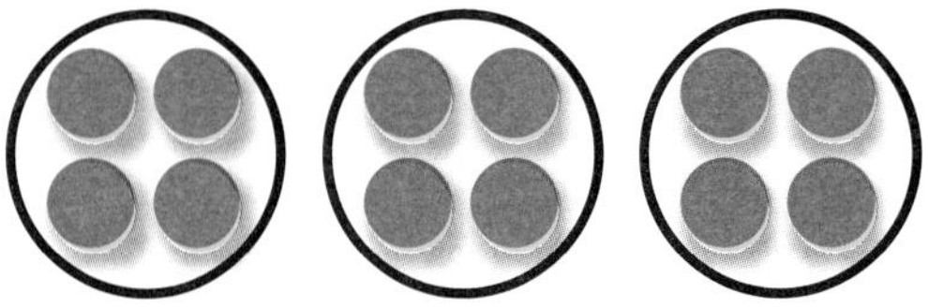

$$12 \div 3 = 4$$

dollar (page 103)

dollar
sign → $1.00   one dollar
↑
decimal point

doubles (page 7)

$$3 + 3 = 6$$

doubles plus one (page 7)

$$3 + 4 = 7$$

edge (page 261)

edge →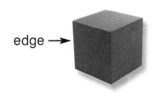

equal groups (page 411)

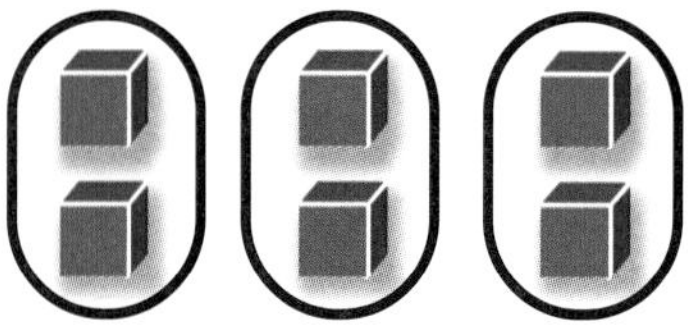

3 groups of 2
$$2 + 2 + 2 = 6$$

equal parts (page 335)

The parts of this rectangle
are equal.

equal sign (page 3)

$$3 + 1 = 4$$
↑
equal sign

equal to (page 61)

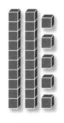

25   =   25

estimate (page 177)

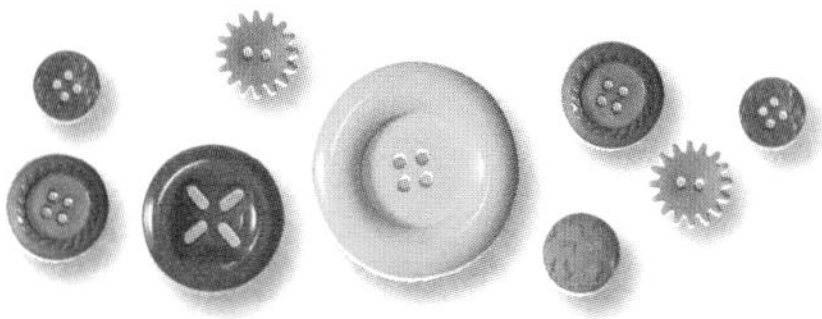

about 10 buttons

even numbers (page 65)

0, 2, 4, 6, 8, 10 . . .

face (page 259)

face →

fact family (page 25)

6 + 7 = 13   7 + 6 = 13

13 − 6 = 7   13 − 7 = 6

flip (page 249)

foot (page 273)

A **foot** is 12 inches.

fractions (page 337)

one-half   one-third   one-fourth   one-sixth

$\frac{1}{2}$ $\frac{1}{3}$ $\frac{1}{4}$ $\frac{1}{6}$

gram (page 291)

This clip weighs about 1 gram.

greater than > (page 61)

63 is **greater than** 29.

63 > 29

half-dollar (page 99)

50¢   50 cents

half-hour (page 125)

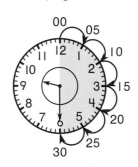

hour (page 125)

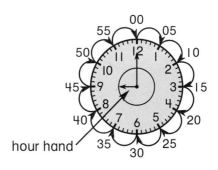

hour hand

hundreds (page 307)

2 hundreds

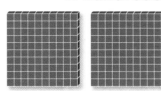

200

© Harcourt

458

inch (page 271)

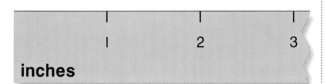

inches

kilogram (page 291)

This book weighs about
1 **kilogram**.

less than < (page 61)

29 is **less than** 63.

29 < 63

line of symmetry (page 245)

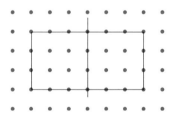

liter (page 287)

A **liter** is a little more than a quart.

meter (page 275)

A **meter** is 100 centimeters.

minutes (page 125)

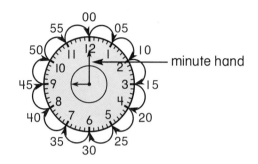

minute hand

multiplication sentence
(page 417)

$$4 \times 3 = 12$$

multiply (page 413)

$$2 \times 3 = \mathbf{6} \leftarrow \text{product}$$

nickel (page 97)

5¢   5 cents

number sentence (page 13)

$$6 + 8 = 14$$

odd numbers (page 65)

1, 3, 5, 7, 9, 11 . . .

ones (page 45)

2 **ones**

© Harcourt

order property (page 3)

$$6 + 3 = 9$$
$$3 + 6 = 9$$

ordinal numbers (page 59)

first   **second**   **third**

ounce (page 289)

This weighs about 1 **ounce**.

oval (page 241)

P.M. (page 137)

The time between noon
and midnight.

pattern (page 69)

30, 40, 50, 60, 70 . . .

Count by tens.

penny (page 97)

1¢   1 cent

perimeter (page 277)

2

2   2

2

$$2 + 2 + 2 + 2 = 8$$

pictograph (page 85)

Classmates Who Have Pets	
birds	👤 👤
cats	👤
dogs	👤 👤 👤 👤
fish	👤

Key: Each 👤 stands for 2 children.

picture graph (page 75)

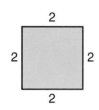

Our Favorite Breakfast Foods	
cold cereal	🥣 🥣 🥣 🥣 🥣
hot cereal	🥣
pancakes	🥞 🥞 🥞
toast	🍞 🍞 🍞 🍞

pint (page 285)

2 cups = 1 **pint**

pound (page 289)

This weighs 1 **pound**.

pyramid (page 257)

quart (page 285)

4 cups = 1 **quart**

quarter (page 99)

25¢   25 cents

rectangle (page 241)

rectangular prism (page 257)

regroup (page 161)

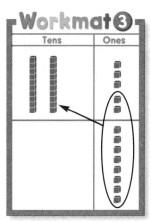

round (page 177)

To estimate to the closest ten.

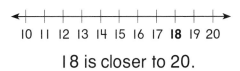

18 is closer to 20.

side (page 243)

← side

skip-count (page 67)

5, 10, 15, 20, 25 . . .

© Harcourt

slide (page 251)

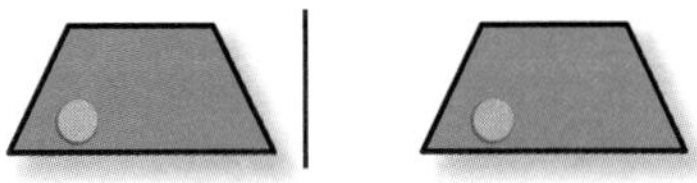

sphere (page 257)

square (page 241)

subtract (page 19)

$6 - 2 = 4$

sum (page 3)

$6 + 9 = 15$ ⬅— **sum**

table (page 79)

Our Favorite Sandwiches	
cheese	III
bologna	ℍℍ II
hamburger	ℍℍ I
tuna	III

tally marks (page 79)

temperature (page 293)

thermometer

The **temperature** is 30°F.

ten frame (page 9)

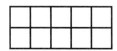

tens (page 45)

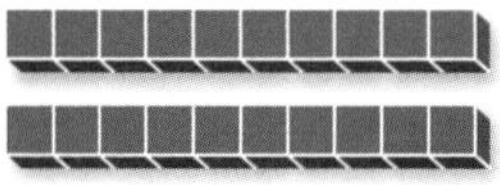

triangle (page 241)

turn (page 249)

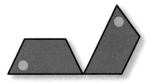

zero property (page 3)

$5 + 0 = 5$

© Harcourt

© Harcourt

463